ETHNOGRAPHY
Principles in Practice

ETHNOGRAPHY
Principles in Practice

MARTYN HAMMERSLEY
PAUL ATKINSON

TAVISTOCK PUBLICATIONS
LONDON AND NEW YORK

First published in 1983 by
Tavistock Publications Ltd
11 New Fetter Lane,
London EC4P 4EE
Reprinted 1986

Published in the USA by
Tavistock Publications
in association with Methuen, Inc.
29 West 35th Street,
New York, NY 10001

© 1983 Martyn Hammersley and
Paul Atkinson

Printed in Great Britain at the
University Press, Cambridge

British Library Cataloguing in
Publication Data
Hammersley, Martyn
Ethnography
1. Ethnology
I. Title   II. Atkinson, Paul
572   GN316

ISBN 0-422-77150-3
ISBN 0-422-77160-0 Pbk

Library of Congress Cataloging in
Publication Data
Hammersley, Martyn.
Ethnography, principles in
practice.
Bibliography: p.
Includes indexes.
1. Ethnology-Methodology.
2. Ethnology —
Field work.   3. Social Sciences —
Field work.
I. Atkinson, Paul   II. Title.
GN 345-H35   1983   306'.01'8
83-683
ISBN 0-422-77150-3
ISBN 0-422-77160-0 (pbk.)

The more ancient of the Greeks (whose writings are lost) took up . . . a position . . . between the presumption of pronouncing on everything, and the despair of comprehending anything; and though frequently and bitterly complaining of the difficulty of inquiry and the obscurity of things, and like impatient horses champing at the bit, they did not the less follow up their object and engage with nature, thinking (it seems) that this very question – viz., whether or not anything can be known – was to be settled not by arguing, but by trying. And yet they too, trusting entirely to the force of their understanding, applied no rule, but made everything turn upon hard thinking and perpetual working and exercise of the mind.

(Francis Bacon 1620)

The whole of science is nothing more than a refinement of everyday thinking.   (Albert Einstein 1936)

Science is self-conscious commonsense.

(W.V. Quine 1960)

Contents

Acknowledgements

This book has taken us somewhat longer to write than we initially anticipated, but it would have taken even longer without the aid and encouragement of numerous other people. We thank the following colleagues for much help in clarifying our ideas: Sara Delamont, Anne Murcott, and other members of the Ethnography Group in the Department of Sociology, University College, Cardiff; Andy Hargreaves, Phil Strong, Peter Woods, and members of the Ethnography Research Group, The Open University. We must also express our gratitude to Meryl Baker, Stella Riches, Myrtle Robins, and Lilian Walsh for typing (and retyping!) various drafts of the manuscript.

Preface

We began thinking about this book while working together on some materials for an Open University course on Research Methods in Education and the Social Sciences. It seemed to us that within sociology in particular ethnography was in great danger of becoming ossified into a narrow and insular tradition, cut off from mainstream social science. Most ethnography texts have presented it as a distinct paradigm in conflict with, or at best paralleling, other theoretical and methodological approaches.

For us, this represents a betrayal of the spirit of ethnography, of what in this book we have come to call the principle of reflexivity. Ethnography is simply one of the several research methods available to social scientists; one that, like the others, has important strengths but also certain characteristic weaknesses. Of course, ethnography has come to be associated with some distinctive methodological ideas, such as the importance of understanding the perspectives of the people under study, and of observing their activities in everyday life, rather than relying solely on their accounts of this behaviour or experimental simulations of it. However, these ideas are not the only important methodological principles in social research, nor do they privilege ethnography over other methods in any absolute way. While it is tempting to react against the tendency of some methodologists to treat ethnography as outside science by constructing an 'alternative paradigm', which places it at the centre and banishes these other methods to the margins, this is a misguided response. It claims too much, while yet conceding ground to those who seek to identify science exclusively with experimentation and quantification. Methods must be selected according to purposes; general claims about the superiority of one technique over another have little force.

In writing this book we have sought to steer a course between an abstract, methodological treatise and a practical 'cookbook'. This is because for us methodology and method, like social theory and empirical research, feed into one another. Neither can be discussed effectively in isolation. In the opening chapter we outline some of the different methodological frameworks through which ethnography has been viewed, and spell out the implications of what we take to be the most important feature of social research: its reflexivity, the fact that it is part of the social world it studies. Subsequent chapters focus on more concrete aspects of ethnographic research, advocating and illustrating the reflexive point of view.

In writing this book we have had two rather different audiences in mind. On the one hand, there are practitioners of ethnography, of whatever degree of experience, student and professional. It is to them that our argument about the fruitfulness of thinking about ethnography in terms of reflexivity, rather than the more common framework of naturalism, has been primarily directed. At the same time, we have tried to write a book that is accessible to those with little or no knowledge of ethnographic techniques, though such readers might be well advised to begin at Chapter 2 and read the first chapter later (for example after Chapter 9). In this way the methodological questions tackled in Chapter 1 can be placed in their proper context.

1

What is ethnography?

Over the last few years there has been a growth of interest in ethnography among researchers in many different fields, both theoretical and practical. This stems largely from a disillusionment with the quantitative methods that have for long held the dominant position in most of the social sciences. However, it is in the nature of opposition movements that their cohesion is more negative than positive: everyone agrees, more or less, on what must be opposed, but there is less agreement on the nature of the alternative. Thus, across the numerous fields in which ethnography, or something very like it, has come to be proposed, one finds considerable diversity in prescription and practice. There is disagreement as to whether ethnography's distinctive feature is the elicitation of cultural knowledge (Spradley 1980), the detailed investigation of patterns of social interaction (Gumperz 1981), or holistic analysis of societies (Lutz 1981). Sometimes ethnography is portrayed as essentially descriptive, or perhaps as a form of story-telling (Walker 1981); occasionally, by contrast, great emphasis is laid on the development and testing of theory (Glaser and Strauss 1967; Denzin 1978).

As will become clear later, for us ethnography (or participant observation, a cognate term) is simply one social research method, albeit a somewhat unusual one, drawing as it does on a wide range of sources of information. The ethnographer participates, overtly or covertly, in people's daily lives for an extended period of time, watching what happens, listening to what is said, asking questions; in fact collecting whatever data are available to throw light on the issues with which he or she is concerned.

In many respects ethnography is the most basic form of social research. Not only does it have a very long history (Wax 1971), but it also bears a close resemblance to the routine ways in which people make sense of the world in everyday life. Some commentators regard this as its basic strength, others see it as a fundamental weakness. Ethnography has sometimes been dismissed as quite inappropriate to social science, on the grounds that the data and findings it produces are 'subjective', mere idiosyncratic impressions that cannot provide a solid foundation for rigorous scientific analysis. Others argue that only through ethnography can the meanings that give form and content to social processes be understood. 'Artificial' methods such as experiments and survey interviews are rejected on the grounds that these are incapable of capturing the meaning of everyday human activities. Indeed, the very notion of a science of social life explaining human behaviour in causal terms may be rejected.

All social researchers feel the tension between conceptions of science modelled on the practices of natural science on the one hand, and ideas about the distinctiveness of the social world and the implications of this for how it should be studied on the other. Often this tension is presented as a choice between two conflicting paradigms (Wilson 1971; Johnson 1975; Schwartz and Jacobs 1979). While the names given to these paradigms often differ, there is considerable overlap in content among the various accounts. Following much precedent we shall call these paradigms 'positivism' and 'naturalism'; the former privileging quantitative methods, the latter promoting ethnography as the central, if not the only legitimate, social research method.

In our view, statements about paradigms are best viewed as attempts to reconstruct the logic-in-use (Kaplan 1964) of social research. From this point of view, and especially as regards ethnography, neither positivism nor naturalism is entirely satisfactory. Indeed, in our view they share a fundamental misconception: they both maintain a sharp distinction between social science and its object. We shall try to show that once one recognizes the reflexive character of social research, that it is part of the world it studies, many of the issues thrown up by the dispute over positivism become easier to resolve, and the specific contribution to be made by ethnography emerges more clearly.

Positivism and naturalism

We shall begin by examining positivism and naturalism and their implications for ethnography. It should perhaps be pointed out, however, that while the ideas we group together under these headings have a certain affinity, we do not pretend that social scientists can be divided straightforwardly into two groups on this basis. Indeed, even those whose work we cite as exemplifying one or another feature of the two perspectives by no means always adhere to the perspective *in toto*. Rather than produce straightforward descriptions of the methodological views of particular groups of social scientists, we have sought to capture two influential trends in thinking about the nature of social science in general, and of ethnography in particular. We shall use these throughout the book as benchmarks to fix our own position.

Positivism has a long history in philosophy, but it reached its apogee in the 'logical positivism' of the 1930s and 1940s (Kolakowski 1972). This movement had a considerable influence upon social scientists, notably in promoting the status of experimental and survey research and the quantitative forms of analysis associated with them. Where earlier, in both sociology and social psychology, qualitative and quantitative techniques had generally been used side by side, often by the same researcher, there was now a tendency for distinct methodological traditions to be formed and for those legitimated by positivism to become dominant. In these disciplines the distinction between qualitative and quantitative methods gradually metamorphosed into an epistemological chasm.

Today, the term 'positivism' is used in a confusing variety of ways. Indeed, in the last ten years, among social scientists, it has become little more than a term of abuse. For present purposes the major tenets of positivism can be outlined as follows (for more detailed discussions see Keat and Urry 1975; Giddens 1979; and Cohen 1980):

1. *Physical science, conceived in terms of the logic of the experiment, is the model for social research.* While positivists do not claim that all the methods of the physical sciences are the same, they do argue that these share a common logic. This is the logic of the experiment where quantitatively measured variables are manipulated in order to identify the relationships among them. This logic, it is argued, is the defining feature of science.

2. *Universal laws.* Positivism has come to adopt a characteristic conception of explanation, usually termed the 'covering law' model. Here events are explained in deductive fashion by appeal to universal laws that posit regular relationships between variables held to obtain across all circumstances. However, it is the statistical version of this model, whereby the relationships have only a high *probability* of applying across all circumstances, that has generally been adopted by social scientists and this has encouraged great concern with sampling procedures, especially in survey research. Given this model, a premium is placed on the generalizability of findings.

3. *Neutral observation language.* Finally, epistemological and/or ontological priority is given to phenomena that are directly observable; any appeal to intangibles runs the risk of being dismissed as metaphysical nonsense. Scientific theories must be founded upon – tested by appeal to – descriptions that simply correspond to the state of the world, involving no theoretical assumptions and thus being beyond doubt. This foundation could be sense data, as in traditional empiricism, or as with later versions, the realm of the 'publicly observable': the movement of physical objects, such as mercury in a thermometer, which can be easily agreed upon by all observers. Because observation in the social world is rarely as straightforward as reading a thermometer, this concern with a theoretically neutral

observation language has led to great emphasis being given to the standardization of procedures of observation. This is intended to facilitate the achievement of measurements that are stable across observers. If measurement is reliable in this sense, it is argued, it provides a sound, theoretically neutral base upon which to build.

Central to positivism, then, is a certain conception of scientific method, modelled on the natural sciences, and in particular on physics (Toulmin 1972). Method here is concerned with the testing of theories. A sharp distinction is drawn between the context of discovery and the context of justification (Reichenbach 1938 and 1951). It is the procedures employed in the latter that are held to mark science off from commonsense, the aim being to replace the latter with a body of scientific knowledge.

The most important feature of scientific theories is that they are open to, and subjected to, test: they can be confirmed, or at least falsified. This process of testing involves comparing what the theory says should occur under certain circumstances with what actually does occur; in short comparing it with 'the facts' (Goode and Hatt 1952). These facts are collected by means of methods that, like the facts they collect, are regarded as theory-neutral; otherwise, it is assumed, they could not provide a test of the theory. In particular, every attempt is made to eliminate the effects of the observer by developing an explicit, standardized set of experimental or interview procedures. This allows replication by others so that an assessment of the reliability of the findings can be made (Moser and Kalton 1971). In survey research, for example, the behaviour of interviewers is specified down to the wording of questions and the order in which they are asked. In experiments the behaviour of the experimenter and the instructions he or she gives to subjects are closely specified. If it can be ensured that each experimental subject or survey respondent in a study and its replications is faced with the same set of stimuli, then, it is argued, their responses will be commensurable. Where such explicit and standardized procedures are not employed, as in participant observation, then, so the argument goes, it is impossible to know how to interpret the responses since one has no idea what they are responses to. Such research, it is claimed, can do no more than speculate about causal relationships since no basis for testing hypotheses is available.

In reaction against mounting positivist criticism over the last forty years, ethnographers have developed an alternative view of the proper nature of social research, often termed 'naturalism' (Blumer 1969; Lofland 1967; Matza 1969; Denzin 1971; Schatzman and Strauss 1973; Guba 1978; but see also Williams 1976).

Naturalism proposes that, as far as possible, the social world should be studied in its 'natural' state, undisturbed by the researcher. Hence, 'natural', not 'artificial' settings like experiments or formal interviews, should be the primary source of data. Furthermore, the research must be carried out in ways that are sensitive to the nature of the setting. A key element of naturalism is the demand that the social researcher adopt an attitude of 'respect' or 'appreciation' toward the social world. In Matza's words, naturalism is 'the philosophical view that remains true to the nature of the phenomenon under study' (1964:5). This is counterposed to the positivists' primary and prior commitment to a conception of scientific method reconstructed from the experience of natural scientists:

> 'Reality exists in the empirical world and not in the methods used to study that world; it is to be discovered in the examination of that world . . . Methods are mere instruments designed to identify and analyze the obdurate character of the empirical world, and as such their value exists only in their suitability in enabling this task to be done. In this fundamental sense the procedures employed in each part of the act of scientific inquiry should and must be assessed in terms of whether they respect the nature of the empirical world under study – whether what they signify or imply to be the nature of the empirical world is actually the case.'
>
> (Blumer 1969:27-8)

A first requirement of social research according to this view, then, is fidelity to the phenomena under study, not to any particular set of methodological principles, however strongly supported by philosophical arguments. Moreover, social phenomena are regarded as quite distinct in character from natural phenomena. Here naturalism draws on a wide range of philosophical and sociological ideas: symbolic interactionism, phenomenology, hermeneutics, linguistic philosophy, and ethnomethodology. From very different starting points these various traditions argue that the social world cannot be understood in terms of causal relationships or by the subsumption of social events under universal laws. This is because human actions are based upon, or infused by, social meanings: intentions, motives, attitudes, and beliefs. Thus, for example, at the heart of symbolic interactionism is a rejection of the stimulus-response model of human behaviour which is built into the methodological arguments of positivism. In the view of interactionists, people *interpret* stimuli, and these interpretations, continually under revision as events unfold, shape their actions. The same physical stimulus can mean different things to different people and, indeed, to the same person at different times.

On this argument, using standardized methods in no way ensures the commensurability of the data produced. In fact quite the reverse occurs. Interpretations of the same set of experimental instructions or interview questions will undoubtedly vary among people and across occasions. According to naturalism, in order to understand people's behaviour we must use an approach that gives us access to the meanings that guide that behaviour. Fortunately, the capacities we have developed as social actors can give us such access. As participant observers we can learn the culture or subculture of the people we are studying. We can come to interpret the world in the same way as they do.

The need to learn the culture of those we are studying is most obvious in the case of societies other than our own. Here, not only may we not know *why* people do what they do, often we do not even know *what* they are doing. We are in much the same position as Schutz's (1964) stranger. Schutz notes that in the weeks and months following the immigrant's arrival in the host society, what he or she previously took for granted as knowledge about that society turns out to be unreliable if not obviously false. In addition, areas of ignorance previously of no importance come to take on great significance, overcoming them being necessary for the pursuit of important goals, perhaps even for the stranger's very survival in the new environment. In the process of learning how to participate in social situations in the new society, the stranger gradually acquires an inside knowledge of it, which supplants his or her previous 'external' knowledge. Schutz argues that by virtue of being forced to come to understand the culture of the host society in this way, the stranger acquires a certain objectivity not available to culture members. The latter live inside the culture, quite unable to see it as anything but a reflection of 'how the world is'. They are not conscious of the fundamental assumptions, many of which are distinctive to that culture, that shape their vision.

As Schutz points out, the experience of the stranger is not restricted to those moving to live in a different society. Movement among groups within a single society can produce the same effects, though generally in a milder form. According to the naturalist account, the value of ethnography as a social research method is founded upon the existence of such variations in cultural patterns across and within societies, and their significance for understanding social processes. Ethnography exploits the capacity that any social actor possesses for learning new cultures, and the objectivity to which this process gives rise. Even where he or she is researching a familiar group or setting, the participant observer is required to treat it as 'anthropologically strange' in an effort to make explicit the assumptions he or she takes for granted as a culture member. In this way the culture is turned into an object available for study. Through marginality, in perspective and perhaps also in social position, naturalism proposes that it is possible to construct an account of the culture under investigation that captures it as external to, and independent of, the researcher; in other words, as a natural phenomenon. In fact, the *description* of cultures becomes the primary goal. The search for universal laws is rejected in favour of detailed descriptions of the concrete experience of life within a particular culture and of the social rules or patterns that constitute it. Attempts to go beyond this, to explain particular cultural forms, are discouraged. As Denzin (1971:168) notes 'the naturalist resists schemes or models which over-simplify the complexity of everyday life'.

In short, then, naturalism presents ethnography as the pre-eminent if not exclusive social research method. This is because any account of human behaviour requires that we understand the social meanings that inform it. People interpret stimuli in terms of such meanings, they do not respond merely to the physical environment. Such understanding requires that we learn the culture of those we are studying. This cannot be done by following standardized procedures; it is a natural process analogous to the experience of any stranger learning the culture of a group. The task becomes cultural description; anything more is rejected as imposing the researcher's own arbitrary and simplistic categories on a complex reality. The centrality of meaning also has the consequence that people's behaviour can only be understood in context. For this reason 'natural' settings must be investigated: we cannot understand the social world by studying artificial simulations of it in experiments or interviews. To restrict the investigation of social behaviour to such settings is to discover only how people behave in experimental and interview situations.

Problems with naturalism

The origins of the contrasting positions on the nature of social research we have outlined can be traced back as far as differences in view between Plato and Aristotle (von Wright 1971; Levy 1981). However, it is only in the last fifty years that these ideas have generated distinct research traditions within some social science disciplines. Nineteenth-century investigators, such as Mayhew (1861), LePlay (1879), and Booth (1902–3), treated quantitative and qualitative techniques as complementary. Even the sociologists of the Chicago School, often represented as thoroughly interactionist in outlook and arch-exponents of participant observation, employed both 'case-study' and 'statistical' methods. While there were recurrent debates among them regarding the relative advantages and uses of the two sorts of technique, there was general agreement on the value of both (Harvey 1982). It was only later, with the rapid development of statistical methods and the growing influence of positivist philosophy, that survey research came to be regarded by some of its practitioners as a self-sufficient methodological tradition. (In social psychology the process started rather earlier and the experiment became even more dominant.)

Within sociology, naturalism emerged as a reaction against the development of the survey research tradition, the construction of an alternative paradigm designed to protect ethnography and other qualitative techniques from the positivist critique. The pioneer in the 1940s and 1950s was Herbert Blumer (Blumer 1969), while in the 1960s the trend was strengthened by the renaissance of interpretive sociology. Even in anthropology, where ethnography has always been the staple research method, a similiar, if milder, tendency to the establishment of distinct research traditions can be found (Pelto and Pelto 1978). In social psychology it is only relatively recently that the dominance of the experiment has been seriously threatened (Harré and Secord 1972; Cronbach 1975; Rosnow 1981).

Undoubtedly, many of the naturalists' criticisms of positivism are well-founded. Indeed, the force of some of them has been recognized by experimentalists and survey researchers themselves. The serious problems involved in drawing inferences from responses under experimental conditions, or from what is said in interviews, to what people do in everyday life, have come to be listed under the heading of 'ecological validity' (Brunswik 1956; Bracht and Glass 1968). In most of the physical sciences the generalizability of findings across time and space presents few problems. Chemical substances, for example, do not usually behave differently inside and outside the walls of laboratories. However, this seems to be a serious problem in the study of human behaviour. As a little reflection on everyday life makes clear, people do behave, and are expected to behave, differently according to context (Deutscher 1973).

One aspect of the problem of ecological validity – the effects of researchers and the procedures they use on the responses of the people studied – has been subjected to considerable investigation (Orne 1962; Rosenthal 1966; Hyman 1954; Sudman 1974; Schuman 1982). Similarly, recognition of the difficulties involved in interpreting the meaning of people's responses has led to calls for the extension of pilot work of a broadly ethnographic kind in surveys and of 'unstructured' debriefing interviews on experiments. There have even been calls for participant observation to be used as a supplement or complement to these methods (Crowle 1976).

Of course, those working in the experimental and survey traditions do not usually draw the same conclusions from naturalist criticisms as would the naturalist. They are understandably reluctant to abandon experiments and surveys in favour of exclusive reliance on ethnography. Even less are they inclined to accept naturalism's rejection of causal explanation, and in our view they are quite correct in this. While many of them have yet to realize the full implications of what is valid in naturalism, they are certainly wise not to embrace it *in toto*.

Naturalists are right to point to the dangers of drawing inferences from what people say and do in research settings to what they do in everyday settings, but the problem of ecological validity is more subtle than they suppose. Not only are 'artificial' settings by no means *necessarily* ecologically unrepresentative in relevant respects, but also the results of research carried out in 'natural' settings may be ecologically invalid too. Owing to the influence that a participant observer may have on the setting studied, and/or the effects of temporal cycles within the setting (Ball 1983), the conclusions he or she draws from the data are by no means necessarily valid for that setting at other times. For similar reasons, findings produced by participant observation in one setting may not be true for other settings of 'the same type'.

At a deeper level, the very notion of 'natural' and 'artificial' settings is misleading. Even to make this distinction is to take the positivists' rhetoric for reality, to treat them as if they really had succeeded in becoming Martians, viewing society from outside (Davis 1973). 'Artificial' settings set up by researchers are still part of society. Indeed, the real force of the naturalist critique of experiments and survey interviews is precisely that they are social occasions subject to all those processes of symbolic interpretation and social interaction to be found elsewhere in society, and which threaten constantly to undermine positivist attempts to manipulate variables.

This ambivalence on the part of naturalism over the nature of 'artificial' settings is a symptom of a general problem. It reflects a conflict between the account of social research it presents, bordering on a naive realism, and its view of social actors, derived from symbolic interactionism and other forms of interpretive sociology.

Where positivism stresses hypothesis-testing, and in particular the role of 'crucial experiments', naturalism portrays research as a process of exploration. There is a strong parallel here with the views of some early natural scientists:

> 'In the early days of science, it was believed that the truth lay all around us . . . was there for the taking . . . waiting, like a crop of corn, only to be harvested and gathered in. The truth would make itself known to us if only we would *observe* nature with that wide-eyed and innocent perceptiveness that mankind is thought to have possessed in those Arcadian days before the Fall . . . before our senses became dulled by prejudice and sin. Thus the truth is there for the taking only if we can part the veil of prejudice and preconception and *observe things as they really are. . . .*'
>
> (Medawar 1979:70)

Rather than importing methods from the physical sciences, naturalism argues, we must adopt an approach that respects the nature of the social world, which allows it to reveal its nature to us. This argument sometimes takes on a political dimension because the objects under investigation in social research are people who have their own views about the world, views that through their actions also shape the character of that world. Interactionist theory notes how some powerful groups are able to impose their 'definitions of reality' on others, and this analysis is applied to social research itself, the conclusion being drawn that science should not assist in the oppression of people in this way. In response to this the research task comes to be defined as understanding the perspectives of social actors, and in particular those of 'underdogs' (Becker 1967; Gouldner 1968).

While forming a useful antidote to positivism's preoccupation with hypothesis-testing, this inductivist methodology is fundamentally misconceived. After all, how can we discover the nature of the social world without employing some method? Indeed, is not discovering the nature of social phenomena precisely the goal of social science? While some methods may be more structured and selective than others, all research, however exploratory, involves selection and interpretation. Even in a very small-scale setting we could not begin to describe everything, and any description we do produce is inevitably based on inferences. Thus, for example, when setting out to describe a culture, we operate on the basis of the assumption that there are such things as cultures, and have some ideas about what they are like; and we select out for analysis the aspects of what is observed that we judge to be 'cultural'. While there may be nothing wrong with such cultural description, the kind of empiricist methodology enshrined in naturalism renders the theory implicit and thus systematically discourages its development and testing.

One of the most significant assumptions built into naturalism is that all perspectives and cultures are rational. Understanding a culture becomes the first requirement and any attempt to explain it in terms of material interests or ideological distortion is regarded as incompatible with such understanding. Here the quite different issues of intelligibility and validity are confused. Views do not have to be true to be intelligible, though of necessity we do assume in all science that the truth is intelligible. Here, naturalism takes over the common, but erroneous, view that only false beliefs can be explained sociologically, and in this case the outcome is a thoroughgoing relativism. While the usual consequence of relativism – the erosion of any possibility of knowledge – is avoided, the cost is nevertheless very high: social research is limited to cultural description. Anything more would imply that the cultures under study were false, being the product of social causation rather than of cultures members actively constructing reality.

This is a paradoxical conclusion. While culture members freely and legitimately engage in checking claims against facts and frequently employ causal explanations to account for one another's behaviour, the social scientist is debarred from this on the grounds that it would 'distort reality'. Naturalism's escape from relativism is secured, then, by applying quite different theories to the way in which social researchers on the one hand and culture members on the other make sense of the social world. The restriction placed on social research limiting it to cultural description serves to keep these two theories apart, to prevent them from coming into collision.

What we have here, in effect, is the retention of the distinction between science and commonsense that lies at the heart of positivism. While naturalism conceptualizes both science and commonsense in very different ways and reverses their status and power, the distinction nevertheless remains. It is a distinction that has little to recommend it, however. It is the social scientists' equivalent of that between professional and lay knowledge adopted by many occupations. Of course, the question of who is judged a professional and who a layperson is relative to a particular occupation, but the contrast between science and commonsense, like other devices used by professionals to highlight their expertise against a background of lay ignorance, obscures that relativity. Indeed, the distinction between science and commonsense, whether used by positivism or naturalism, tends to imply that science is quite separate from society and that scientists, *qua* scientists, are quite different from other people.

Reflexivity

The distinction between science and common-sense, between the activities of the researcher and those of the researched, lies at the heart of both positivism and naturalism. It is this that leads to their joint obsession with eliminating the effects of the researcher on the data. For one, the solution is the standardization of research procedures; for the other it is direct experience of the social world, in extreme form the requirement that ethnographers 'surrender' themselves to the cultures they wish to study (Wolff 1964; Jules-Rosette 1978). Both positions assume that it is possible, in principle at least, to isolate a body of data uncontaminated by the researcher, either by turning him or her into an automaton or by making him or her a neutral vessel of cultural experience. However, searches for empirical bedrock of this kind are futile; all data involve theoretical assumptions (Hanson 1958).

The first and most important step towards a resolution of the problems raised by positivism and naturalism is to recognize the reflexive character of social research: that is, to recognize that we are part of the social world we study (Gouldner 1970; Borhek and Curtis 1975; and Hammersley 1982b). This is not a matter of methodological commitment, it is an existential fact. There is no way in which we can escape the social world in order to study it; nor, fortunately, is that necessary. We cannot avoid relying on 'common-sense' knowledge nor, often, can we avoid having an effect on the social phenomena we study. There is, though, as little justification for rejecting all common-sense knowledge out of hand as there is for treating it as all 'valid in its own terms': we have no external, absolutely conclusive standard by which to judge it. Rather, we must work with what knowledge we have, while recognizing that it may be erroneous and subjecting it to systematic inquiry where doubt seems justified. Similarly, instead of treating reactivity merely as a source of bias, we can exploit it. How people respond to the presence of the researcher may be as informative as how they react to other situations.

However distinctive the purposes of social science may be, the methods it employs are merely refinements or developments of those used in everyday life. This is obvious in the case of ethnography, and perhaps also in the historian's use of documents (Barzun and Graff 1970), but it is equally true of other methods. As a 'structured conversation', the interview is by no means unique to social research. While the journalistic interview, the social work interview, the market research interview, and the social science interview each carry distinctive features, they are clearly overlapping varieties of a single interactional format. The same applies, if perhaps less obviously, to the experiment. While few people apart from scientists use laboratory experiments, the general device of experimentation is widespread. As Medawar (1979:69) explains, 'in the original Baconian sense, an experiment is a contrived, as opposed to a natural experience or happening – is a consequence of "trying things out" '. Experiments are questions put to the world: 'what would happen if . . .?' Such experimentation is common in everyday life and the 'genuine' laboratory experiment is simply a refinement of this. Furthermore, experimentation is founded upon the more basic principle of the testing of hypotheses through comparison of cases. It is predictions that are tested, but these need not even relate to future events, let alone to those that are open to manipulation by the researcher. They are predictions only in the sense that they antecede the researcher's knowledge of their truth (Reilly 1970).

We are arguing, then, that the testing of hypotheses is by no means restricted to science. And, indeed, the role of hypothesis-testing has been noted in a variety of areas, including perception (Gregory 1970) and language learning (Chomsky 1968). It even plays a major role in the process that naturalism places at the very˙ heart of social research: understanding the actions of others. In observing people's behaviour we derive hypotheses from our cultural knowledge to describe and explain their actions, and we test these out against further information. Thus, for example, if we know something about school classrooms we can guess that a pupil raising his or her hand may be indicating that he or she is offering to answer a teacher's question, volunteering to do some chore, or owning up to some misdemeanour. To find out which of these applies, or whether some other description is more appropriate, we have to investigate the context in which the action occurs; that is, we have to generate possible meanings from the culture for surrounding or other apparently relevant actions. Having done that, we must then compare the possible meanings for each action and decide which form the most plausible underlying pattern. Thus, to take a simple example, if the teacher has just asked a question, we might conclude that the pupil is offering to provide the answer. If, however, the teacher chooses someone else to answer who successfully provides an answer and yet the original pupil keeps his or her hand up, we might suspect that the original intention had not been to answer the question but that he or she has something else to say. However, it may be that the pupil is dreaming and has not realized the question has been answered, or it may be that he or she thinks the answer provided was incorrect or has something to add to it. These alternative hypotheses can, of course, be tested by further observations and perhaps also by asking the pupil involved.

The moral to be drawn is that all social research takes the form of participant observation: it involves participating in the social world, in whatever role, and reflecting on the products of that participation. Irrespective of the method employed, it is not fundamentally different from other forms of practical everyday activity, though of course it is closer in character to some than to others. As participants in the social world we are still able, at least in anticipation or retrospect, to observe our activities 'from the outside' as objects in the world. Indeed, it is this capacity that allows us to co-ordinate our actions. While there are differences in purpose and perhaps also in refinement of method, science does not employ cognitive equipment of an essentially different kind from that available to non-scientists.

The fact of reflexivity has some important methodological implications, it seems to us. For one thing, it makes implausible attempts to found social research upon epistemological foundations independent of common-sense knowledge. As Rescher (1978:20) notes, the search for 'absolutely certain, indefeasible, crystalline truths, totally beyond the possibility of invalidation . . . represents one of the great quixotic quests of modern philosophy'. This is a view that corresponds closely to the 'critical commonsensism' of Peirce (Reilly 1970; Almeder 1980).

The same argument counts against efforts to set up alternative social research paradigms founded upon contrasting epistemological or ontological assumptions. It leads us to view social science as sharing much in common with natural science while yet treating both as merely the advance guard of common-sense knowledge. If paradigms play an important role in science, their character is almost certainly less all-encompassing than Kuhn and some of those who have taken up his ideas often suggest (Keat and Urry 1975). Moreover, differences in view about the nature of social research are merely reconstructions of its logic; they are hypotheses subject to evaluation against the evidence currently available and against further evidence that will become available in the future. As hypotheses, they must not be treated as matters of ultimate commitment even if, for the purposes of practical scientific work, they are taken as true until further notice.

Reflexivity has implications for the *practice* of social research too. Rather than engaging in futile attempts to eliminate the effects of the researcher, we should set about understanding them; a point that Schuman has recently made in relation to social surveys.

'The basic position I will take is simple: artifacts are in the mind of the beholder. Barring one or two exceptions, the problems that occur in surveys are opportunities for understanding once we take them seriously as facts of life. Let us distinguish here between the simple survey and the scientific survey. . . . The simple approach to survey research takes responses literally, ignores interviewers as sources of influence, and treats sampling as unproblematic. A person who proceeds in this way is quite likely to trip and fall right on his artifact. The scientific survey, on the other hand, treats survey research as a search for meaning, and ambiguities of language and of interviewing, discrepancies between attitude and behaviour, even problems of non-response, provide an important part of the data, rather than being ignored or simply regarded as obstacles to efficient research.'

(Schuman 1982:23)

In short, 'what is an artifact if treated naively reflects a fact of life if taken seriously' (1982:24). In order to understand the effects of the research and of research procedures, we need to compare data in which the level and direction of reactivity varies. Once we abandon the idea that the social character of research can be standardized out or avoided by becoming a 'fly on the wall' or a 'full participant', the role of the researcher as active participant in the research process becomes clear. He or she is the research instrument *par excellence*. The fact that behaviour and attitudes are often not stable across contexts and that the researcher may play an important part in shaping the context becomes central to the analysis. Indeed, it is exploited for all it is worth. Data are not taken at face value, but treated as a field of inferences in which hypothetical patterns can be identified and their validity tested out. Different research strategies are explored and their effects compared with a view to drawing theoretical conclusions. What is involved here is the adoption of an experimentalist mentality, in the general sense outlined earlier. Theories are made explicit and full advantage taken of any opportunities to test their limits and to assess alternatives. Such a view contrasts sharply with the image of social research projected by naturalism, though it is much closer to other models of ethnographic research such as 'grounded theorizing' (Glaser and Strauss 1967), 'analytic induction' (Cressey 1950; Denzin 1978), and the strategy model to be found alongside naturalism in the work of Schatzman and Strauss (1973).

The third and final conclusion we wish to draw from reflexivity is that the theories we develop to explain the behaviour of the people we study should also, where relevant, be applied to our own activities as researchers and should aid the development of research strategies. The first step required for this – the collection of data about the research process – has been under way since Whyte added his methodological appendix to *Streetcorner Society* in 1955 (Whyte 1981). Recently, though, this trend has become stronger, and a large number of research biographies have appeared in the last ten or twelve years. The subsequent stage of applying existing theories or developing new ones to make sense of this data has, however, hardly begun in a systematic way (though see, for example, Berreman 1962 and Martin 1981). We shall try to illustrate the potentialities of this at various points throughout this book.

Having argued that social research shares much more in common with other kinds of social activity than is customarily assumed, it is clearly also important for us to say where we think its distinctiveness lies. We must ask what the purpose of social research is, or, as Garfinkel (1981:vii) puts it, 'if social science is the answer, what is the question?'

We have seen that positivism and naturalism address this issue in very different ways. For positivism it is the discovery of universal laws, or at least explanations of particular phenomena framed in terms of universal laws, that is the goal. For naturalism, on the other hand, the only legitimate task is cultural description.

In our view the development and testing of theory is the distinctive function of social theory; it is this that marks it off from journalism and literature, even though it shares much in common with these other pursuits (Strong 1982). Moreover, the idea of relationships between variables that, given certain conditions, hold across all circumstances seems essential to the very idea of theory (Willer 1967). Quantification, as an aid to precision, goes along with this too; though this is not to excuse the indiscriminate quantification that positivism has sometimes encouraged.

Nevertheless, in several important respects the positivist

model is misleading and naturalism instructive. For one thing, we would want to insist that the mere establishment of a relationship among variables, while providing a basis for prediction, does not constitute a theory. A theory must include reference to mechanisms or processes by which the relationship among the variables identified is generated. Moreover, such reference must be more than mere speculation, the existence and operation of these 'intervening variables' must be described (Keat and Urry 1975). Equally, while formalized theories are the goal, we must not allow this to blind us to the value of more informal theories, or to regard theorizing as restricted to social scientists. As we noted earlier, there is no clear-cut distinction to be drawn between theory and fact, nor is common-sense knowledge limited to one end of the theoretical–empirical continuum (Kaplan 1964).

However, it is positivism's conception of the research process, of how the goal of theory is to be achieved, that is most deficient. Reliance is placed upon the hypothetico-deductive method in which, as we saw, all the emphasis is given to the testing of theory. Indeed, where theory comes from, or how it is developed, are regarded as unimportant. What is required is that its truth or falsity be ascertained in the most rigorous manner possible.

There has been some disagreement over whether theories can be *proved* valid, and in fact it seems clear that they cannot: there is always the possibility that new facts will appear in the future that will disprove them. The most elegant attempt to resolve this problem is the work of Karl Popper who argues that while theories can never be proven true, they can be falsified since only one contradictory example is required for this (Popper 1972; Magee 1972). On this view the defining feature of science is the attempt to falsify theories. Science proceeds, according to Popper, through the progressive elimination of error.

However, this view makes it very difficult to understand how natural science has been so successful in furthering our understanding of the physical world. As Rescher points out, the idea that the elimination of falsehood results in scientific progress only holds if we assume that there are a limited number of hypotheses to test:

'Once we grant (as Popper time and again insists) that any hypotheses we may actually entertain are but a few fish drawn from an infinite ocean – are only isolated instances of those infinitely many available hypotheses we have not even entertained, none of which are prima facie less meritorious than those we have – then the whole idea of seeking truth by elimination of error becomes pointless. If infinitely many distinct roads issue from the present spot, there is no reason to think that, by eliminating one or two (or n) of these, we come one jot closer to finding the one that leads to the desired destination.'

(Rescher 1978:53–5)

Rescher's argument suggests that we cannot afford to ignore the context of discovery, and indeed he goes on to suggest that there are heuristic procedures available for developing theory.

However, the problem is not simply that an infinite number of hypotheses are available for testing. It seems likely that sociologists *do* make judgements as to the plausibility of particular hypotheses, but we cannot assume, as Peirce (see Rescher 1978) did in the case of the natural sciences, that these will be based on well-founded intuition. Much anthropological and sociological research has been concerned with the way in which beliefs are structured by social processes. Particular emphasis has been placed upon how different groups develop divergent perspectives on the same phenomena and stereotypes of one another. And, of course, if social research is itself part of the social world, we cannot assume that social scientists escape such processes unscathed. Now, there is no implication here that beliefs that are socially produced are necessarily wrong, but the sociology of knowledge does show that the origins of our beliefs, and the sources of the sense of certainty we attach to them, may be different to what we imagine. It also suggests that social scientists must take care not to become straitjacketed by the beliefs that are typical of the social circles in which they move.

The hypothetico-deductive method has also led to the idea that every study must be a test of a hypothesis, as Becker notes in his essay, Life History and the Scientific Mosaic:

'But perhaps the major reason for the relatively infrequent use of [the life history] is that it does not produce the kind of "findings" that sociologists now expect research to produce. As sociology increasingly rigidifies and "professionalizes", more and more emphasis has come to be placed on what we may, for simplicity's sake, call the *single study*. I use the term to refer to research projects that are conceived of as self-sufficient and self-contained, which provide all the evidence one needs to accept or reject the conclusions they proffer, whose findings are to be used as another brick in the growing wall of science – a metaphor quite different than that of the mosaic.'

(Becker 1970:72)

What positivism neglects, then, is the process by which theory is generated and developed, a point made forcefully by Glaser and Strauss (1967) in their attack on 'verificationism'. They demonstrate the importance of the development of theory and the role of systematic comparison in that process. However, in our view, like naturalism, though to a lesser degree, 'grounded theorizing' represents an over-reaction to positivism. At various points in their argument Glaser and Strauss (1967) seem seriously to underrate the importance of testing, some-times implying that 'grounded' theory, once developed, is more or less beyond doubt. Of course, they are correct to recognize that the emerging theory is usually subjected to testing, at least of a weak kind, in the process of development. But systematic and rigorous testing of the developed theory is nevertheless important even though it can never be absolutely conclusive.

In a similar way, Glaser and Strauss also tend to over-react in their rejection of the more descriptive forms of ethnography (see particularly Glaser 1978). Like positivists, they tend to overlook the variety of different functions that research can serve. Indeed, they too seem hooked on the single study model. Description of the perspectives of a particular category or group of people, or of patterns of interaction within a particular type of setting can be extremely valuable, not least because it may open up to challenge the preconceptions that social scientists bring to research. This is made more obvious in the case of 'exotic' societies but the argument also applies, in some ways more strongly, to the study of our own societies.

There are many different layers or circles of cultural

knowledge within any society. Indeed, this is particularly true of modern industrial societies with their complex divisions of labour, multifarious life-styles, ethnic diversity, and deviant communities; and the subcultures and perspectives that maintain, and are generated by, these social divisions. This was, of course, one of the major rationales for Chicago School research. Drawing on the analogy of plant and animal ecology, they set out to document the very different patterns of life to be found in different parts of the city of Chicago, from the 'high society' of the so-called Gold Coast to slum ghettos such as Little Sicily. Later, the same kind of approach came to be applied to the cultures of different occupations and deviant groups, as well as even more diffuse 'social worlds' (Strauss 1978) such as those of art (Becker 1974), surfing (Irwin 1973), or racing (Scott 1968). Describing such 'worlds' tests assumptions and creates theory.

Ethnography as method

Once one begins to recognize the complexity of the scientific enterprise, the different functions that research can serve, and the failings of the single study model, one is in a better position to appreciate the contribution that ethnography can make to social science. It should be clear that we do not regard ethnography as an 'alternative paradigm' to experimental, survey, or documentary research. Rather it is simply one method with characteristic advantages and disadvantages, albeit one whose virtues have been seriously underestimated by many social researchers owing to the influence of positivism.

The value of ethnography is perhaps most obvious in relation to the *development* of theory. Its capacity to depict the activities and perspectives of actors in ways that challenge the dangerously misleading preconceptions that social scientists often bring to research has already been mentioned. Much like Schutz's (1964) stranger, it is difficult for an ethnographer to maintain such preconceptions in the face of extended first-hand contact with the people and settings concerned. Furthermore, while the initial response to such contact may be their replacement by other misconceptions, over time the ethnographer has the opportunity to check out his or her understanding of the phenomena under study. Equally importantly, though, the depiction of perspectives and activities in a setting allows one to begin to develop theory in a way that provides much more evidence of the plausibility of different lines of analysis than is available to the 'armchair theorist', or even the survey researcher or experimentalist.

Also important here is the flexibility of ethnography. Since it does not entail extensive pre-fieldwork design, as social surveys and experiments generally do, the strategy and even direction of the research can be changed relatively easily, in line with changing assessments of what is required by the process of theory construction. As a result, ideas can be quickly tried out and, if promising, followed up. In this way ethnography allows theory development to be pursued in a highly effective and economical manner.

However, the contribution of ethnography is not limited to the phase of theory development. It can also be used to test theory. For example, cases that are crucial for a theory – those where it seems most likely to be proved false – may be examined through ethnography; though this is not always feasible for macro-social theory where the scale of the object under investigation often necessitates survey research. While the fact that, unlike in the experiment, variables cannot be physically manipulated hampers the evaluation of competing hypotheses, it does not rule it out. As we noted earlier, experimentation is itself founded upon the logic of comparison. Moreover, what is lost in terms of the control of variables may be compensated by reduced risk of ecological invalidity. Since it investigates social processes in everyday settings rather than in those set up for the purposes of research, the danger that the findings will apply only to the research situation is generally lessened. In addition, ethnography's use of multiple data sources is a great advantage here. This avoids the risks that stem from reliance on a single kind of data: the possibility that one's findings are method-dependent. The multi-stranded character of ethnography provides the basis for triangulation in which data of different kinds can be systematically compared (see Chapter 8). In our view this is the most effective manner in which reactivity and other threats to validity can be handled.

A good example of the way in which ethnography can be used

to test theory is provided by the work of Hargreaves (1967), Lacey (1970), and Ball (1981) on pupil orientations to school. They argue that the way in which schools differentiate pupils on academic and behavioural criteria, especially via streaming, tracking, and banding, polarizes them into pro- and anti-school subcultures. These subcultures, in turn, shape pupils' behaviour inside and outside school and affect their levels of academic achievement. This theory is tested in examples of three types of secondary school: secondary modern (Hargreaves), grammar school (Lacey), and comprehensive school (Ball). Moreover, in the case of the grammar school, because the pupils entering the school have been strongly committed to school values at their junior schools, a variable at the heart of competing explanations for the process of polarization – home background – is partially controlled. Similarly, in his study of Beachside Comprehensive, Ball examines the effects of a shift from banding to mixed ability grouping, representing a weakening of differentiation, showing that polarization is also weakened. Taken together these studies give us some confidence that the theory is well founded, though they do not provide absolutely conclusive proof. But then no method is able to do that.

Conclusion

We have examined two contrasting reconstructions of the logic of social research and their implications for ethnography. Neither positivism nor naturalism provides an adequate framework for social research. Both neglect its fundamental reflexivity, the fact that we are part of the social world we study, and that there is no escape from reliance on common-sense knowledge and on common-sense methods of investigation. All social research is founded on the human capacity for participant observation. We act in the social world and yet are able to reflect upon ourselves and our actions as objects in that world. By including our own role within the research focus and systematically exploiting our participation in the world under study as researchers, we can develop and test theory without placing reliance on futile appeals to empiricism, of either positivist or naturalist varieties.

Reconstructing our understanding of social research in line

with the implications of its reflexivity also throws light on the function of ethnography. Certainly there is little justification for the view that it represents an alternative paradigm to quantitative research. On the other hand, it has a much more powerful contribution to make to social science than positivism allows. The remainder of this book is devoted to spelling out the implications of reflexivity for ethnographic practice.

2

Research design: problems, cases, and samples

At first blush, the conduct of ethnography is deceptively simple: 'anyone can do it', apparently. Indeed, some authors have reported being given little more research advice than just that before they set out on their fieldwork. Nader, for example, relates how at one time this had become a tradition among North American anthropologists:

> 'Before leaving Harvard I went to see Kluckhohn. In spite of the confidence I had gained from some of my training at Harvard, this last session left me frustrated. When I asked Kluckhohn if he had any advice, he told the story of a graduate student who had asked Kroeber the same question. In response Kroeber was said to have taken the largest, fattest ethnography book off his shelf, and said, "Go forth and do likewise".'
>
> (Nader 1970:98)

Such non-advice seems to rest on the assumption that the conduct of ethnography is unproblematic, and requires little preparation and no special expertise.

One of the reasons for this reluctance to give advice about how to do ethnographic research is awareness of the fact that such research cannot be programmed, that its practice is replete with the unexpected, as any reading of the many published research biographies now available will confirm. When one is carrying out research in settings in which one has little power, and of which one has little previous knowledge, the research cannot be fully designed in the pre-fieldwork phase.

There is, however, another, less legitimate, reason why the advice given to those about to embark upon ethnography is often simply to 'go and do it'. This is the idea, associated with naturalism, that ethnography consists of open-ended observation and description, so that 'research design' is almost superfluous. Here, one useful research strategy is inflated into a paradigmatic approach. Speaking of the study of animal behaviour, Tinbergen (1972:23) remarks that periods of exploratory, intuitive observation are of particular value 'when one feels in danger of getting out of touch with the natural phenomena; of narrowing one's field of vision'. Naturalists in sociology have sometimes appealed to natural history and ethology to legitimate their recommendation of exploratory observation and description (Lofland 1967; Blumer 1969; Speier 1973). It is important to remember, though, that observation in ethology is guided by a relatively well-defined set of assumptions derived from evolutionary theory. Darwin (quoted in Selltiz *et al.* 1959:200) himself remarks at one point: 'How odd it is that anyone should not see that observation must be for or against some view, if it is to be of any service.'

Certainly we must recognize that, much less than other forms of social research, the course of ethnography cannot be predetermined. But this neither eliminates the need for pre-fieldwork preparation nor means that the researcher's behaviour in the field need be haphazard, merely adjusting to events by taking 'the line of least resistance' (Warren 1974). Indeed, we shall argue that research design should be a reflexive process operating throughout every stage of a project.

Foreshadowed problems

Research always begins with some problem or set of issues, from what Malinowski refers to as 'foreshadowed problems':

'Good training in theory, and acquaintance with its latest results is not identical with being burdened with ''preconceived ideas''. If a man sets out on an expedition, determined to prove certain hypotheses, if he is incapable of changing his views constantly and casting them off ungrudgingly under the pressure of evidence, needless to say his work will be worthless. But the more problems he brings with him into the field, the more he is in the habit of moulding his theories according to facts, and of seeing facts in their bearing upon theory, the better he is equipped for the work. Preconceived ideas are pernicious in any scientific work, but foreshadowed problems are the main endowment of a scientific thinker, and these problems are first revealed to the observer by his theoretical studies.'

(Malinowski 1922:8–9)

Sometimes the starting point for research is a well-developed theory from which a set of hypotheses can be derived. Such theories are relatively rare in sociology and anthropology, but perhaps more frequent in social psychology (an example of a participant observation study in this mould is Festinger *et al.* 1956).

Most ethnographic research has been concerned with developing theories rather than with merely testing existing hypotheses, and a number of authors, most notably Glaser and Strauss (1967), have pointed to the advantages to be gained from developing theory through systematic data collection rather than by reliance on 'armchair theorizing'. Nevertheless, as Strauss (1970) himself has shown, considerable progress can sometimes be made in clarifying and developing research problems before fieldwork begins. As an illustration he examines Davis's (1961) research on 'the management of strained interaction by the visibly handicapped':

'Davis's theory is about (1) *strained* (2) *sociable interaction* (3) in *face-to-face* contact between (4) *two persons*, one of whom has a (5) *visible handicap* and the other of whom is (6) *normal* (no visible handicap). . . . The underlined terms in the above sentence begin to suggest what is explicitly or implicitly omitted from Davis's theoretical formulation. The theory is concerned with the visibly (physically) handicapped, not with people whose handicaps are not immedi-

ately visible, if at all, to other interactants. The theory is concerned with interaction between two people (not with more
than two). . . . The interaction occurs in situations termed
"sociable"; that is, the relations between interactants are
neither impersonal nor intimate. Sociable also means interaction prolonged enough to permit more than a fleeting
exchange but not so prolonged that close familiarity
ensues. . . .'

(Strauss 1970:47–8)

Strauss goes on to show that by varying these different elements
of the theory new research questions can be generated.

Often the relevant literature is less developed than in the case
referred to by Strauss, but the absence of detailed knowledge of a
phenomenon or process itself represents a useful starting point
for research. Macintyre (1977) provides an example in her study
of the 'pregnancy careers' of single women:

'Approximately one fifth of all conceptions, and an even
higher proportion of first conceptions, in Britain in the early
1970s were to single women. There were four common outcomes of pregnancy for single women: marriage to the
putative father; induced abortion; remaining single and keeping the baby; and remaining single and giving the baby up for
adoption. It is known that the incidence of these outcomes
has changed from time to time, as have, of course, the relevant social attitudes, social policy and legislation, and these
have been the subject of demographic and historical studies.
*Yet little is known about how these outcomes are reached, or
how these may be affected by social attitudes, policies and
legislation.*'

(Macintyre 1977:9; our emphasis)

Alternatively, the stimulus may be a surprising fact or set of
facts. Thus, Measor (1983) noted that not only did girls tend to
fare worse than boys in science examinations, but that the gap
was even greater in the case of Nuffield science. She set out to
investigate why this was the case through participant observation in Nuffield science lessons and by interviewing both boys
and girls about their attitudes to these lessons.

As this example illustrates, the significance of the initial problem may be not so much theoretical as political or practical, in this case arising from a concern with equality of opportunity for women. Even where the starting point is not current social theory, however, elaboration of the problem soon draws such theory in, as Freilich's work on Mohawk Heroes indicates:

'New Yorkers sometimes read in their newspapers about a unique phenomenon in their midst: the Mohawk Indians who work on the steel structures of various buildings in and around their city. Articles, at times accompanied by pictures of smiling Indians, discuss these ''brave'' and ''sure-footed'' Mohawks. The question of why so many Mohawks work in structural steel is one that is often researched by students enrolled in colleges located in and around New York. In 1956, this problem was, in fact, my first professional research assignment. I used A.F.C. Wallace's paper ''Some Psychological Determinants of Culture Change in an Iroquoian Community'' as the foil in my proposal for research support. Wallace's paper suggested that Mohawks lack a fear of heights, and that this lack of fear explains their involvement with the steel industry. I argued that a negative trait (lack of fear) cannot have specific positive consequences (lead a tribe into steel work). I argued further that there is no functional value in a lack of fear of heights for steel work, and that in actuality the opposite is true: a normal fear of high places leads to caution that saves lives. A more plausible argument seemed to be that Mohawks frequently act *as if* they have no fear of heights. In presenting a subsidiary problem, ''Why these acts of daredevilry?'', I put forth my theoretical belief that socio-cultural factors explain social and cultural phenomena better than do psychological factors. I had a vague notion that Mohawks in steel work represented some kind of cultural continuity. Thus, the questions I posed were (1) why is it good, culturally, for a Mohawk male to be a structural steel worker? and (2) How does such a cultural ''goodness'' relate to Mohawk cultural history?'

(Freilich 1970:185–86)

Social events themselves may also stimulate research, providing an opportunity to explore some unusual occurrence or to test a theory. Notable here are what are sometimes called 'natural experiments': organizational innovations, natural disasters, or political crises that promise to reveal what happens when the limiting factors that normally constrain a particular element of social life are breached. At such times social phenomena that are otherwise taken-for-granted become visibly problematic for the participants themselves, and thus for the observer. Schatzman and Strauss (1955) provide an example in their discussion of the problems of inter-class communication arising subsequent to a tornado. Studying the origins and consequences of organizational innovations is even more common. Ball's (1981) study of Beachside Comprehensive is a recent instance, examining a switch from banding to mixed ability grouping in a secondary school.

Even personal experiences may provide motive and opportunity for research. Once again, though, such experiences are rendered interesting or significant by current theoretical ideas: the stimulus is not intrinsic to the experiences themselves. Good illustrations here are Roth's (1963) work on TB patients, and Kotarba's (1975) work on acupuncturists. (For a collection of essays by other medical sociologists reflecting on their own enforced experience of medical settings, see Davis and Horobin 1977.)

There are no hard and fast rules for deciding how far the initial research problem can be elaborated before the collection of data begins. Exploring the components and implications of a general foreshadowed problem with the help of whatever secondary literature is available is a wise first step. Relevant here are not only research monographs and journal articles but also official reports, journalistic exposés, autobiographies, diaries, and 'non-fiction novels' (see Chapter 6). There comes a point, however, when little more progress can be made without beginning the collection of primary data; though reflection and the use of secondary literature should of course continue beyond that point.

The development of research problems

The aim in the pre-fieldwork phase and in the early stages of data collection is to turn the foreshadowed problems into a set of questions to which a theoretical answer can be given, whether this be a narrative description of a sequence of events, a generalized account of the perspectives and practices of a particular group of actors, or a more abstract theoretical formulation. Sometimes in this process the original problems are transformed or even completely abandoned in favour of others, as Dollard illustrates:

'My original plan was to study the personality of Negroes in the South, to get a few life histories, and to learn something about the manner in which the Negro person grows up. It was far from my wish to make a study of a community, to consider the intricate problem of the cultural heritage of the Negro, or to deal with the emotional structure of a specific small town in the deep South. I was compelled, however, to study the community, for the individual life is rooted in it.

Only a few days of five months in Southerntown had passed before I realized that whites and whiteness form an inseparable part of the mental life of the Negro. He has a white employer, often white ancestors, sometimes white playmates, and he lives by a set of rules which are imposed by white society. The lives of white and Negro people are so dynamically joined and fixed in one system that neither can be understood without the other. This insight put an end to the plan of collecting Negro life histories in a social void.

Negro life histories refer at every point to a total situation, i.e. to Southerntown itself, the surrounding county, the southeastern culture area, and in a strict sense the whole region which is bound to American cotton economy. This observation came as a very unwelcome perception, since it necessitated getting a perspective on the community and the county, and informing myself incidentally on many apparently remote matters. Study of the social context of the lives of Negroes has crowded out the original objective of the research, at least so far as the publication of specific life histories is concerned.'

(Dollard 1937 and 1957:1–2)

Change in research problems stems from several different sources. As with Dollard, it may be discovered that the original formulation of the problem was founded on erroneous assumptions. Equally, it may be concluded that, given the current state of knowledge, the problem is not soluble. Medawar comments:

'Good scientists study the more important problems they think they can solve. It is, after all, their professional business to solve problems, not merely to grapple with them. The spectacle of a scientist locked in combat with the forces of ignorance is not an inspiring one if, in the outcome, the scientist is routed. That is why some of the most important biological problems have not yet appeared on the agenda of practical research.'

(Medawar 1967:7)

Periodically, methodologists rediscover the truth of the old adage that finding the right question to ask is more difficult than answering it (Merton 1959). Much of the effort that goes into theory construction is concerned with formulating and reformulating the research problem in ways that make it more amenable to theoretical solution.

Problems vary in their degree of abstractness. Some, especially those deriving from practical or political concerns, will be 'topical' (Lofland 1976), being concerned with types of people and situations readily identified in everyday language. Others have a more 'generic' cast. Here the researcher is asking questions such as 'Of what abstract sociologically conceived *class* of situation is this particular situation an instance?'; and 'What are the abstract features of this kind of situation?' This distinction between topical and generic research problems is closely related to the distinction between *substantive* and *formal* analyses outlined by Glaser and Strauss:

'By substantive theory, we mean that developed for a substantive, or empirical, area of sociological inquiry, such as patient care, race relations, professional education, delinquency, or research organizations. By formal theory, we mean that developed for a formal, or conceptual, area of sociological inquiry, such as stigma, deviant behaviour, formal organization, socialization, status incongruency, authority and power, reward systems, or social mobility.'

(Glaser and Strauss 1967:32)

In ethnographic research there is frequently a constant interplay between the topical and the generic, or the substantive and the formal. One may begin with some formal analytic notion and seek to extend or refine its range of application in the context of a particular new substantive application. This can be illustrated by reference to the work of Hargreaves, Hester, and Mellor (1975) on deviance in school classrooms. Starting from the formal concepts of 'labelling theory', Hargreaves and his colleagues sought to extend the use of this analytic framework to, and examine its value for, the study of school deviance. They were able to derive from it a sort of 'shopping list' of issues. This list of topics moves the focus of concern from the formal towards the substantive, from the generic towards the topical. Their list reads:

'Rules. What are the rules in schools and classrooms? Which rules are allegedly broken in imputations of deviance? Who makes the rules? Are the rules ever negotiated? How are the rules communicated to members? What justifications are given for the rules, by whom, to whom, and on what occasions? Do teachers and pupils view the rules in the same way? Are some rules perceived as legitimate by some teachers and some pupils? How do members know that certain rules are relevant to (i.e. are "in play" in) a given situation? How do members classify the rules? What differences do members see between different rules? For example, do rules vary in importance?

Deviant acts. How do members link an act to a rule to permit the imputation of deviance? How do teachers know that a pupil has broken a rule? That is, what is the interpretive work undertaken by teachers to permit the categorization of an act as deviant? Similarly, how do pupils know that their acts are deviant?. . .

Deviant persons. How do teachers link deviant acts to persons so that persons are defined as deviant? What is the relationship between different labels? Why is one label used rather than another?. . .

Treatment. What treatments are made by teachers in relation to acts or persons defined as deviants? On what grounds and with what justifications do teachers decide on one treatment rather than another?. . .

Career of the deviant. What is the structure of the career of

the deviant pupil? What are the contingencies of such careers?
How are such careers initiated and terminated?'
(Hargreaves, Hester, and Mellor 1975:23-4)

Such a list of problems clearly draws on the authors' prior
knowledge of sociological work on schools and deviance, and
reflects an interplay between formal and substantive interests.
These questions do not constitute a research hypothesis or set of
hypotheses, nor would they provide a research design as such.
Likewise, one would not expect such a list to be a definitive one:
in some ways it would probably prove to be over-ambitious, and
in others it would probably omit unforeseen problems.

One can also develop research problems by extending the use
of an analytic framework from one substantive area to another.
One of the major perspectives of the study of the Kansas medical
school by Becker *et al.* (1961) is of this sort. They adopt a perspective from industrial sociology – that industrial workers attempt
to set their own 'level and direction of effort' – and apply it to
the topical situation of the medical students who, faced with
overwhelming academic demands, likewise attempt to negotiate manageable levels of effort, and to establish appropriate
directions for their efforts.

Just as one can formulate problems by moving from the formal
to the substantive, so one can move from the substantive to the
formal or generic. This can be illustrated in part from a research
project in which one of us (Atkinson) has been involved.

The project in question has been concerned with the investigation of 'industrial training units', designed to ease the transition from school to working life for 'slow learners'. The research
included a number of strands, including participant observation
in two such industrial units, interviews with a range of officials,
documentary sources, and so on. The project was not simply a
'one-off' case-study, but one of a number of similar pieces of
research being undertaken in Britain. These other projects were
also investigating innovative interventions to facilitate the transition from school.

The formulation of the interests of the research began with
foreshadowed problems that were primarily substantive or
topical in origin. In an exploratory orientation, the research
team began the fieldwork phase with general interests of this

sort: how is the day-to-day work of the unit organized?; how are the students selected and evaluated?; what sort of work do they do, and what sort of work are they being prepared for?

During the course of the fieldwork a number of issues were identified with more precision, and new categories were developed. At the same time, it became apparent that there was a need to formulate these ideas in terms that were more general than their local manifestations in our own project. A more pressing reason for this was the desirability of generating concepts that would permit of principles for, and systematic comparison between, the different research projects in Britain. A research memorandum put the issue in this way:

'During our last meeting . . . we talked about the possibility of developing and working with some general analytic categories. The idea I was putting forward . . . was that evaluation projects were doomed to be little more than one-off, local affairs, unless we were able to work with ideas and frameworks of more general applicability. Such "generalization" would not imply that all projects should work within "the same" research design, or collect "the same" data by "the same" technique. Clearly, particular evaluations must remain sensitive to local conditions and responsive to changing circumstances. Nor should such a suggestion be interpreted as a plea for a straitjacket of predetermined questions and categories. Such categories should only be thought of as "sensitizing" concepts – indicating some broad dimensions for comparison between projects, and for the development of general frameworks to tie together disparate projects and evaluations.'

(Atkinson 1981b)

The issues of comparison and generalization touched on in this memorandum will be developed elsewhere. For the time being we simply wish to illustrate the general rationale for attempting to move from the local to the more generic, in so far as it directs attention towards comparison, and draws on the work of other analysts. We shall not attempt to detail all the ideas drawn on and alluded to in this particular project. The following extracts from the same research memorandum are illustrative of how these ideas were used to categorize some key issues in the research, and to stimulate the posing of further topical questions:

> '*Gatekeepers*. By gatekeepers I mean actors with control over key resources and avenues of opportunity. Such gatekeepers exercise control at and during key phases of the youngster's status passage(s). Such gatekeepers' functions would actually be carried out by different personnel in the different organization settings. . . .
>
> The identification of the general class of "gatekeepers" would then allow us to go on to ask some pertinent questions of a general nature. For instance: What resources do gate-keepers have at their disposal? What perceptions and expectations do gatekeepers have of "clients"? Are these perceptions mutually compatible or are there systematic differences of opinion? Do gatekeepers believe that their expectations of clients are met or not? Do they have an implicit (or even an explicit) model of the "ideal client"?
>
> What is the *information-state* of gatekeepers? For example, what sort of model of the labour market are they operating with? What views of working life do they bring to bear? How accurate are their assessments of the state of local labour markets?
>
> What sort of *routines and strategies* do gatekeepers employ? For instance, what criteria (formal and informal) are used to assess and categorize "clients"? What bureaucratic routines are used (if any)? What record-keeping procedures are used, and how are such data interpreted in practice?'
>
> (Atkinson 1981b)

Closely allied with this outline of 'gatekeepers' as a general sensitizing device, the memorandum also included the following:

> '*Labelling*. This general category clearly overlaps with the gatekeepers' practical reasoning, and with some issues in definitions of client populations.
>
> To what extent is there a danger of self-fulfilling prophecies, as a result of the identification of target populations? To what extent do projects themselves help to crystallise racial, gender or ability categorizations and stereotypes?
>
> Do employers and potential employers operate with stig-

matizing stereotypes? Do projects overcome, or do they help to confirm such stereotypes? What particular aspects of projects and the youngsters do "gatekeepers" such as employers seize on and react to?

Do the youngsters label themselves and each other in accordance with formal or informal labels attached to them?

Are the professionals involved in projects themselves subject to *stigma* in the views of other professionals and agencies?'

(Atkinson 1981b)

Obviously, these extracts from a research memorandum do not constitute even the beginning of an exhaustive analysis for projects aimed at easing the transition to work, or at coping with the problem of youth unemployment. Our reference to it here is an attempt to exemplify one stage in the process whereby ideas are formulated. While many of the questions that are posed here are fairly concrete or topical in content, the general tenor of the document draws attention to generic concepts such as *gatekeepers*, *labelling*, *stigma*, *routines*, *strategies*, *practical reasoning*, and *self-fulfilling prophecies*.

This research memorandum, then, helps to 'freeze' the process of problem formulation during an intermediate stage in a research project. The initial fieldwork has suggested a number of potentially important aspects to be identified more thoroughly, and some potentially useful analytic ideas. Thus, research problems are identified more precisely. At the same time, such identifications permit new research questions to be posed, or for them to be posed more systematically. Hence guidelines for further data collection are also laid down.

One must beware of over-simplifying the distinction between topical and generic levels of analysis. One does not simply progress in a uni-directional way from one to the other. In the conduct of an actual project, one would not expect simply to progress from a series of substantive issues, and end up with one's formal categories or *vice versa*. There will normally be a constant shuttling back and forth between the two analytic modes. Particular substantive issues may suggest affinities with some formal concept that will, in turn, indicate substantive issues as deserving new or further attention, and so forth.

Selecting settings and cases

There is another factor that often plays a significant role in shaping the way in which research problems are developed in ethnography: the nature of the setting chosen for study. This arises because in ethnographic research the development of the research problem is rarely completed before fieldwork begins; indeed, the collection of primary data often plays a key role in that process of development. As a result, though, it is often found that some of the questions into which the foreshadowed problems have become decomposed or transformed are not open to investigation in the setting selected. The researcher is then faced with the choice of either dropping these questions from the investigation or re-starting the research in a setting where they *can* be investigated. While on occasion the importance of a problem may lead to the latter course being adopted, generally researchers stay in the original setting and select problems for investigation in the light of its characteristics. After all, as in the case of Hargreaves, Hester, and Mellor's (1975) work, more questions are usually generated than can be tackled in a single study. Moreover, moving to another setting not only involves further delay and renewed problems of access, but there is also no guarantee that the new setting will turn out to be an appropriate setting in which to investigate the preferred problem. Everett Hughes is reported to have remarked, only half jokingly, that one should select the research problem for which the setting one has chosen is the ideal site!

Whatever their stage of development before data collection begins, the foreshadowed problems will specify a range of types of setting in which research might usefully be carried out. Sometimes, as in the case of research on 'natural experiments' and other kinds of 'opportunistic research' (Riemer 1977), the selection of a setting for study hardly arises. The research problem and the setting are closely bound together. Usually, however, the issue is not so easily resolved. Often, it is advisable to 'case' possible research sites with a view to assessing their suitability, the feasibility of carrying out research there, and how access might best be accomplished should they be selected (Schatzman and Strauss 1973:19). This involves collecting and subjecting to preliminary analysis any documentary evidence available about the setting, interviewing anyone who can be easily contacted who has experience or knowledge of the setting, and perhaps making brief visits to the setting, covertly or overtly.

'Casing the joint' in this fashion may not only provide information about settings in which the research might be carried out, but also feeds into the development and refinement of the research problem. It may be discovered that what had been assumed to be a homogeneous category of people must be broken down into a number of sub-types who have different characteristics and who are likely to be found in very different places. Warren provides an example:

'The first decision that must be made by a researcher who wishes to study the gay community – unless he has unlimited time and money to spend – is *which* gay community he wishes to study: the world of exclusive private gay clubs for businessmen and professionals? or the dope addict transvestites so vividly depicted in *Last Exit To Brooklyn*? or the sado-masochistic leather boys? Any extended preliminary observation will make it objectively obvious that ''the'' gay community is divided – fairly loosely at the boundaries – into a hierarchy linked to some extent with status and class criteria in the ''real'' world.'

(Warren 1972:144)

The role of pragmatic considerations must not be underestimated in the choice of a setting. While by no means absent in hypothesis-testing research, they are likely to play a very important role in research concerned with theory development. This is because here the criteria specifying suitability are usually much less determinate: there is generally a very wide range of relevant settings. As a result, contacts with personnel promising easy access, the scale of the travel costs likely to be involved, and the availability of documentary information, etc. are often major considerations in narrowing down the selection. (See, for example, Fox's 1964 discussion of her choice of Belgium as the site for a study of European medical research.)

Sometimes, the search for an appropriate setting can take unpredictable turns. Dingwall's (1981) account of the development of his work on health visitor training may not be an extreme example. Dingwall recounts that as an undergraduate sociology student he became particularly interested in the 'new sociology of education' (Young 1971; Gorbutt 1972), with its characteristic stress on the sociology of knowledge. His initial idea, therefore, was to attempt to study the socialization of teachers from this theoretical perspective. Having been persuaded against this by a supervisor, Dingwall turned towards nurses as an alternative professional group who might lend themselves to such a study. An approach to a local nursing training school proved negative. (The refusal was couched in terms very familiar to many of us: that as a result of the Briggs Committee everything would shortly be changed, and hence research was inappropriate at that time.) Finally, Dingwall made a successful attempt to gain access to health visitor training, partly through the advice and sponsorship of a staff member who was contributing to the School of Health Visitors' teaching. Dingwall acknowledges that at the time the suggestion was made that he study health visitors, he had 'no idea what a health visitor was'.

It is important, however, not to confuse the choice of a setting with the selection of a case for study. The vocabulary of studying 'fields' and 'settings' is widely used in talking and writing about ethnography. The main source of this tendency to regard natural settings as the object of study is of course naturalism, though it is often traced further back, for example to the Chicago School:

> '[The sociology of Chicago] was nursed as a cartographic exercise, studying Little Sicily, the Jewish ghetto, Polonism, the Gold Coast, the slums, Hobohemia, rooming-house districts and the gangs of the city. Each of these areas was treated as a symbolic world which created and perpetuated a distinctive moral and social organisation. Each was subjected to an interpretative analysis which attempted to reproduce the processes by which that organisation was brought into being. They were collectively identified *natural areas*: "natural" because they were themselves part of the natural evolution and selection which shaped society; because they were different from the structures produced by planning and science, and because they represented a unit which allegedly framed American thinking on social and political life.'
>
> (Rock 1979:92)

In other sociological contexts, too, similar appeals are made to models of relatively self-contained groups or 'communities'. The anthropological tradition has, for instance, tended to lay stress on the investigation of small-scale 'face-to-face' societies and local collectivities (such as 'the village'). This, and the cognate tradition of 'community studies', has often rested on a Gemeinschaft-like view of the local society, emphasizing its internal stability and its relative discreetness.

But settings are not naturally occurring phenomena, they are constituted and maintained through cultural definition and social strategies. Their boundaries are not fixed but shift across occasions, to one degree or another, through processes of redefinition and negotiation.

There is another reason too why it is potentially misleading to talk of 'studying a setting'. As we noted in Chapter 1, it is not possible to give an exhaustive account of any object. In producing descriptions we always rely on theoretical criteria of selection and inference. There is an important sense, then, in which even in the most descriptively oriented study the case investigated is not isomorphic with the setting in which it takes place. A setting is a named context in which phenomena occur that might be studied from any number of angles; a case is those phenomena seen from one particular theoretical angle. Some features of the setting will be given no attention at all, and even those phenomena that are the major focus will be looked at in a way that by no means exhausts their characteristics. Moreover, a setting may contain several cases. Thus, for example, in studying the effects of various kinds of external examinations on secondary school teaching, it will be particular examination courses within the school that constitute the cases under investigation rather than the school as a whole. Conversely, a case may not be contained within the boundaries of a setting, it may be necessary to go outside of the setting to collect information on important aspects of it. In studying gangs among male prisoners (Jacobs 1974), it may be necessary to explore their links with groupings outside if the manner in which they came to be formed and in which they continue to recruit new members is to be understood.

While it may seem innocent enough, the naturalistic conception of studying fields and settings discourages the systematic and explicit selection of aspects of a setting for study, as well as movement outside of it to follow up promising theoretical leads. It is important to remember that the process of identifying and defining the case under study proceeds side by side with the refinement of the research problem and the development of the theory.

One of the limitations often raised in connection with ethnographic work is that because only a single case, or at any rate a small number of cases, is studied, the representativeness of the findings is always in doubt. This is an important point. However, it is a problem that also arises with experimental research and one to which there is no easy answer. While it is true that the more cases studied in which similar results are obtained, the more confident we can be about our conclusions, statistical sampling techniques do not resolve the issue. This is because the universe of cases being sampled is infinite, comprising all the cases that fall within the scope of the theory that have occurred, or will occur in the future. We cannot be sure that a random sample of the cases currently available for study would be representative of this universe. This problem arises from the fact that the claims made by theories are conditionally universal (Willer 1967); they are intended to apply to all circumstances in which the conditions specified in the theory hold.

The study of a large, randomly selected sample of cases is not necessarily the most useful approach, then. Indeed, as we noted in Chapter 1, the selection of critical cases may be more fruitful. But the strategic selection of cases can take other forms too, for example what Glaser and Strauss (1967) call 'theoretical sampling'. As we noted earlier, the primary concern of these authors is the generation and elaboration of theory. They argue that the selection of cases should be designed to generate as many categories and properties of categories as possible and to relate categories to one another. They recommend two complementary strategies: minimizing the differences between cases to highlight basic properties of a particular category; and then subsequently maximizing the differences between cases in order to increase the density of the properties relating to core categories, to integrate categories and delimit the scope of the theory. As an illustration they cite their research on the awareness contexts surrounding patients dying in hospital:

'Visits to the various medical services were scheduled as follows: I wished first to look at services that minimized patient awareness (and so first looked at a premature baby service and then a neurosurgical service where patients were frequently comatose). I wished next to look at dying in a situation where expectancy of staff and often of patients was great and dying was quick, so I observed on an Intensive Care Unit. Then I wished to observe on a service where staff expectations of terminality were great but where the patient's might or might not be, and where dying tended to be slow. So I looked next at a cancer service. I wished then to look at conditions where death was unexpected and rapid, and so looked at an emergency service. While we were looking at some different types of services, we also observed the above types of service at other types of hospitals. So our scheduling of types of service was directed by a general conceptual scheme – which included hypotheses about awareness, expectedness and rate of dying – as well as by a developing conceptual structure including matters not at first envisioned. Sometimes we returned to services after the initial two or three of four weeks of continuous observation, in order to check upon items which needed checking or had been missed in the initial period.'

(Glaser and Strauss 1967:59)

The appropriate strategy to adopt in selecting cases will depend very much on the stage research has reached in the relevant theoretical area, and the selection strategy may also change over the course of the research project. In the early phases of generating theory, which cases are chosen for investigation may not matter greatly. Later on in the process of developing and testing theory it may come to take on considerable importance.

Sampling within the case

Selecting cases for investigation is not the only form of sampling involved in social research. Equally important is sampling *within* cases. In ethnography, decisions must be made about where to observe and when, who to talk to and what to ask, as well as about what to record and how. In this process we are not only deciding what is and is not relevant to the case under study but also sampling from the data available in the case. Very often this sampling is unwitting, but it is important to make the criteria employed as explicit and as systematic as possible, so as to try to ensure that the case has been adequately sampled.

There are three major dimensions along which sampling within cases occurs: time, people, and context. Time may seem a dimension of obvious importance in social life, but it has often been neglected. Attitudes and activities often vary over time in ways that are highly significant for social theory. Berlak *et al.* provide an example from their research on 'progressive' primary schools in England:

> 'During our first weeks in the English schools we gradually began to understand that the images of the schools conveyed in the literature were to some extent distorted. The way in which this understanding developed is exemplified by our experience during the first weeks of our study of Mr Thomas's classroom. In his classroom, in a school in an affluent sub-urban area, we observed thirty children on a Wednesday morning who, after a brief discussion with the teacher, went about their work individually: some began to work on "maths", others to study spelling or to write original stories in much the way [that the literature describes]. We observed no teacher behavior on that morning which appeared to direct the children to what they were to do. It appeared that the children were choosing to learn, did their work carefully, and were pursuing their own interests. However, during the following days, we observed events and patterns which appeared to account for the behavior observed on that Wednesday morning. On the following Monday morning we observed Mr Thomas set work minimums in each subject of the week. . . . On the following Friday morning we saw him collect the children's work "diaries" where each child had recorded in detail the work he had completed during the week. Over the week-end, Mr Thomas and, as we were to later discover, sometimes the head, checked each record book and wrote comments in the diaries such as "good", "more maths", or the ominous "see me". Such items, which explained some of the apparently spontaneous classroom behavior, had not appeared in the literature.'
>
> (Berlak *et al.* 1975:218)

The general issue of the social construction and distribution of time is quite beautifully demonstrated in Zerubavel's (1979) study of time in hospitals. In Zerubavel's work, the organization of time is not an incidental feature or a background to a substantive focus on other organizational matters. Rather, it is an exercise, in the tradition of Simmel, on the formal category of time itself:

> 'Following the methodological guidelines which I derived from Simmel's formal sociology, I focused my observations on only one aspect of hospital life, namely, its temporal structure, deliberately ignoring – for analytical purposes – the history of the hospital, its national reputation, the quality of its patient care, its architectural design and spatial organization, its finances, the religious and ethnic makeup of its staff, and so on.'
>
> (Zerubavel 1979:xvii)

Zerubavel's is thus an unusually sparse ethnography. Yet the single-mindedness of his observations and his formal analyses enable him to reveal the complex patterning of temporal orders within the organization of daily life in the hospital. He foreshadows their diversity in the Introduction:

> 'The list of sociological aspects of temporality which can be discussed within the context of hospital life is almost endless: the temporal structure of patients' hospital careers; the relations between time and space; deadlines and strategies of beating the schedule; the temporal relations among the various hospital units; considerations of rate, speed, sequence, and timing in hospital work; the impact of organizational time on hospital personnel's life outside the hospital; and so on.'
>
> (Zerubavel 1979:xxi)

To follow Zerubavel's example, think hypothetically about the casualty department of an urban general hospital. Any systematic study here would almost certainly reveal different patterns of work and activity according to the time of day or night, and according to the day of the week. The nature of the referrals and emergency presentations would vary too. Saturday nights would probably be characterized by very different rates and patterns of admission from Sunday nights, and so on. Time in our casualty department would also relate to changing shifts of nursing staff, rotations among junior doctors, and so forth. Very similar considerations would apply in many other settings in factories, prisons, educational settings, and residential homes, for example.

It should be apparent, therefore, that any attempt to represent the entire range of persons and events in the case under study will have to be based on adequate coverage of the various temporal divisions. On the other hand, it is impossible to conduct fieldwork round the clock, and some degree of time sampling must be attempted. It may be possible to undertake the occasional period of extended fieldwork, but these are hard to sustain. (These remarks do not apply in quite the same way to anthropological fieldwork, where the ethnographer is in principle 'in play' all day, every day: though even here, the fieldworker will need to 'escape' periodically in order to write up notes, file material, and simply relax.) In any event, long uninterrupted periods of fieldwork are not always to be encouraged. The production of decent field notes, the indexing and filing of material, writing memoranda and reflexive notes are all time-consuming and demanding activities. Very long periods of observation will thus become quite unmanageable. The longer the time between observation and recording, the more troublesome will be the recall and recording of adequately detailed and concrete descriptions. Long bursts of observation, uninterrupted by periods of reflexive recording, will thus result in data of poor quality.

Hence, all ethnographers have to resist the very ready temptation to try to see, hear, and participate in everything that goes on. A more selective approach will normally result in data of better quality, provided the periods of observation are complemented by periods of productive recording and reflection. Rather than attempting to cover the entire working day, for instance, one may be able to build up an adequate representation by following the sort of strategy outlined by Schatzman and Strauss:

'If the researcher elects to observe work around the clock, he can first observe a day shift for several days, then evenings and then nights, for a period of consecutive days until he is reasonably familiar with all three shifts. Or he may cover events at any given sub-site by "overlapping" time on consecutive dates – for example, 7:00 A.M. to 9:00 A.M., 8:00 A.M. to 10:00 A.M., 9:00 A.M. to 11:00 A.M. – and over a period of days cover the organization around the clock.'

(Schatzman and Strauss 1973:39)

Over and above these procedures for establishing adequate coverage, the researcher will probably identify particularly salient periods and junctures: the changeover between shifts, for instance, might prove crucial in the organization of work, the sharing of information, and so on. Such crucial times should then come in for particular attention.

Similar considerations to those outlined above will also apply to larger-scale temporal dimensions, such as seasonal or annual cycles, and patterns of recruitment of new cohorts, although overall constraints of time and resource will obviously prove limiting here.

Hitherto we have referred primarily to issues relating to fieldwork in organizations and the like. It should also be apparent that similar considerations might apply to fieldwork in less formally defined settings. The patterns of urban life, 'relations in public', the use of public settings, and patterns of deviant activity all follow temporal dimension: the seasons, the days of the week, and the time of day or night all play their part. Likewise, it may be important to pay some attention to special occasions, such as seasonal festivals and carnivals, ceremonies and rituals, rites of passage, and social markers of status passage.

In organizing this sampling of time, it is as important to sample the routine as it is to observe the extraordinary. The purpose of such systematic data collection procedures is to ensure as full and representative a range of coverage as possible, not just to identify and single out the superficially 'interesting' events.

No social setting will prove socially homogeneous, and the adequate representation of the *people* involved in a particular case will normally require some sampling (unless the whole population of relevant actors can be studied adequately and in equal depth). The sampling of persons may be undertaken in terms of fairly standard 'face-sheet' demographic criteria. That is, depending on the particular context, one may sample persons by reference to categories of gender, race, age, occupation, educational qualifications, and so on. However, face-sheet categories are of importance only as they are relevant to the emerging theory or to rival theories, and they will usually be complemented by other categories of theoretical relevance. Such emergent categories may be either 'member-identified categories' or 'observer-identified categories'. The distinction is drawn from Lofland (1976), as is the terminology. 'Member-identified categories' refers to typifications that are employed by members themselves, that is, they are 'folk' categories that are normally encapsulated in the 'situated vocabularies' of a given culture. 'Observer-identified categories' are types constructed by an observer.

Some cultures are particularly rich in member-generated categories. Spradley (1970), for instance, in his work on tramps identifies the following taxonomy of terms that are used to iden-tify major types: ding, bore car tramp, bindle stiff, working stiff, airedale, home guard tramp, mission stiff, and rubber. The taxonomy also includes the sub-types harvest tramp, tramp miner, fruit tramp, construction tramp, sea tramp, nose diver, and professional nose diver.

Similarly, in her study of a women's prison, Giallombardo (1966) documents the following collection of labels that the pris-oners themselves use to categorize the inmates: snitchers, inmate cops, and lieutenants; squares, jive bitches; rap buddies, homeys; connects, boosters; pinners; penitentiary turnouts, lesbians, femmes, stud broads, tricks, commissary hustlers, chippies, kick partners, cherries, punks, and turnabouts. These labels are applied on the basis of 'the mode of response exhibited by the inmate to the prison situation and the quality of the inmates' interaction with other inmates and staff' (Giallam-bardo 1966:270). In particular, the identifications reflect styles of sexual response.

On the other hand, the observer may erect hypothetical types, on the basis of the fieldwork. In a study of waiting behaviour, for instance, Lofland identified the following key types:

'1. *The sweet young things*. Generally a female. Once having taken a position, normally a seated one, she rarely leaves it. Her purpose is straight; potentially suggestive or reveal-ing "slouching" is not dared.

2. *The Nester.* Having once established a position, such persons busy themselves with arranging and rearranging their props, much in the manner of a bird building a nest.
3. *The Investigator.* Having first reached a position, the investigator surveys his surroundings with some care. Then . . . he leaves his position to begin a minute investigation of every inanimate object in sight.
4. *The Seasoned Urbanite* . . . is easy and relaxed . . . within the confines of legitimate setting use and proper public behaviour.
5. *The Maverick* . . . is a non-style. . . . Its users are those who either do not know, are not able, or do not care to protect themselves in public settings. . . . There are three types . . .; children . . .; the constantly stigmatised . . .; and eccentrics. . . .'

(Lofland 1966 in Lofland 1971:35)

Whether the sampling of persons takes place on the basis of member-identified or observer-identified categories (and often both are used), the process is inextricably linked with the development of the theory and the collection of data, the two together providing the categories in terms of which sampling takes place.

Taking account of variations in *context* is as important as sampling across time and people. Within any setting people may distinguish between a number of quite different contexts that require different kinds of behaviour. Some of these will be fairly obvious, others less so. In schools, for example, it is well known that the behaviour of teachers often differs sharply between classrooms and staffrooms (Woods 1979; Hammersley 1980). This contrast is an example of a more abstract distinction between frontstage and backstage regions developed by Goffman:

'A back region or backstage may be defined as a place, relative to a given performance, where the impression fostered by the performance is knowingly contradicted as a matter of course. There are, of course, many characteristic functions of such places. It is here that the capacity of a performance to express something beyond itself may be painstakingly fabricated; it is here that illusions and impressions are openly constructed. Here stage props and items of personal front can be stored in a kind of compact collapsing of whole repertoires of actions and characters. Here grades of ceremonial equipment, such as different types of liquor or clothes, can be hidden so that the audience will not be able to see the treatment accorded them in comparison with the treatment that could have been accorded them. Here devices such as the telephone are sequestered so that they can be used "privately". Here costumes and other parts of personal front may be adjusted and scrutinized for flaws. Here the team can run through its performance, checking for offending expressions when no audience is present to be affronted by them; here poor members of the team, who are expressively inept, can be schooled or dropped from the performance. Here the performer can relax; he can drop his front, forgo speaking his lines, and step out of character.'

(Goffman 1959:114–15)

Goffman illustrates his argument by reference to a wide range of settings from hotel restaurants to shipyards.

It is important, however, not to mistake places for contexts. We must remember, again following Goffman (1963), that architectural structures are merely props used in the social drama, they do not determine behaviour in a direct fashion. What we think of, for example, as 'staffroom behaviour' may also occur in other parts of a school where conditions are right, or even in the bar of a local public house. Conversely, behaviour typical of the staffroom may not occur while visitors, or even the headteacher, are there. If we are to ensure that we are not led into false generalizations about attitudes and behaviour within a case through contextual variability, we must identify the contexts in terms of which people in the setting act, recognizing that these are social constructions not physical locations, and try to ensure that we sample across all those that are relevant.

Variations among people, occasions, and contexts may or may not be significant for the emerging theory of course. Where they are, the result will be either a redefinition of the research problem or a reconstruction of the theory. In other words, the variation may be rendered irrelevant by redrawing the boundaries of the case in line with a redefinition of the research problem, or the theory may be developed in such a way as to account for it (Cressey 1950).

Up to this point we have talked for the most part as though research design decisions in ethnography are based solely on theoretical and methodological criteria. This is of course highly misleading. Even more than with other social research methods, issues of practicability play a major role in this kind of research. The cases we might wish to select may not be open to study, for one reason or another; and even if they are, effective strategies for gaining access to the necessary data will need to be developed. Similarly, not all the people we wish to observe or talk to, nor all the contexts we wish to sample, may be accessible; certainly not at the times we want them to be. The problem of gaining access to data is particularly serious in ethnography since one is operating in settings where the researcher generally has little power, and people have pressing concerns of their own that often give them little reason to co-operate. It is to this problem that we turn in the next chapter.

3

Access

The problem of obtaining access to the necessary data looms large in ethnography. It is often at its most acute in initial negotiations to enter a setting and during the 'first days in the field'; though the problem persists, to one degree or another, throughout the data collection process.

In many ways, gaining access is a thoroughly practical issue. As we shall see, it involves drawing on the interpersonal resources and strategies that we all tend to develop in dealing with everyday life. But the process of achieving access is not *merely* a practical matter. Not only does its achievement depend upon theoretical understanding, often disguised as 'native wit', but the discovery of obstacles to access, and perhaps of effective means of overcoming them, themselves provide insights into the social organization of the setting.

The work of Barbera-Stein (1979) provides a good illustration of this. Barbera-Stein's fieldwork was undertaken in several different therapeutic or day-care centres for pre-school children. Her original research design foundered because access was denied to several settings. She writes in retrospect of her experience of access negotiation:

'The access negotiations can be construed as involving multiple views of what is profane and open to investigation vs. what is sacred or taboo and closed to investigation unless the appropriate respectful stance or distance is assumed.'

(Barbera-Stein 1979:15)

She ties this observation to particular settings and particular activities in them:

'I had requested permission to observe what the psychoanalytic staff considered sacred. In their interactions with emotionally disturbed children, they attempted to establish effective bonds modelled after the parent-child bond. This was the first step in their attempts to correct the child's faulty emotional development. This also was the principal work of the social workers at the day-care centre as well. Consistent with the above are the restrictions which were placed on my formal access to the day-care centre. Formal access to the day-care centre initially was made contingent upon my not observing on Tuesdays and Thursdays, when the social workers engaged the children in puppet play sessions. Puppet play was used as a psychological projective technique in monitoring and fostering the emotional development of the children.'

(Barbera-Stein 1979:15)

Even after eight months of fieldwork, and after some renegotiation, access to such 'sacred' puppet-play sessions was highly restricted. Barbera-Stein was allowed to observe only three sessions and was forbidden to take notes.

In contrast, Barbera-Stein herself assumed that interactional data on families in the home would be highly sacred, and did not initially request access to such information. In fact it turned out that this was not regarded as problematic by the social workers, as they viewed working with families as their stock-in-trade, and it was an area in which they were themselves interested. This latter experience illustrates, incidentally, that while one must remain sensitive to issues of access to different domains, it is unwise to allow one's plans to be guided entirely by one's own presuppositions concerning what is and is not accessible.

Newby's research on farmworkers provides another example of how access problems can be turned into data, and also used as a source of analytic insights:

'The necessity to approach farmworkers via the farmer was already telling one something about the social situation of the workers . . . namely, that they were socially invisible to many inhabitants in the locality, and that the employer *was* a significant other in their lives.'

(Newby 1977a:115)

Negotiating access and data collection are not, then, distinct phases of the research process. They overlap significantly. Much can be learned from the problems involved in making contact with people as well as from how they respond to the researcher's approaches.

Entry to settings

Access is not simply a matter of physical presence or absence. It is far more than a matter of the granting or withholding of permission for research to be conducted. Perhaps this can be illustrated by reference to research where too literal a notion of access would be particularly misleading. It might be thought that problems of access could be avoided if one were to study 'public' settings only, such as streets, shops, public transport vehicles, bars, and similar locales. In one sense this is true. Anyone can, in principle, enter such public domains; that is what makes them 'public'. No process of negotiation is required for that. On the other hand, things are not necessarily so straightforward. In many settings, while physical *presence* is not in itself problematic, appropriate *activity* may be so.

Amongst other things, public domains may be marked by styles of social interaction involving what Goffman (1971) terms 'civil inattention'. Anonymity in public settings is not a contingent feature of them, but is worked at by displays of a studied lack of interest in one's fellows, minimal eye contact, careful management of physical proximity, and so on. There is, therefore, the possibility that the fieldworker's attention and interest may lead to infringements of such delicate interaction rituals. Similarly, much activity in public settings is fleeting and transient. The fieldworker who wishes to engage in relatively protracted observations may therefore encounter the problem of managing 'loitering', or having to account for himself or herself in some way.

Some examples of such problems are provided in Karp's (1980) account of his investigation of the 'public sexual scene' in and around Times Square in New York, particularly in pornographic bookshops and cinemas. Admittedly, this is a very particular sort of public setting in that a good deal of what goes on may be 'disreputable' and the behaviour in public correspondingly guarded.

Karp tried various strategies for achieving access and initiating interaction. He tried to negotiate openly with some bookshop managers, but failed. (He reports that some colleagues subsequently suggested that in view of the sexual nature of the business that was going on, introducing himself as a professor at Queens College was not a propitious start to his negotiations!) Similarly, after a while, regulars on the street interpreted his hanging around in terms of his being a hustler, or a cop. He also reports failure to establish relationships with prostitutes, although his field notes seem to display a rather clumsy and naive approach to this.

Karp resolved his problems to some extent by realizing that they directly paralleled the interactional concerns of the participants themselves, and he was able to draw on his access troubles for analytical purposes in that light. He quotes a research note to this effect:

'I can on the basis of my own experience substantiate, at least in part, the reality of impression-management problems for persons involved in the Times Square sexual scene. I have been frequenting pornographic bookstores and movie theatres for some nine months. Despite my relatively long experience I have not been able to overcome my uneasiness during activity in these contexts. I feel, for example, nervous at the prospect of entering a theatre. This nervousness expresses itself in increased heartbeat. I consciously wait until few people are in the vicinity before entering; I take my money out well in advance of entering; I feel reticent to engage the female ticket seller in even the briefest eye contact.'

(Karp 1980:94)

In the face of such interactional constraints, Karp decided to resort to observation alone, with minimal participation beyond casual conversation. He concludes by pointing out that such public settings may be as constraining for a researcher as any organizational setting.

To a considerable extent Karp's is an account of relative failure to establish and maintain working 'presence' and relationships, although he learns from his problems. One should not conclude from his experience, however, that 'loitering' can never lead to workable research conditions. West writes on the value of such apparently casual approaches:

'I met both . . . referred delinquents and others by frequenting their hangouts, such as stores, pool halls, restaurants, and alleys, and by trying to strike up casual acquaintanceship over bottles of pop, by joining games, chatting amicably, and other methods. Some boldness and a tough-skinned attitude to occasional personal rejection were helpful, in addition to skills in repartee, sports, empathy, and sensitivity. I recall few incidents of outright rebuff. I generally made frequent "rounds" of a chosen neighbourhood, perhaps twice daily at the beginning: stopping at a corner, walking down frequented streets, dropping into stores, playing a game of pool, watching baseball games, or drinking pop at a restaurant. After leaving each location, I surreptitiously jotted down names or descriptions of teenagers met or noticed, then proceeded on. After a few visits or perhaps a couple of weeks, I became recognised as something of a regular, and usually had managed to strike up conversations with a few youngsters.'

(West 1980:34)

Liebow (1967) also describes how successfully he was able to initiate research by 'hanging about'. In the course of his account Liebow illustrates a number of important aspects of negotiating access. He was engaged to participate in a study of 'child-rearing practices among low income families in the District of Columbia', and charged with collecting field material on low-income males, to complement material gathered from family interviews. Once Liebow had read through the project literature, the director suggested a likely neighbourhood for Liebow to 'get his feet wet'. Liebow recounts how he set out into this neighbourhood. On the first day he witnessed a scuffle between a policeman and a woman, and fell into conversation with some of the onlookers. This led into several hours of talk with a young man. This he wrote up, and in retrospect, he comments:

> 'I had not accomplished what I set out to do, but this was only the first day. And, anyway, when I wrote up this experience that evening, I felt that it presented a fairly good picture of this young man and that most of the material was to the point. Tomorrow, I decided, I would get back to my original plan – nothing had been lost. But tomorrow never came. . . .'
>
> (Liebow 1967:238)

The 'original plan' that Liebow was cherishing initially was to do several small studies, 'each covering a strategic part of the world of the low-income male': a neighbourhood study, a labour union, and a bootleg joint, perhaps supplemented by some life-histories and genealogies. In the event, however, rather than getting his 'feet wet' in the first neighbourhood he tried,

> 'I went in so deep that I was completely submerged and any plan to do three or four separate studies, each with its own neat, clean boundaries, dropped forever out of sight. My initial excursions into the street – to poke around, get the feel of things, and to lay out the lines of any fieldwork – seldom carried me more than a block or two from the corner where I started. From the very first weeks or even days, I found myself in the middle of things: the principal lines of my field work were laid out, almost without my being aware of it. For the next year or so, and intermittently thereafter, my base of operations was the corner carry-out across the street from my starting point.'
>
> (Liebow 1967:236–37)

On the second day of his fieldwork, Liebow returned to the scene of his first encounter. Again he fell into conversation, with three 'winos' in their forties, and a younger man 'who looked as if he had just stepped out of a slick magazine advertisement . . .' (1967:238–39). This younger man was Tally Jackson, who acted as Liebow's sponsor and confidant, and on whose social circle the research came to be focused.

Now Liebow's study is an impressive and important contribution to urban ethnography, but there are danger signals in his account of the fieldwork. It may or may not have been a good idea to abandon his original, somewhat vague, intentions of conducting several small, related projects. On the other hand, it may not have been such a good idea to have, as it appears, surrendered himself so thoroughly to the chance meeting with Tally and its consequences. As Liebow himself remarks, 'the principal lines of my fieldwork, were laid out, *almost without my being aware of it*' (1967:237) (our emphasis). Here, rather than the research problem being transformed in response to opportunities arising in the course of the research and the research design being modified accordingly, Liebow seems to have abandoned systematic research design altogether.

Nevertheless, Liebow's research illustrates the significance of informal 'sponsorship'. Tally vouchsafed for him, introduced him to a circle of friends and acquaintances, and so provided access to data. The most famous of such 'sponsors' in the field is undoubtedly 'Doc' who helped in Whyte's study of 'corner boys' (Whyte 1981). Whyte's methodological appendix is a classic description of the serendipitous development of a research design, and the influence of Doc was a major determinant in its evolution. Doc agreed to offer Whyte the protection of friendship, and coached him in appropriate conduct and demeanour.

Liebow's and Whyte's contacts with their sponsors were quite fortuitous. However, sponsorship of a similiar kind may be gained through the mobilization of existing social networks, based on acquaintanceship, kinship, occupational membership, and so on. Hoffman (1980) provides insight into the way in which such networks can be used, while drawing attention once more to the relationship between problems of access and the quality of the data subsequently collected. Hoffman's research was concerned with a locally influential elite – members of boards of hospital directors in Quebec. In the first place she notes a general problem of access to such an elite:

> 'Introducing myself as a sociology graduate student, I had very limited success in getting by the gatekeepers of the executive world. Telephone follow-ups to letters sent requesting an interview repeatedly found Mr X "tied-up" or "in conference". When I did manage to get my foot in the door, interviews rarely exceeded a half hour, were continually interrupted by telephone calls (for "important" conferences,

secretaries are usually asked to take calls) and elicited only ''front work'' (Goffman 1959), the public version of what hospital boards were all about.'

(Hoffman 1980:46)

During one interview however, Hoffman's informant discovered that he knew members of her family. This gave rise to a very different sort of interview, and very different data:

'The rest of the interview was dramatically different than all my previous data. I was presented with a very different picture of the nature of board work. I learned, for example, how board members used to be recruited, how the executive committee kept control over the rest of the board, how business was conducted and of what it consisted, and many other aspects of the informal social organization of board work.'

(Hoffman 1980:46-7)

Abandoning her original research design – based on interviewing a representative example from different institutions – Hoffman therefore started to select informants on the basis of social ties. She began with direct personal contacts, and then asked those acquaintances to refer her to other informants and so on. This strategy, she concludes, produced 'more informative and insightful data'.

Hoffman graphically juxtaposes typical responses to illustrate the point:

'Response to an Unknown Sociologist	Response to a Known Individual
Board Member A	Board Member B

Q. *How do you feel in general about how the board has been reorganized?*

I think the basic idea of participation is good. We need better communication with the various groups. And I think they probably have a lot to offer.	This whole business is unworkable. It's all very nice and well to have these people on the board, they might be able to tell us something here and there, or describe a situation, but you're not going to run a hospital on that!

Q. *How is the new membership working out? Do they parti-*
   cipate? Any problems?

. . . oh yes, Mr X (orderly) participates. He asked something today, now what was it? Sometimes they lack skill and experience, but they catch on. There is no problem with them. We get along very well.	Mr X (orderly) hasn't opened his mouth except for a sandwich. . . . But what *can* he contribute? . . . You could rely on the old type of board member . . . you knew you could count on him to support you. You didn't have to check up all the time. But these new people, how do you know how they will react? Will they stick behind you? And there is the problem of confidentiality. Everything you say you know will be all over the hospital ten minutes after the meeting. You can't say the same things anymore. You have to be careful in case someone interpretes you as being condescending or hoity-toity.'

(Hoffman 1980:48-9)

Hoffman tends to portray the issue of access here in terms of 'penetrating informants' 'fronts', and clearly contrasts the two varieties of data in terms of aiming for 'better' and more truthful accounts. This can be problematic: 'frankness' may be as much a social accomplishment as 'discretion', and we shall return to the problem of the authenticity of accounts later. But Hoffman's discussion dramatically focuses attention on the relationships between 'access', the fieldworker's perceived identity, and the data that can be gathered.

In a similar vein, Loizos (1975:302) describes how he built upon kinship in selecting the village of 'Kalo' in Cyprus for his fieldwork. His father had been born there, hence 'This made it possible for me to be classified as a *chorianos*, fellow-villager (although a rather odd one)'. Despite his own lack of Greek and the great social distance between himself and the villagers, Loizos found that many of them felt a considerable obligation to help him in the fieldwork. To that extent, while in many ways that of the typical novice fieldworker, Loizos's position in the village was a privileged one.

Gatekeepers

Hoffman's account takes us towards those 'formal', 'private' settings where boundaries are clearly marked, are not easily penetrated, and may be policed by 'gatekeepers'. In formal organizations, for example, initial access negotiations may be focused on formal permission that can legitimately be granted or withheld by key personnel. Although not necessarily the case, such gatekeepers are often the ethnographer's initial point of contact with such research settings.

It should be said, though, that the relevant gatekeepers are not always obvious. Indeed, the distinction between sponsors and gatekeepers is by no means clear-cut. Even in formal bureaucratic organizations it is not always obvious whose permission needs to be obtained, or whose good offices it might be advisable to secure. Gouldner reports precisely this kind of problem in his research on the Oscar Center gypsum plant. He recounts that the research team

'made a "double-entry" into the plant, coming in almost simultaneously by way of the Company and the Union. But it soon became obvious that we had made a *mistake*, and that the problem had *not* been to make a double-entry, but a *triple-*entry; for we had left out, and failed to make *independent* contact with a distinct group – the management of that particular plant. In a casual way, we had assumed that main office management also spoke for the local plant management and this, as a moment's reflection might have told us, was not the case. In consequence our relations with *local* management were never as good as they were with the workers or the main office management.'

(Gouldner 1954:255–56)

Knowing who has the power to open up or block off access, or who consider themselves and are considered by others to have the authority to grant or refuse access, is, of course, an important aspect of sociological knowledge about the setting. However, this is not the catch-22 situation it might appear. For one thing, as we argued in Chapter 1, research never starts from scratch, it always relies on common-sense knowledge to one degree or another. We may already know sufficient about the setting to be able to judge what the most effective strategy is likely to be for gaining entry. If we do not, we can 'case' the setting beforehand, for example by contacting people with knowledge of it or of other settings of a similar type. This will normally solve the problem, though as Whitten (1970) found out in his research on negro communities in Nova Scotia, there is no guarantee that the information provided is sound. Whitten was told by local people that he should phone the councillor for the largest settlement, that to try to meet him without phoning would be rude. He did so, 'with disastrous results':

> 'I introduced myself as an anthropologist from the United States, interested in problems encountered by people in rural communities in different parts of the Americas. Following procedures common in the United States and supported by educated Nova Scotians, I said that I was particularly inter-ested in Negro communities kept somewhat outside of the larger social and economic system. I was told, politely, but firmly, that the people of the rural Dartmouth region had had enough of outsiders who insulted and hurt them under the guise of research, that the people of the region were as human as I, and that I might turn my attention to other communities in the province. I was asked why I chose ''Negroes'' and when I explained that Negroes, more than others, had been excluded from full participation, I was again told that the people of rural Nova Scotia were all alike, and that the colored people were tired of being regarded as somehow different, because there was no difference.'
>
> (Whitten 1970:371)

Whitten discovered that he had made two basic mistakes:

> 'First, when Nova Scotians tell one to first call the official responsible for a community, they are paying due respect to the official, but they do not expect the investigator to take this

advice. They expect that the investigator will establish an enduring contact with someone who can introduce him to the official. Crucial to this procedure is that the investigator be first known to the person who will make the introduction, for the middleman may be held responsible for the investigator's mistakes. The recommendation to call relieves anyone from the responsibility for the call, and hence it is not expected that a person will follow this advice. Second, it is not expected that one will use the term Negro in referring to Nova Scotians ethnically identified as colored. The use of ethnic terminology (including the term colored) is reserved for those who are already a part of the system. . . .

The most effective way to approach an official, we found, is to recognize no ethnic distinctions whatsoever, thereby forcing the official to make the preliminary distinction (e.g. between colored community and white community). By so doing the investigator is in a position to immediately inquire as to the significance of ethnicity. Had we acted a bit more slowly, and ignored ethnic differences, we might have succeeded in gaining early entrée, but we erred by assuming that we knew the best way to do things in Anglo-America. By talking too much, and not reflecting carefully on the possible connotations attached to our ''instructions'', our work bogged down for a time.'

(Whitten 1970:371–72)

Whether or not they grant entry to the setting, gatekeepers will generally, and understandably, be concerned as to the picture of the organization that the ethnographer will paint, and they will have practical interests in seeing themselves and their colleagues presented in a favourable light. At least, they will wish to safeguard what they perceive as their legitimate interests. Gatekeepers may therefore attempt to exercise some degree of surveillance and control, either by blocking off certain lines of inquiry, or by shepherding the fieldworker in one direction or another.

As an illustration of one way in which gatekeepers may try to influence things, Bogdan and Taylor report:

'We know one novice who contacted a detention home in order to set up a time to begin his observation. The supervisor with whom he spoke told him that he wouldn't be interested in visiting the home that day or the next because the boys would just be making Hallowe'en decorations. He then suggested which times of the day would be best for the observer to "see something going on". The observer allowed himself to be forced to choose from a limited number of alternatives when he should have made it clear that he was interested in a variety of activities and times.'

(Bogdan and Taylor 1975:44–5)

Although Bogdan and Taylor report this as happening to a novice, it often remains a problem for even the most experienced fieldworker. (In this instance, the ethnographer needs to explain that he or she is willing or even eager to sample the mundane, the routine, or perhaps the boring aspects of everyday life.)

One of the difficulties regularly faced in this context arises from the fact that it is often precisely the most sensitive things that are of most *prima facie* interest. Periods of change and transition, for example, may be perceived as troublesome by the participants themselves, and they may wish, therefore, to steer observers away from them: the conflict of interest arises from the fact that such disruptions can be particularly fruitful research opportunities for the fieldworker.

Mackay (1967) notes this possibility in recounting his period of access negotiation and initial encounters in a school in British Columbia. After initial agreement was reached with the principal,

'The principal indicated that he now had to approach the teachers and discuss it with them and would be in contact when this was done. There followed an interval of about ten days which was explained to have been necessary because one of the teachers was sick (and) another was recovering from a period of intense emotional stress. Since the negotiations for entry into the school were carried on at the beginning of the school year perhaps the teachers did not want others present when student control was still problematic. (This same attitude may be reflected in the teachers' suggestion to the observer as Christmas neared that they did not want observations to take place just before the Christmas break. At this time of year formal teaching is at a minimum and students are

involved in making decorations for the room and getting prepared for the Christmas assembly. These activities are
presumably not supervised as closely as activities during formal teaching and the teachers may not want their students
seen at these times.)'

(Mackay 1967:80–1)

At the outset, of course, Mackay could have had no way of
knowing the actual reason for the delay in his fieldwork getting
underway. But his awareness of the possibility of the teachers'
reluctance clearly gave him some potential understanding of
their sensitivities, and could conceivably have proved a valuable
clue in understanding subsequent events, such as the teachers'
later reticence at Christmas.

The issue of 'sensitive' periods is something that Ball (1980)
explicitly remarks on in the context of a discussion of initial
encounters in school classrooms. He notes that researchers have
tended to devote attention to classrooms where patterns of interaction are already well established. Hence there is a tendency to
portray classroom life in terms of fixed, static models. The pictures of classroom interaction with which we are familiar, Ball
argues, may be artefacts of the preferred research strategy. He
goes on to note:

'The problem is that most researchers, with limited time and
money available to them, are forced to organise their
classroom observations into short periods of time. This
usually involves moving into already established classroom
situations where teachers and pupils have considerably
greater experience of their interactional encounters than does
the observer. Even where the researcher is available to moni-
tor the initial encounters between a teacher and pupils, the
teacher is, not unreasonably, reluctant to be observed at this
stage.

But the reasons for the teacher's reluctance are exactly the
reasons why the researcher should be there. These earlier
encounters are of crucial significance not only for understanding what comes later but in actually providing for what
comes later.'

(Ball 1980:143–44)

Here, then, Ball neatly draws attention to a particular problem of access, and shows how this is not simply a 'practical' matter of organizing the fieldwork (though it is that too), but also bears on issues of theory, and the question of representativeness.

To deceive or not to deceive

Sometimes, of course, it may be judged that the relevant gate-keepers will almost certainly block entry altogether. Here, resort may be made to secret research (see Bulmer 1982 on the ethical issues). Holdaway (1982) provides an example from his work on the police. As a serving officer who was seconded to university to read sociology and returned to the force wishing to do research on it, Holdaway was faced with six options:

> 'A. Seek the permission of the chief officer to research, giving full details of method and intention.
> B. Seek permission as above, so phrasing the research description that it disguised my real intentions.
> C. Seek permission of lower ranks, later requesting more formal acceptance from senior officers.
> D. Do no research.
> E. Resign from the police service.
> F. Carry out covert research.
>
> I chose the final option without much difficulty. From the available evidence, it seemed the only realistic option; alternatives were unrealistic or contained an element of the unethical which bore similarity to covert observation. I believe that my senior officers would have either refused permission to research or obstructed me. Option B is as dishonest a strategy as covert research, if the latter is thought dishonest. For example, if I were a Marxist and wanted to research the police and declared my Marxism, I know that I would be denied research access; yet to "front" myself in a different research guise is surely dishonest. Option C could not have been managed. D denies the relevance of my studies and Option E would have been its logical progression – yet I felt an obligation to return to the police who had financed my study.'
>
> (Holdaway 1982:63)

Holdaway was in the unusual position of knowing the setting he wanted to research, and the gatekeepers who could give him permission to do the research, very well indeed. Often, however, judgements that access to a setting is impossible are less well-founded. There are many settings to which one might expect entry to be blocked but that have been shown to be accessible, at least to some degree. For example, Fielding (1982) approached the National Front for permission to carry out research on their organization, and received it, though he felt it necessary to supplement official access with covert observation. Similarly, Chambliss recounts how he gained access to the world of organized crime:

> 'I went to the skid row, Japanese, Filipino, and Black sections of Seattle dressed in truck driver's clothes. . . . Sitting in the bar of a café one day I noticed several people going through a back-door. I asked the waitress, Millie – a slight, fortyish ex-prostitute and sometime-drug-user with whom I had become friends, where these people were going:
>
> MILLIE: To play cards.
> ME: Back there?
> MILLIE: Yes, that's where the poker games are.
> ME: Can I play?
> MILLIE: Sure. Just go in. But watch your wallet.
>
> So I went, hesitantly, through the back door and into a large room which had seven octagonal, green felt covered tables. People were playing five card stud at five of the tables. I was immediately offered a seat by a hand gesture from the cardroom manager. I played – all the time watching my wallet as I had been advised.
>
> I went back every day for the next week. . . . In conversation with the cardroom manager and other players I came to realize (discover?) what any taxicab driver already knew: that pornography, gambling, prostitution, and drugs were available on practically every street corner. So I began going to other cafés, card-rooms, and bars. I played in many games and developed a lot of information just from casual conversation.
>
> Within a week I was convinced that the rackets were highly organized. The problem became one of discovering how, and

by whom. I was sitting talking to Millie on the 30th of the month when a man I recognized as a policeman came through the door and went into the manager's office. I asked Millie what he was doing:

MILLIE: He's the bag man.
ME: The what?
MILLIE: The bag man. He collects the payoff for the people downstairs.
ME: Oh.

I spent the next two months talking informally to people I met at different games, in pornography shops, or on the streets. I soon began to feel that I was at a dead end . . . . I had discovered the broad outlines of organized crime in Seattle, but how it worked at the higher level was still a mystery. I decided it was time to "blow my cover".

I asked the manager of the cardroom I played in most to go to lunch with me. I took him to the faculty club at the University of Washington. This time when he saw me I was shaven and wore a shirt and tie. I told him of my "purely scientific" interests and experience and, as best I could, why I had deceived him earlier. He agreed to help. Soon I began receiving phone calls: "I understand you are interested in Seattle. Did you ever think to check Charles Carroll's brother in law?" And there was one honest-to-God clandestine meeting in a deserted warehouse down at the wharf. . . .

Over the next ten years I pursued this inquiry, widening my contacts and participating in an ever larger variety of rackets. As my interests in these subjects and my reliability as someone who could be trusted spread, I received more offers to "talk" than I had time to pursue.'

(Chambliss 1975:36–8)

The work of Holdaway, Fielding, and Chambliss raises the question of deception in negotiations over access. Where the research is secret to all those under study and to gatekeepers too, the problem of access may be 'solved' at a stroke, providing the deception is not discovered; though the researcher has to live with the moral qualms, anxieties, and practical difficulties to which the use of this strategy may lead. However, research carried out without the knowledge of anyone in, or associated with, the setting is quite rare. Much more common is that some people are kept in the dark while others are taken into the researcher's confidence.

What is at issue here, though, is not just whether permission to carry out the research is requested, and from whom, but also *what* those concerned are told about it. Some commentators recommend that an explicit research bargain, spelling out in full the purposes of the research and the procedures to be employed, be made with all those involved, right from the start. Often, though, this is neither possible nor desirable. Given the way in which research problems may change over the course of fieldwork, the demands likely to be made on people in the setting and the policy implications and political consequences of the research are often a matter for little more than speculation at the outset. There is also the danger that the information provided will influence the behaviour of the people under study in such a way as to invalidate the findings. While often it may be judged that the chances of this are small given the other pressures operating on these people, there are instances where it may be critical. Had Festinger *et al.* (1956) informed the apocalyptic religious group they were studying not only that the research was taking place but also about the hypothesis under investigation, that would almost certainly have undermined the validity of their research.

The other argument for not always providing a full account of one's purposes to gatekeepers and others at the beginning of the research is that unless one can build up a trusting relationship with them relatively rapidly, they may refuse access in a way that they would not do later on in the fieldwork. Once people come to know the researcher as a person who can be trusted to be discreet in handling information within the setting, and who will honour his or her promises of anonymity in publications, access may be granted that earlier would have been refused point blank. On this argument it is sometimes advisable not to request at the outset the full access to data one will eventually require but to leave negotiation of what seem to be the more delicate forms of access till field relationships have been established.

Nevertheless, while telling the 'whole truth' in negotiating entry for research, as in most other social situations, may not always be a wise or even a feasible strategy, deception should be avoided wherever possible, not just for ethical reasons, but also because it can rebound badly later on in the fieldwork. Indeed, sometimes it may be necessary to warn gatekeepers or sponsors of possible consequences of the research to avoid problems subsequently, as Geer notes from her research on American colleges:

> 'In colleges of high prestige, the researcher may be hampered in his negotiations because the administrators cannot imagine that anything harmful to the college could be discovered. In this case, it is up to the researcher to explain the kinds of things that often turn up – homosexuality, for example, or poor teaching. The administrator can sometimes be drawn into a scientific partnership. By treating him as a broad-minded and sophisticated academic, one gradually works him around to a realization that although the study may be threatening, he and his college are big enough to take it. It may seem unnecessary to prepare administrators for the worst in this fashion, but it prepares the ground for the shock they may get when they see the manuscript at the end of a study. Administrators may attempt to prevent publication or feel that the college has been exploited and similar research should not be authorized. However, the administrator who has committed himself to a generous research bargain is more likely to be proud of the results.'
>
> (Geer 1970:83)

Negotiating access is a balancing act. Gains and losses now and later, as well as ethical and strategic considerations, must be traded off against one another in whatever manner is judged to be most appropriate, given the purposes of the research and the circumstances in which it is to be carried out.

Obstructive and facilitative relationships

Seeking the permission of gatekeepers or the support of sponsors is often an unavoidable first step in gaining access to the data. Furthermore, the relationships established with such people can have important consequences for the subsequent course of the

research. Berreman, discussing his research on a Pahari village
in the Himalayas, reports:

> 'We were introduced (to the villagers) by a note from a non-
> Pahari wholesaler of the nearest market town who had long
> bought the surplus agricultural produce of villagers and had,
> as it turned out, through sharp practices of an obscure nature,
> acquired land in the village. He asked that the villagers treat
> the strangers as "our people" and extend all hospitality to
> them. As might have been expected, our benefactor was not
> beloved in the village and it was more in spite of his inter-
> cession than on account of it that we ultimately managed to
> do a year's research in the village.'
>
> (Berreman 1962:6)

Even the most friendly and co-operative of gatekeepers or
sponsors will shape the conduct and development of the
research. To one degree or another, the ethnographer will be
channelled in line with existing networks of friendship and
enmity, territory and equivalent 'boundaries'. Having been
'taken up' by a sponsor, the ethnographer may find it difficult to
achieve independence from such a person, finding the limits of
his or her research bounded by the social horizon of a sponsoring
group or individual. Such social and personal commitments
may, like gatekeepers' blocking tactics, close off certain
avenues of inquiry. The fieldworker may well find him- or herself involved in varieties of 'patron–client' relationship with
sponsors, and in so doing find influence exerted in quite
unforeseen ways. The ambiguities and contingencies of sponsorship and patronage are aptly illustrated by two similar studies
from rural Spain (Barrett 1974; Hansen 1977).

Barrett reports that the members of his chosen village,
Benabarre, were initially reserved. This was partially breached
when a village baker started to take Barrett round and introduce
him to others. However the big breakthrough came when the
village was visited by a Barcelona professor who was descended
from a Benabarre family. The professor was interested in
Barrett's work and spent a good deal of time with him:

> 'Nothing could have had a more beneficial effect on my rela-
> tions with the community. Don Tomás enjoys immense

respect and popularity among the villagers, and the fact that he found my work significant was a behavioural cue to a great many people. The reasoning was apparently that if I were someone to beware of, Don Tomás would not be fooled; if *he* believed I was the genuine article, then I must be! The response was immediate. Doors which until then had been closed to me opened up; new people greeted me on the streets and volunteered their services.'

(Barrett 1974:7)

Barrett realized that this was not simply a lucky breakthrough, it was also an important clue to social relationships in the village. Hierarchical relationships were of fundamental importance. Initially, Barrett had avoided close association with the 'upper crust' families:

'I thought that if there were polarization between the social strata this might make it more difficult later to win acceptance among the peasants. It was virtually the opposite! The fact that I was *not* associating with those who were considered my peers was simply confusing, and made it vastly more difficult to place me in the social order. Once Don Tomás extended his friendship, and introduced me to other families of similar social rank, this served almost as a certificate of respectability.'

(Barrett 1974:8)

Hansen's experiences in rural Catalonia are equally revealing about the hierarchical assumptions of village life:

'Initially, the interviewing process went very slowly because I was overly polite and solicitous about seeking interviews with people I hardly knew. I made the error of being too formal, which made these people suspicious of me. My mistake was brought home to me forcefully by one of the few nobles remaining in the Alto Panadés, whom I had interviewed by chance. He explained in no uncertain terms that I was behaving like a servant or client to these individuals when my own wealth, looks and education meant that I was superior to them. Therefore, he said, I should command them to give me interviews. He proceeded to accompany me to more than twenty bourgeois landholders, and ordered them to give me what I wanted, on the spot, including details of business scandals, etc. All complied, some with obeisance towards the Count, and all with both deference and expansiveness toward me. The Count checked all their answers to see if they were concealing vital information. Astonished and embarrassed as I was, the Count had a point. After these twenty interviews, I was swamped by volunteers. It had suddenly become fashionable to be interviewed by *el distinguido antropólogo norteamericano.'*

(Hansen 1977:163–64)

Gatekeepers, sponsors, and the like (indeed, most of the people who act as hosts to the research) will operate in terms of expectations about the ethnographer's identity and intentions. As the examples of Hansen and Barrett make clear, these can have serious implications for the amount and nature of the data collected.

Many hosts have highly inaccurate, and lurid, expectations of the research enterprise, especially of ethnographic work. Two closely related models of the researcher tend to predominate in this context, 'the expert' and 'the critic'. Both images can conspire to make the gatekeeper uneasy as to the likely consequences of the research, and the effects of its conduct.

The model of the 'expert' often seems to suggest that the social researcher is, or should be, a person who is extremely well informed as to 'problems' and their 'solutions'. The expectation may be set up that the ethnographer seeking access is claiming such expertise, and is expecting to 'sort out' the organisation or community. This view therefore leads directly to the second image, that of the 'critic'. Gatekeepers may expect the ethnographer to try to act as an evaluator.

Under some circumstances, these expectations may have favourable connotations. Evaluation by experts, leading to improvements in efficiency, interpersonal relations, planning, and so on, may have at least the overt support of those at the top (though not necessarily of those in subordinate positions). On the other hand, the expectation of expert critical surveillance may create anxieties on the part of gatekeepers. Even if permission for the research is not withheld altogether, gatekeepers may, as we have suggested, attempt to guide the research in directions they prefer, or away from potentially sensitive areas.

On the other hand, it may be very difficult for the ethnographer to establish credibility if hosts expect some sort of 'expertise'. Such expectations clash with the fieldworker's actual or cultivated ignorance and incompetence. Smigel (1958), for instance, has commented on the propensity of lawyers to try to 'brush off' researchers who appear to be legally ill-informed, a point confirmed to some extent by Mungham and Thomas (1981). Ethnographers are sometimes conspicuous for an apparent lack of activity as well. This, too, can militate against their being treated seriously by their hosts.

From a variety of contexts researchers report hosts' suspicions and expectations often proving barriers to access. Such suspicions may be fuelled by the very activities of the fieldworker. Barrett (1974), for instance, remarks on how the inhabitants of his Spanish village interpreted his actions. He was not sensitive to the possibility that villagers might be frightened by someone making notes, when they did not know what was being written down. Rumours about him included beliefs that he was a communist spy, a CIA agent, a protestant missionary, or a government tax agent.

As we noted early on in this chapter, the problem of access is not resolved once one has gained entry to a setting, since this by no means guarantees access to all the data available within it. Not all parts of the setting will be equally open to observation, not everyone may be willing to talk, and even the most willing informant will not be prepared, or perhaps even able, to divulge all the information available to him or her. If the data required to develop and test the theory are to be acquired, negotiation of access is therefore likely to be a recurrent preoccupation for the ethnographer. Negotiation here takes two different but by no means unrelated forms. On the one hand, explicit discussion with those whose activities one wishes to study may take place, much along the lines of that with sponsors and gatekeepers. But the term 'negotiation' also refers to the much more wide-ranging and subtle process of manoeuvring oneself into a position from which the necessary data can be collected. The ethnographer's negotiation of a role in the setting, and the implications of different roles for the nature of the data collected, will be examined in the next chapter.

4

Field relations

Like gatekeepers and sponsors, people in the field will also seek
to place or locate the ethnographer within their experience. This
is necessary, of course, for them to know how to deal with him or
her. Some individuals and groups have little or no knowledge of
social research. As with Barrett (1974), anthropologists are frequently suspected, initially at least, of being government spies,
tax inspectors, police informers, etc. Den Hollander provides an
example of an apparently more favourable initial identification
that nevertheless proved to be an insurmountable obstacle to his
research:

> 'In a town in southern Georgia (1932) it was rumoured after a
> few days that I was a scout for a rayon concern and might help
> to get a rayon industry established in the town. My denial
> reinforced the rumour, everyone tried to convince me of the
> excellent qualities of the town and its population – the
> observer had turned into a fairy godmother and serious work
> was no longer possible. Departure was the only solution.'
>
> (Den Hollander 1967:13)

Even where people in a setting are familiar with research,

there may be a serious mismatch between their expectations of the researcher and his or her intentions. Like gatekeepers, they too may view the researcher as expert or critic. Furthermore they may be, or consider themselves to be, very sophisticated in their knowledge of research methodology without being familiar with ethnography. Where this is the case they may challenge the legitimacy of the research and the credentials of the researcher.

Whether or not people have knowledge of social research, they are often more concerned with what kind of person the researcher is than with the research itself. They will try to gauge how far he or she can be trusted, what he or she might be able to offer as an acquaintance or friend, and perhaps also how easily he or she could be manipulated or exploited. (For a striking analysis of this process see Edgerton 1965.) The management of 'personal front' (Goffman 1955) is important here. As in other situations where identities have to be created or established, much thought must be given to 'impression management'. Impressions of the researcher that pose an obstacle to access must be avoided or countered as far as possible, while those that facilitate it must be encouraged; within the limits set by ethical considerations.

Impression management

Personal appearance can be a salient consideration, as Liebow notes:

> 'Almost from the beginning, I adopted the dress and something of the speech of the people with whom I was in most frequent contact, as best I could without looking silly or feeling uncomfortable. I came close in dress (in warm weather, tee or sport shirt and khakis or other slacks) with almost no effort at all. My vocabulary and diction changed, but not radically. . . . Thus, while remaining conspicuous in speech and perhaps in dress, I had dulled some of the characteristics of my background. I probably made myself more accessible to others, and certainly more acceptable to myself. This last point was forcefully brought home to me one evening when, on my way to a professional meeting, I stopped off at the carry-out in a suit and tie. My loss of ease made me clearly aware

that the change in dress, speech, and general carriage was as important for its effect on me as it was for its effect on others.'

(Liebow 1967:255–56)

Liebow here stresses that while his demeanour and dress tended to reduce the social differences between himself and his companions, he did not strive to become exactly like them. Howard Parker, writing about his work with adolescent deviants, makes a very similar point:

'Dress regulations were not unduly strict, and a dark pair of cord jeans and a leather jacket were as acceptable as all-blue denim or combinations of leather, cord and denim. I never attempted to copy dress style completely, adapting only to the extent of blunting differences. My own black shirt, black jeans, burgundy leather, style was always acceptable and indeed my leather (acquired locally at a very reasonable price!) became a bit of a joke and it was agreed that I most probably not only slept in it but copulated in it also. "There's a leather going in the Block, Parker lad, 'bout time you went mod isn't it? They'll give you a needle at the Royal hospital to get that old one off" (*Joey*).'

(Parker 1974:216)

Such forms of dress, then, can 'give off' the message that the ethnographer seeks to maintain the position of an acceptable marginal member. They thus declare the essential affinity between researcher and hosts, without any attempt on the part of the former to ape the style of the latter. Such considerations apply particularly under conditions of overt research, where an explicit research role must be constructed. Under conditions of secret research, of course, the fieldworker will be much more sharply constrained to match his or her personal front to that of the other participants.

Patrick's research on a Glasgow gang reveals the difficulty of 'passing' in this way:

'Clothes were another major difficulty. I was already aware of the importance attached to them by gang members in the school and so, after discussion with Tim, I bought . . . a midnight-blue suit, with a twelve-inch middle vent, three-inch flaps over the side pockets and a light blue handkerchief with

a white polka dot (to match my tie) in the top pocket. . . .
Even here I made two mistakes. Firstly, I bought the suit outright with cash instead of paying it up, thus attracting both
attention to myself in the shop and disbelief in the gang when I
innocently mentioned the fact. Secondly, during my first
night out with the gang, I fastened the middle button of my
jacket as I was accustomed to. Tim was quick to spot the mistake. The boys in the gang fastened only the top button; with
this arrangement they can stand with their hands in their
trouser pockets and their jackets buttoned – ''ra gallous
wae''.'

(Patrick 1973:13, 15)

There can be no clear prescription for dress other than to commend a degree of self-consciousness over self-presentation. A
mistake over such a simple matter can jeopardize the entire
enterprise. Having gained access to the Edinburgh medical
school, for instance, Paul Atkinson (1976, 1981a) went to see one
of the influential gatekeepers for an 'informal' chat about the
actual fieldwork. He was dressed extremely casually (as well
as having very long hair). He had absolutely no intention of
going onto the hospital wards looking like that. But the
gatekeeper was taken aback by his informal appearance, and
started to get cold feet about the research altogether. It took a
subsequent meeting, after a hair-cut and the donning of a lounge
suit, to convince him otherwise.

To some extent we have already touched on more general
aspects of self-presentation. Speech and demeanour will require
monitoring, though, as we have seen, it is not necessarily
desirable for them to be matched to those of participants. The
researcher must judge what sort of impression he or she wishes to
create, and manage appearances accordingly. Such impression
management is unlikely to be a unitary affair, however. There
may be different categories of participants, and different social
contexts, which demand the construction of different 'selves'. In
this, the ethnographer is no different in principle from social
actors in general, whose social competence requires such sensitivity to shifting situations.

The construction of a working identity may be facilitated in
some circumstances if the ethnographer can exploit relevant

skills or knowledge he or she already possesses. Parker illustrates the use of social skills in the course of his work with a Liverpool gang. He wrote that:

> 'blending in was facilitated by certain basic skills. One of the most important involved being "quick": although I was regarded as normally "quiet" and socially marginal, this placidity is not always a good idea. Unless you are to be seen as something of a "divvy" you must be able to look after yourself in the verbal quickfire of the Corner and the pub. . . . Being able to kick and head a football reasonably accurately was also an important aspect of fitting into the scheme. Again, whilst I was "no Kevin Keegan" and indeed occasionally induced abuse like "back to Rugby Special", I was able to blend into a scene where kicking a ball around took up several hours of the week. I also followed The Boys' football team closely each week and went to "the match" with them when I could. This helped greatly. Indeed when everyone realized I supported Preston (as well as Liverpool, of course) it was always a good joke since they were so often getting beaten. "Why don't you play for them they couldn't do any worse?"; "Is there a blind school in Preston?" (*Danny*).'
>
> (Parker 1974:217–19)

One sort of expertise, of a rather different sort, that anthropologists often find themselves trading on is that of superior technical knowledge and resources. Medical knowledge and treatment constitutes one form of this. The treatment of common disorders, usually by simple and readily available methods, has long been one way in which anthropologists in the field have succeeded in ingratiating themselves. This can create problems, of course, as McCurdy (1976) found out, with surgery time capable of taking up the whole day. Nevertheless, this is one way in which the fieldworker can demonstrate that he or she is not an exploitative interloper, but has something to give. Legal advice, the writing of letters, and the provision of 'lifts', for example, can perform the same role, though the value of pure sociability should not be underestimated. Indeed, the researcher must often try to find ways in which 'normal' social intercourse can be established. One often has to try to find some neutral ground with participants, where mundane small-talk can take place. It may be very threatening to hosts if one pumps them *constantly* about matters relating directly to research interests. Especially in the early days of field negotiations it may be advantageous to find more 'ordinary' topics of conversation with a view to establishing one's identity as a 'normal', 'regular', 'decent' person.

Beynon (1983) comments on this aspect of his ethnography in an urban secondary school for boys, in his attempts to establish rapport with the teaching staff:

> 'Although I did not consciously search these out, I stumbled upon topics in which they and I shared a certain degree of interest to serve as a backcloth, a resource to be referred to for "starters", or for "gap fillers" to keep the conversational door ajar.'
>
> (Beynon 1983:40)

Needless to say, such 'neutral' topics are not actually divorced from the researcher's interests at hand, since they can throw additional and unforeseen light on informants, and yield fresh sources of data.

Beynon also lists as a 'way-in' his own local connections:

> 'being regarded as "a local" was an important step forward, especially when it became known that I lived within comfortable walking distance of Victoria Road. This considerably lessened the sense of threat which some felt I posed.'
>
> (Beynon 1983:41)

This would not lessen such 'threats' in all cases, however. In some settings the participants might feel less threatened by a 'stranger', and feel more uneasy about the possible significance of an observer's local knowledge. The same applies to another of Beynon's 'ways in':

> 'More significantly by far, however, was my own background in teaching and experience in secondary schools, which I unashamedly employed to show staff that I was no stranger to teaching, to classrooms, and to school life in general. I was too old to adopt the now-familiar ethnographic persona of "naive student", and found it best to present myself as a former teacher turned lecturer/researcher.'
>
> (Beynon 1983:41)

Beynon goes on to quote the following exchange, which illustrates how such experience was a 'bonus' in his particular circumstances. At the same time, the extract illustrates a reaction to the attentions of a research worker typical of many settings.

> 'MR. BUNSEN: Where did you teach in London?
>
> J.B.: South London and then Hertfordshire.
>
> MR. PIANO: (who had been reading the Staff notice board) Good Lord, I didn't realise you were one of us! I thought you were one of the ''experts'' who never taught, but knew all about it.
>
> J.B.: I don't know all about it, but I have taught.
>
> MR. PIANO: How long?
>
> J.B.: Ten years, in a Grammar and then a Comprehensive.
>
> MR. PIANO: That's a fair stretch. Well, well, I can start thumping them now!'
>
> (Beynon 1983:42)

We can note in passing the common resentment on the part of some occupational practitioners, and especially teachers, of detached, often invisible 'experts'; though a fieldworker's willingness to stay and learn can often overcome such hostilities, irrespective of prior membership or expertise.

Beynon himself goes on to note that the employment of such strategies in establishing 'mutuality' was more than him pandering for the teachers' approval. Not only did such exchanges facilitate the collection of data, but they were 'data' in their own right. He also notes some feelings of personal disquiet, wondering whether he was unduly exploitative in offering 'friendship' in return for data.

The problem that the ethnographer often faces in such circumstances is deciding how much self-disclosure is appropriate or fruitful. It is hard to expect 'honesty' and 'frankness' on the part of participants and informants, whilst never being frank and honest about oneself. Nevertheless, just as in many everyday situations, one often has to suppress or play down one's own personal beliefs, commitments, and political sympathies. Again, this is not necessarily a matter of gross deception. The normal requirements of tact, courtesy, and 'interaction ritual' in general (Goffman 1972), mean that in some ways 'everyone has to lie' (Sacks 1975). For the researcher this may be particularly a matter of self-conscious impression management, and may thus become an ever-present aspect of social interaction in the field. One cannot bias the fieldwork by talking only with people one finds most congenial or politically sympathetic: one cannot choose one's informants on the same basis as one chooses friends (for the most part) (Hammersley 1983c).

The fieldworker may find him- or herself being 'tested' and pushed towards disclosure, particularly when the group or culture in question is founded upon beliefs and commitments (such as religious convictions, political affiliations, and the like). Here the process of negotiating access and rapport may be a matter of progressive initiation. The fieldworker may find the management of disclosure a particularly crucial feature of this delicate procedure. The same may apply with particular force to the investigation of deviance, where deviants may require reassurance that the ethnographer does not harbour feelings of disapproval, nor intends to initiate action against them.

There are, of course, aspects of personal front that are not open to 'management' and that may limit the negotiation of identities in the field, and these include so-called 'ascribed' characteristics. Although it would be wrong to think of the effects of these as absolutely determinate or fixed, such characteristics as gender, age, and ethnic identification may shape relationships with gatekeepers, sponsors, and people under study in important ways.

The researcher cannot escape the implications of gender: no position of genderless neutrality can be achieved. This is a feature of social research that has recently come under close scrutiny, in part as a consequence of the Women's Movement (see for example Roberts 1981). In the context of field research, Golde's (1970) collection of papers by women anthropologists highlights a number of recurrent themes that relate specifically to gender, some of which have been further amplified by Warren and Rasmussen (1977). (Revealingly, the issue of gender as such has only been raised in relation to female fieldworkers; the implications of gender have always been there, but have rarely been rendered visible and available for reflection.)

Common cultural stereotypes of females can work to their advantage in some respects. In so far as women are seen as unthreatening, then they may gain access to settings and information with relative ease. By the same token, however, their gender may limit women's access to particular domains – the domestic world of fellow women, children, the elderly, and so on. Male researchers may find it equally difficult to gain access to the world of women, especially in cultures where there is a strong division between the sexes.

Easterday *et al.* (1977) also remark on some of the ways in which female researchers may enter into field relationships, comparing different settings that are marked by varieties of sex roles. (Their paper is, incidentally, a useful example of how the systematic comparison of researchers' own experiences can potentially lead to a more general understanding of the research process, rather than the one-off autobiographical account.) In male-dominated settings, for instance, women may come up against the male 'fraternity', from which they are excluded; women may also find themselves the object of 'hustling' from male hosts; they may be cast in the role of the 'go-fer' runner of errands, or may be adopted as a sort of mascot. These possibilities all imply a lack of participation, or non-serious participation on the part of the woman. Not only will the female researcher find it difficult to be taken seriously by male hosts, but other females may also display suspicion and hostility in the face of her intrusion. Easterday *et al.* (1977) also recognize that for such reasons, female researchers may find advantageous trade-offs. The 'hustling' informant who is trying to impress the researcher may prove particularly forthcoming to her, and males may be manipulated by femininity. In some circumstances it may be easier for females to present themselves as socially acceptable incompetents, in many ways the most favourable role for a participant observer to adopt in the early stages of fieldwork.

There can be little doubt that much of the particular character of ethnographic writing has been coloured by the (male) gender of the great majority of writers. In her commentary on urban studies, Lyn Lofland has drawn attention to the 'thereness' of women; that is, like domestic servants, they are present, but as part of the background and are rarely taken notice of:

'There is really nothing in urban sociology on women quite comparable to the finely textured, closely grained, empirically loving, portrayal of "the boys' world" in Suttles' *The Social Order of the Slum* (1968), or of "corner boys and college boys" in Whyte's *Street Corner Society* (1955), or of "cats" in Finestone's *Cats, Kicks and Colour* (1967), or of "negro streetcorner men" in Liebow's *Tally's Corner* (1967), or of "urban nomads" in Spradley's *You Owe Yourself a Drunk* (1970).'

(Lofland 1975:145)

Lofland is too astute a sociologist to attribute such emphases to gender bias alone; she also implicates particular analytic preoccupations and assumptions concerning the formulation of 'social problems'. Her essay is a valuable discussion of an important sociological blind spot.

Ethnicity, like gender, sets its limits and poses its problems. Ethnicity is, of course, not merely a matter of physical characteristics, but also implies matters of culture, power, and personal style. Keiser (1970), reflecting on his work with the 'Vice Lords', a Chicago street gang, notes that it was difficult for him, as a white man, to establish relationships with black informants. While some were willing to accept him as a 'white nigger', others displayed strong antagonisms.

On the other hand, belonging to a different ethnic or even national group can sometimes have distinct advantages. Hannerz (1969), discussing his research on a black ghetto area in the United States, points out that while one of his informants jokingly suggested that he might be the real 'blue-eyed blond devil' that the Black Muslims talked about, his Swedish nationality distanced him from other whites.

Papanek (1964) draws attention to the two aspects of the fieldworker's identity we have referred to above. Reflecting on her experience in studying purdah, she points out that as a woman she had access to the world of women, which no man could ever attain, while her own foreignness helped to remove her from the most restricting demands of female modesty. As an outsider, the woman fieldworker in such a culture may be able to establish relatively 'neutral' roles *vis-à-vis* men in a way that no female *member* of the society could. (This view is endorsed by Jeffery (1979) on the basis of her own work on women in purdah.) The 'foreign' woman may almost become an 'honorary man'

(Warren and Rasmussen 1977). This latter is particularly the case if the researcher is no longer young.

Age is another important aspect of the fieldworker's persona. Although it is by no means universally true, there appears to be a tendency for ethnography to be the province of younger research workers. In part this may be because the younger person has more time to commit to the fieldwork (often for a higher degree); in part it may suggest that junior people find it easier to adopt the 'incompetent' position of the 'outsider' or 'marginal' person. This is not to imply that ethnography is properly restricted to younger investigators, but one must at least entertain the possibility that age will have a bearing on the kinds of relationships established and the data collected. The junior research student may well establish quite different working relationships from those available to, say, the middle-aged professor.

Honigmann (1970) illustrates the effects that age can have in comparing his research on the Kaska Indians at the age of thirty with his work on the Eskimos of Baffin Island which he carried out when he was forty-nine:

> 'Many experiences, both social and professional, brought special rewards, and consequently our stay in Frobisher Bay was not unpleasant, but there was not the kind of pleasurable excitement that in Western Canada had come from identifying with the community and participating intensely in the libidinous tenor of its behaviour. In Frobisher Bay I danced with my wife, except for old-fashioned group dances, joined no illicit drinking parties, and in the tavern drank carefully and watched the clock in order to have time to catch the last bus back to Apex [the suburb where he lived]. Perhaps by the time I reached Frobisher Bay I had lost some of the adaptability I possessed in my youth, and perhaps this limited the behaviour I could adopt in participant observation. Changes that time had brought in my professional status may also have been a factor, for my age seems to have alienated me from the younger men and women, especially those deviant from the larger society's norms.'
>
> (Honigmann 1970:61–2)

However, the effects of age, as of all personal characteristics, must not be overestimated. It is often possible to overcome them as Corsaro (1981) found in his research on nursery schoolchildren:

'Two four-year-old girls (Betty and Jenny) and adult researcher (Bill) in a nursery school:

BETTY: You can't play with us!
BILL: Why?
BETTY: Cause you're too big.
BILL: I'll sit down. (sits down)
JENNY: You're still too big.
BETTY: Yeah, you're "Big Bill"!
BILL: Can I just watch?
JENNY: OK, but don't touch nuthin!
BETTY: You just watch, OK?
BILL: OK.
JENNY: OK, Big Bill?
BILL: OK.

(Later Big Bill got to play.)'

(Corsaro 1981:117)

In the course of fieldwork, then, people who meet, or hear about, the researcher will cast him or her into certain identities on the basis of 'ascribed characteristics', as well as aspects of appearance and manner. This 'identity work' (Goffman 1959) must be monitored for its effects on the kinds of data collected. At the same time, the ethnographer will generally try to shape the nature of his or her role, as it is emerging in the setting, in such a way as to try to ensure that access to the necessary data is achieved.

Field roles

In the early days of fieldwork, the conduct of the ethnographer is often little different from the sort of activity that any layperson engages in when faced with the practical need to make sense of a particular social setting. Consider the position of the novice or recruit – a freshman student, a military rookie, a person starting a new job, say – who finds him- or herself in relatively strange surroundings. How do such novices get to 'know the ropes' and become 'old hands'? Obviously, there is nothing magical about this process of learning. Novices watch what other people are doing, ask other people to explain what is going on, try things out for themselves – occasionally making mistakes – and so on. The novice thus acts like a social scientist: making observations and inferences, asking informants, constructing hypotheses, and acting on them.

When studying an unfamiliar setting, the ethnographer is also a novice. Wherever possible he or she must put him- or herself into the position of being an 'acceptable incompetent', as Lofland (1971) neatly describes it. It is only through watching, listening, asking questions, formulating hypotheses, and making blunders that the ethnographer can acquire some sense of the social structure of the setting and begin to understand the culture of participants.

The crucial difference between the 'lay' novice and the ethnographer in the field is that the latter attempts to maintain a self-conscious awareness of what is learned, how it has been learned, and the social transactions that inform the production of such knowledge. As we saw in Chapter 1, it is an important requirement of ethnography that we suspend a wide range of common-sense and theoretical knowledge in order to minimize the danger of taking on trust misleading preconceptions about the setting and the people in it. 'Strange' or 'exotic' settings quickly demolish the ethnographer's faith in his or her preconceptions just as Schutz's (1964) stranger finds that what he or she knows about the new country will not suffice for survival in it.

Laura Bohannon (under the *nom de plume* Elenore Bowen) has written a vivid, semi-fictionalized account of her own initial encounters with an African culture. She captures the sense of alienation and 'strangeness' experienced by the fieldworker, and a feeling of being an 'incompetent':

'I felt much more like a backward child than an independent young woman. My household supported me, right or wrong against outsiders, but made their opinions known after the fact, and so obviously for my own good that I could not be justifiably angry. I felt even less like a trained and professional anthropologist pursuing his researches. I was hauled around from one homestead to another and scolded for my lack of manners or for getting my shoes wet. Far from having docile informants whom I could train, I found myself the spare-time amusement of people who taught me what they considered it good for me to know and what they were interested in at the moment, almost always plants or people.'

(Bowen 1954:40–1)

She documents the personal and emotional difficulties of coming to terms with such estrangement, but it is apparent from her account that this is integral to the process of learning. For instance, in the following account of a form of greeting that is exchanged when people meet on a path:

'The situation allows of fine calculation. To play fair, both should walk on at an even rate: a sudden sprint of speed may disconcert the other party, but such stratagems are resorted to only by the inexperienced or by those greedy for social victory at any price. A nervous eye and a half-open mouth indicate arrival within the six yards leeway zone of possible greeting. Whoever then first says "Where are you going?" should be answered in full; the loser, that is, must fill with explanation the time it takes to pass one another and walk on to just that point at which the winner can hear, "And where are you going?" as he walks out of earshot and out of the obligation to reply.

At first, everyone beat me to the draw. By the time I had skill enough to have a fifty-fifty chance, I had discovered refinements of the game. One far beyond my ability at that point and not altogether within the rules anyhow, was to begin a really interesting story of where one was going and why, timed to make the point of the story coincide with walking out of hearing. The other, also my own invention, was made in ignorance on that market day's walk. The reply to the path greeting is a simple phrase which means "I'm going travelling" only when one adds one's destination; otherwise the same phrase means "I'm walking" – not running or riding. At first I was unable to explain where I was going; later, I didn't always want to. Then, the greetings went like this:

"Where are you going?"
"I'm *walking*."

''So I see. *Where* are you going?''

''I'm *walking*. Where are *you* going?''

Half the time the victim of this unorthodox approach was flustered enough to answer and thus forfeit the information he had won by asking first.'

(Bowen 1954:35–6)

Bowen's comments here show how she came to understand this particular fragment of local 'interaction ritual' (Goffman 1972) through a process of trial-and-error, and to progress from incompetence to a (somewhat idiosyncratic) expertise in manipulating the 'rules of the game'.

This process of estrangement is what is often referred to as 'culture shock' and it is the stock-in-trade of social and cultural anthropology. That confrontation of the ethnographer and the 'alien' culture is the methodological and epistemological foundation of the anthropological enterprise, whether it be from the point of view of a romantically-inspired search for exotic cultures, or the less glamorous sort of encounter such as described by Chagnon, from his fieldwork among the Yanomamö.

Chagnon (1977) describes, with engaging frankness, how he set off into 'the field' with a mixture of assumptions. On the one hand, he confesses to a Rousseau-like expectation as to his future relations with the Yanomamö: that they would like him, even adopt him, and so on. At the same time, by virtue of his seven years of training as an anthropologist, he carried with him a considerable load of social-scientific assumptions: as he puts it, that he was about to encounter 'social facts' inhabiting the village, all eager to recount their genealogies to him. In contrast to his romantic phantasies, and his social-scientific assumptions, he did not encounter a collection of social facts, nor indeed were his chosen people the noble or welcoming savages of his imagination. Quite the reverse:

'I looked up and gasped when I saw a dozen burly, naked, filthy, hideous men staring at us down the shafts of their drawn arrows! Immense wads of green tobacco were stuck between their lower teeth and lips making them look even more hideous, and strands of dark green slime dripped or hung from their noses. . . . I was horrified. What sort of welcome was this for the person who came here to live with you and learn your way of life, to become friends with you?'

(Chagnon 1977:4)

It is worth noting in passing here that Chagnon's self-revelation shows not only the 'culture clash' of the Westerner encountering an 'exotic' culture, but also the problem of the social scientist who expects to uncover 'social facts', 'rules', 'institutions', 'organizations', and so on by direct observation of the social world. This is perhaps one of the hardest lessons to learn at the outset. One does not 'see' everyday life laid out like a sociology or anthropology textbook, and one cannot read off analytic concepts directly from the phenomena of everyday life. Some researchers, setting out on fieldwork, may even feel a sense of betrayal when they discover this, or alternatively experience a panic of self-doubt, believing themselves to be inadequate research workers because their observations do not fall neatly into the sorts of categories suggested by the received wisdom of 'the literature'.

In researching settings that are more familiar, it is, of course, much more difficult to suspend one's preconceptions, whether these derive from social science or from everyday knowledge. One reason for this is that what one finds is so obvious. Becker provides a classic example:

> 'We may have understated a little the difficulty of observing contemporary classrooms. It is not just the survey method of educational testing or any of those things that keeps people from seeing what is going on. I think, instead, that it is first and foremost a matter of it all being so familiar that it becomes impossible to single out events that occur in the classroom as things that have occurred, even when they happen right in front of you. I have not had the experience of observing in elementary and high school classrooms myself, but I have in college classrooms and it takes a tremendous effort of will and imagination to stop seeing only the things that are conventionally "there" to be seen. I have talked to a couple of teams of research people who have sat around in classrooms trying to observe and it is like pulling teeth to get them to see or write anything beyond what "everyone" knows.'
>
> (Becker 1971:10)

Another problem with settings in one's own society is that one may not be allowed to take on a novice role. We noted in the previous chapter how researchers are sometimes cast into the role of expert or critic. Moreover, ascribed characteristics, notably age, and latent identities – as in the case of Beynon's (1983) research on teachers – may reinforce this. In studying such settings the ethnographer is faced with the difficult task of rapidly acquiring the ability to act competently, which is not always easy even within familiar settings, while simultaneously privately struggling to suspend for analytic purposes precisely those assumptions that must be taken for granted in relations with participants.

The 'acceptable incompetent' is not, then, the only role that ethnographers may take on in the field, and, indeed, even where it is adopted it is often abandoned, to one degree or another, as the fieldwork progresses. There have been several attempts to map out the various roles that ethnographers may adopt in settings. Junker (1960) and Gold (1958), for example, distinguish between the 'complete participant', 'participant-as-observer', 'observer-as-participant', and 'complete observer' (see *Figure 1*).

Figure 1 Theoretical social roles for fieldwork

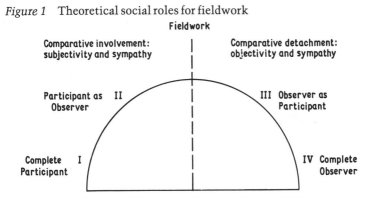

Source: Junker 1960:36. (Reproduced by permission of Chicago University Press.)

In the 'complete participant' role, the ethnographer's activities are wholly concealed. Here the researcher may join an organization or group – Alcoholics Anonymous (Lofland and Lejeune 1960), Pentecostalists (Homan 1980), an army unit (Sullivan *et al.* 1958), a mental hospital (Rosenhahn 1982) – as though they were ordinary members but with the purpose of carrying out research. Alternatively, complete participation may occur where the putative researcher is already a member of the group or organization that he or she decides to study. This was the case with Holdaway's (1982) research on the police, and Dalton's (1959) work on 'Men Who Manage'. An extreme example is Bettelheim's (1970) account of life in German concentration camps.

'Complete participation' is, then, approximated in some circumstances. Some commentators have suggested that it is the ideal to which researchers should aim. Jules-Rosette (1978), for instance, has argued for the necessity of 'total immersion' in a native culture. That is, not simply 'passing' as a member but actually *becoming* a member. In Jules-Rosette's case this was accompanied by conversion to the Apostolic Church of John Maranke, an indigenous African movement. This indeed is the criterion Jules-Rosette demands for what she calls 'reflexive ethnography': a usage of the term 'reflexive' that is very different from our own (for yet a third view, see Sharrock and Anderson 1980).

To the inexperienced, 'complete participation' might seem very attractive. Such identification and immersion in the setting may appear to offer safety: one may travel incognito, obtain 'inside' knowledge, and avoid the trouble of access negotiations. There is some truth in this, and indeed in some settings complete participation may be the only strategy by which the data required can be obtained. However, 'passing' as a member over a protracted period may place great strain on the fieldworker's dramaturgical capacities; and should the ethnographer's cover be 'blown', then the consequences could be disastrous, both for the researcher personally and for the completion of the fieldwork project.

More fundamentally still, the strategy of 'complete participation' will normally prove extremely limiting. The range and character of the data that can be collected will often prove restricted in practice. The participant will, by definition, be implicated in existing social practices and expectations in a far more rigid manner than the known researcher. The research activity will therefore be hedged round by these pre-existing social routines and realities. It will prove hard for the fieldworker to arrange his or her actions in order to optimize data collection possibilities. Some potentially fruitful lines of inquiry may be rendered practically impossible, in so far as the complete participant has to act in accordance with existing role expectations.

This is a point well made by Pollert (1981) in relation to her study of female factory workers. She discusses the possible strategy of obtaining a factory job herself. In the first place, the management of her chosen industrial setting would not permit it, but:

> 'Second, had I got a job, the advantages of experiencing for myself what it felt like, and possibly becoming very close to a small work-group around me, would have been heavily outweighed by the disadvantages of restricted movement, abiding by the rules preventing entry into other departments (without permission), and losing the privileges of the outsider, of speaking to other employees in the factory, including chargehands, supervisors and managers.'
>
> (Pollert 1981:6)

The limitations of complete participation are also indicated by Gregor (1977). During the early days of fieldwork in a Brazilian Indian village, Gregor and his wife attempted – in the interests of 'good public relations' – to live out their lives as villagers:

> 'Unfortunately we were not learning very much. Each day I would come back from treks through the forest numb with fatigue, ill with hunger, and covered with ticks and biting insects. My own work was difficult to pursue, for fishing and hunting are serious business and there is no time to pester men at work with irrelevant questions about their mother's brothers. Meanwhile, my wife was faring little better with the women.'
>
> (Gregor 1977:28)

Hence Gregor and his wife stopped 'pretending' that they were 'becoming' Brazilian villagers, and turned to systematic *research* activity, collecting data for census material, genealogies, residence patterns, hammock arrangements, and so on.

In contrast to the 'complete participant', the 'complete observer' has no contact at all with those he or she is observing. Observation may take place through a one-way mirror. Covert observation from a window of public behaviour in the street (Lofland 1973) also falls into this category, and perhaps also research like that by Karp (1980) on the 'public sexual scene' in Times Square.

Paradoxically, complete observation shares many of the advantages and disadvantages of complete participation. In their favour they can both minimize problems of reactivity: in neither case will the ethnographer interact *as a researcher* with members being studied. On the other hand, there may be severe limits on what can and cannot be observed and the questioning of participants may be impossible. Adopting either of these roles alone would make it very difficult to generate and test theory in a rigorous manner, though both may be useful strategies to adopt during particular phases of the fieldwork, and in some situations may be unavoidable.

Most field research involves roles somewhere between these two poles. Whether the distinction between participant-as-observer and observer-as-participant is of any value is a moot point. Indeed, in examining this distinction a serious problem with Junker's (1960) typology arises: it runs together several dimensions of variation that are by no means necessarily related. One of these, touched on in the previous chapter, is the question of secrecy and deception. Another is the issue of whether the ethnographer takes on a role already existing in the field or negotiates a new role; though no hard and fast distinction can be made here, and indeed we should beware of treating the roles already established in the setting as rigid and fixed in character (Turner 1962).

Nevertheless, there is an important point at issue. In secret research one has little option but to take on an existing role, though it may be possible to extend and modify it somewhat to facilitate the research (Dalton 1959). Sometimes even in open research there may be no choice but to take on an established role, as Freilich (1970) found out in his research on Mohawk steelworkers in New York. Having become adopted as a friend of one of the Mohawks, he tried to revert to the role of anthropologist. As he remarks:

> 'It was soon clear that any anthropological symbol was tabu . . . I could use no pencils, notebooks or questionnaires. I

even failed in attempts to play the semianthropologist. For example I tried saying, ''Now that is really interesting; let me write that down so that I don't forget it''. Suddenly my audience became hostile, and the few words I jotted down cost me much in rapport for the next few days.'

(Freilich 1970:193)

Generally, though, in open research the ethnographer has some choice over whether or not to take on one of the existing roles in the field. Thus, for example, in research on schools, ethnographers have sometimes adopted the role of teacher (see for example Hargreaves 1967 and Lacey 1976), sometimes not; though they have rarely taken on the role of pupil (but see Corsaro 1981 and Llewellyn 1980).

Decisions about the role to adopt in a setting will depend on the purposes of the research and the nature of the setting. In any case, anticipation of the likely consequences of adopting different roles can rarely be more than speculative. Fortunately, shifts in role can often be made over the course of fieldwork. Indeed, there are strong arguments in favour of moving among roles so as to allow one to discount their effects on the data. In studying nursery-school children, Corsaro (1981) not only sought to become a participant in the children's games, but also during a later phase of the research he used a one-way mirror to observe their behaviour. Similarly, Sevigny (1981), studying art classes in a college, collected data by surreptitiously taking on the role of student, by acting as tutor, as well as adopting a variety of researcher roles.

Different roles within a setting can be exploited, then, in order to get access to different kinds of data, as well as to acquire some sense of the various kinds of bias characteristic of each.

Managing marginality

There is a third dimension of variation in research roles built into the typology developed by Junker and Gold: from the 'external' view of the observer to the 'internal' view of the participant. The 'complete participant' gets access to inside information and experiences the world in ways that may be quite close to the ways other participants experience it. In this way greater access to participant perspectives may be achieved. At the same time, there is the danger of 'going native'. Not only may the task of analysis be abandoned in favour of the joys of participation, but even where it is retained bias may arise from 'over-rapport'. Miller outlines the problem in the context of a study of local union leadership:

> 'once I had developed a close relationship to the union leaders I was committed to continuing it, and some penetrating lines of inquiry had to be dropped. They had given me very significant and delicate information about the internal operation of the local [union branch]: to question closely their basic attitudes would open up severe conflict areas. To continue close rapport and to pursue avenues of investigation which appeared antagonistic to the union leaders was impossible. To shift to a lower level of rapport would be difficult because such a change would induce considerable distance and distrust.'

(Miller 1952:98)

Having established friendly relations Miller found the possibilities of data collection limited. Indeed, he suggests that the leaders themselves might have fostered such close relationships as a strategy to limit his observations and criticisms. Miller also notes that over-rapport with one group leads to problems of rapport with others: in his study, his close rapport with union leaders limited his rapport with rank and file members.

The question of rapport applies in two senses, both of which may be glossed as issues of 'identification'. In the sort of case outlined by Miller, one may be identified with particular groups or individuals so that one's social mobility in the field, and relationships with others, become impaired. More subtly, perhaps, is the danger of 'identifying with' such members' perspectives, and hence of failing to treat these as problematic.

One recent British ethnography that appears to many readers to be flawed by such 'partial perspectives' is Paul Willis's (1977) study of working-class adolescent boys. Willis's work is based primarily on conversations with twelve pupils who display 'anti-school' attitudes. These particular working-class boys describe themselves as 'lads' and distinguish themselves from those they call the 'ear'oles', who subscribe to the values of the school. The 'lads' see little chance of obtaining 'middle-class' jobs, and enthusiastically seek working-class employment. Willis argues that the counter-culture 'fits' with the culture of the workplace for manual workers, even suggesting that the more conformist pupils are less well adapted to the culture of working-class jobs.

There are two senses in which 'over-rapport' seems to be indicated in Willis's treatment of these youngsters. In the first place he seems to have devoted his attention almost entirely to the 'lads'; in many respects to have taken over their views without question in the analysis. Hence, the book becomes as much a celebration of the 'lads' as anything else: Willis seems unable or unwilling adequately to distance himself from the 'lads'' accounts. Second, the 'lads' are endorsed by Willis since he treats them more or less as spokesmen for 'the working class'. While Willis explicitly recognizes that working-class culture is variable, he nonetheless seems to identify the 'lads'' views, or some of them, as representative of the working class in general. Since the 'ear'oles' or conformists are also from working-class backgrounds, this is problematic, to say the least. It seems clear that Willis is guilty of 'identifying' with his chosen twelve, and his work is deeply flawed as a result.

In a striking parallel, Stein (1964) provides a reflexive account of his own identification with one set of workers, the miners in the gypsum plant he studied with Gouldner (1954):

'Looking back now I can see all kinds of influences that must have been involved. I was working out authority issues, and clearly I chose the open expression of hostile feelings that was characteristic in the mine rather than the repression that was characteristic on the surface. I came from a muddled class background which involved a mixture of lower-, upper-, and middle-class elements that I have not yet been able to disentangle fully. The main point is that I associate working-class settings with emotional spontaneity and middle-class settings with emotional restraint. I never quite confronted the fact that the surface men were as much members of the working class as were the miners. . . .

The descriptive writing became an act of fealty since I felt that writing about life in this setting was my way of being loyal to the people living in it. This writing came more easily than most of my other writing. But the efforts at interpreting the miners' behavior as a product of social forces, and especially seeing it as being in any way strategic rather than spontaneous, left me with profound misgivings.'

(Stein 1964:20-1)

The 'complete observer' generally escapes the danger of 'going native' of course, but only at the risk of failing to understand the perspective of participants. Moreover, this is not simply a matter of missing out on an important aspect of the setting: it may well lead to serious misunderstanding of the behaviour observed.

While ethnographers may adopt a variety of roles, the aim throughout is to maintain a more or less marginal position. As Lofland (1971:97) points out, the researcher generates 'creative insight' out of this marginal position of simultaneous insider-outsider. The ethnographer must be intellectually poised between 'familiarity' and 'strangeness', while socially he or she is poised between 'stranger' and 'friend' (Powdermaker 1966; Everhart 1977). He or she is, in the title of the collection edited by Freilich (1970), a 'marginal native'.

Marginality is not an easy position to maintain, it engenders a continual sense of insecurity. Johnson (1976), for instance, has recorded in some detail his emotional and physical reactions to the stresses of fieldwork. Some of his fieldnotes document his response with remarkable frankness:

'Every morning around seven forty-five, as I'm driving to the office, I begin to get this pain in the left side of my back, and the damn thing stays there usually until around eleven, when I've made my daily plans for accompanying one of the workers. Since nearly all of the workers remain in the office until around eleven or twelve, and since there's only one extra chair in the two units, and no extra desks as yet, those first two or three hours are sheer agony for me every damn day. Trying to be busy without hassling any one worker too much is like playing Chinese checkers, hopping to and fro, from here to there, with no place to hide.'

(Johnson 1976:152-53)

The physical symptoms that Johnson describes are perhaps rather extreme examples of fieldwork stress. But the phenomenon in general is by no means unusual: many fieldworkers report that they experience some degree of discomfiture by virtue of their 'odd', 'strange', or 'marginal' position. Some flavour of this can be gleaned from Wintrob's (1969) psychological appraisal of the anxieties suffered by anthropologists in the field: it is based on the experiences of a number of graduate students, and published autobiographical accounts.

Wintrob identifies a number of sources of stress, including what he glosses as the 'dysadaptation syndrome', which includes a wide range of feelings – incompetence, fear, anger, frustration. He cites one graduate student's account:

'I was afraid of everything at the beginning. It was just fear, of imposing on people, of trying to maintain a completely different role than anyone else around you. You hem and haw before making a leap into the situation. You want to retreat for another day. I'd keep thinking: am I going to be rejected? Am I really getting the data I need? I knew I had to set up my tent but I'd put it off. I'd put off getting started in telling people about wanting to give a questionnaire. I was neatly ensconced in . . .'s compound (an area of tents comprising one kin group). Everybody there knew what I was doing. I found it hard to move over to the other camp (a few miles away). I rationalised that a field worker shouldn't jump around too much.'

(Wintrob 1969:67)

Malinowski's own diaries reveal many such indications of stress and anxiety: indeed they are a remarkable document for what they reveal about his ambivalent feelings towards the Trobriand Islanders, his own intense self-absorption, and his preoccupation with his own well-being (Malinowski 1967). In a similar vein, Wax (1971) has provided an excellent account of her difficulties in working in a relocation centre for Japanese Americans after the Second World War. Wax describes her initial difficulties with collecting data, in the face of (understandable) suspicion and hostility: 'At the conclusion of the first month of work I had obtained very little data, and I was discouraged, bewildered and obsessed by a sense of failure' (1971:70).

We do not wish to convey the impression that the experience of fieldwork is one of unrelieved misery: for many it is often a matter of intense personal reward and satisfaction. Yet the stress experienced by the 'marginal native' is a very common aspect of ethnography, and it is an important one. In so far as he or she resists over-identification or surrender to 'hosts', then it is likely that there will be a corresponding sense of 'betrayal', or at least of divided loyalties. Lofland (1971:108–09) draws attention to the 'poignancy' of this experience. There is a sense of schizophrenia that the disengaged/engaged ethnographer may suffer. But this feeling, or equivalent feelings, should be managed for what they are. They are not necessarily something to be avoided, or to be replaced by more congenial sensations of comfort. The comfortable sense of being 'at home' is a danger signal. From the perspective of the 'marginal' reflexive ethnographer, there can thus be no question of total commitment, 'surrender', or 'becoming'. There must always remain some part held back, some social and intellectual 'distance'. For it is in the 'space' created by this distance that the analytic work of the ethnographer gets done. Without that distance, without such analytic space, the ethnography can be little more than the autobiographical account of a personal conversion. This would be an interesting and valuable document, but not an ethnographic study.

Ethnographers, then, must strenuously avoid feeling 'at home'. If and when all sense of being a 'stranger' is lost, one may have allowed the escape of one's critical, analytic perspective. The early days of fieldwork are proverbially problematic, and may well be fraught with difficulties: difficult decisions concerning fieldwork strategy have to be made, working relationships may have to be established quickly, and social embarrassment is a real possibility. On the other hand, it would be dangerous to assume that this is just a difficult phase that the researcher can simply outgrow, after which he or she can settle down to a totally comfortable, trouble-free existence. While social relations and working arrangements will get sorted out, and gross problems of strangeness will be resolved, it is important that this should not result in too cosy a mental attitude.

Everhart (1977) illustrates the danger from his research on college students and teachers:

> 'saturation, fieldwork fatigue, and just plain fitting in too well culminated, toward the end of the second year, in a diminishing of my critical perspective. I began to notice that events were escaping me, the significance of which I did not realize until later. For example, previously I had recorded in minute detail the discussions teachers had on categorizing students and those conversations students had on labeling other students. While these discussions continued and were especially rich because of the factors that caused these perspectives to shift, I found myself, toward the end of the study, tuning out of such discussions because I felt I had heard them all before when, actually, many dealt with dimensions I had never considered. On the one hand I was angry at myself for not recording and analyzing the category systems, on the other hand I was tired and found it more natural to sit with teachers and engage in small talk. The inquisitiveness had been drained from me.'
>
> (Everhart 1977:13)

This is not to deny that there will be occasions, many occasions, when one will need to engage in social interaction for primarily social and pragmatic reasons, rather than in accordance with the research interests and strategies. Rather, the point is that one should never surrender oneself entirely to the setting or to the moment. In principle, one should be constantly on the alert, with more than half an eye on the research possibilities that can be seen or engineered from any and every social situation.

If one does start to feel at ease, and the research setting takes on the appearance of routine familiarity, then one needs to ask oneself some pertinent questions. Is this sense of ease a reflection of the fact that the research is actually finished? Have all the necessary data already been collected? (Obviously in theory there is always something new to discover, unforeseen events to investigate, unpredictable outcomes to follow up, and so on; but the line has to be drawn somewhere.) This is always a useful question to ask: there is no point in hanging on in the field to no good purpose, just for the sake of being there, just 'for interest', or from a lack of confidence that one has enough information.

Sometimes you will tell yourself that you are done: that you should either finish the fieldwork, or that you should now move on to a new social setting. Alternatively, it may be the case that a sense of familiarity has been engendered by sheer laziness. Further questions may be in order, if the research does not seem to be finished. Do I feel at ease because I am being too compliant? That is, am I being so 'nice' to my hosts that I *never* get them to confront any potentially troublesome or touchy topics? Likewise, does my social ease mean that I am avoiding some people, and cultivating others with whom I feel more comfortable? In many social contexts, we find ourselves in need of formal or informal sponsors, helpful informants, and so forth. But it is important not to cling to them. From time to time one should evaluate whether the research is being unduly limited by such a possibility. In general, it is well worth pausing to consider whether a sense of comfort and familiarity may be an artefact of laziness, and a limitation imposed on the research by a failure to go on asking new questions, by a reluctance ever to go against the grain, a fear of ever making mistakes, and an unwillingness to try to establish new or difficult social relationships. It is possible to carve out an inhabitable niche in the field during the early stages of a project: it is important not to stay there, and never try one's wings in other contexts.

In Chapter 1 we argued that the role of the researcher in generating the data collected must be recognized. Rather than seeking, by one means or another, to eliminate reactivity, its effects should be monitored and, as far as possible, brought under control. By systematically modifying one's role in the field, different kinds of data can be collected whose comparison may greatly enhance interpretation of the social processes under study. Relevant here is the use of interviewing and the analysis of documents, and these are the subject of the next two chapters.

5

Insider accounts:
listening and
asking questions

It is a distinctive feature of social research that the 'objects' it studies are in fact 'subjects', and themselves produce accounts of their world. As we saw in Chapter 1 this fact is interpreted rather differently by positivism and naturalism. For the former these common-sense accounts are subjective and must be replaced by science; at most they are simply social products to be explained. For naturalism, by contrast, common-sense knowledge constitutes the social world: it must be appreciated and described, not subjected to critical scrutiny as to its validity, nor explained away.

We argued in Chapter 1 that these paradigms share the mistaken assumption that only false beliefs can be explained sociologically, though the conclusions they draw from this are diametrically opposed. Once we reject this assumption, it becomes clear that there are two equally important ways in which accounts, both those of the researcher and of the people under study, can be interpreted. On the one hand they can be read for what they tell us about the phenomena to which they refer. Everyone is a participant observer, acquiring knowledge about the social world in the course of participation in it. Such participant knowledge on the part of people in a setting is an important resource for the ethnographer. However skilful he or she is in negotiating a role that allows observation of events, some information will not be available at first hand. Indeed, some people may be cultivated (Bigus 1972) and even 'trained' (Paul 1953) as informants.

At one time the use of informants seems to have been the staple research method in cultural anthropology. The central concern was the collection of 'specimens' of primitive life, whether material artefacts or myths and legends, as an extract from the field diary of Franz Boas illustrates:

> 'I had a miserable day today. The natives held a big potlatch again. I was unable to get hold of anyone and had to snatch at whatever I could get. Late at night I did get something (a tale) for which I had been searching–"The Birth of the Raven"
> . . . . The big potlatches were continued today, but people found time to tell me stories'
> (Rohner 1969:38, quoted in Pelto and Pelto 1978:243)

As Pelto and Pelto remark: 'Most anthropologists today would be overjoyed at the prospect of observing a full-blown potlatch and would assume that crucially important structural and cultural data could be extracted from the details of the ceremony' (1978:243). While in more recent times ethnographers evince rather different priorities and have come to place more reliance on their own observations, considerable use is still made of informants, both to get information about activities that for one reason or another cannot be directly observed, and to check inferences made from observations.

Accounts are also important, though, for what they tell us about those who produce them. We can use the accounts given by people as evidence of the perspectives of particular groups or categories of actor to which they belong. Indeed, knowledge of these perspectives may form an important element of the theory being developed. Here the mode of analysis is that of the sociology of knowledge (Curtis and Petras 1970; Borhek and Curtis 1975); though there is much work outside the boundaries of that discipline that is also relevant. Particularly important is ethnomethodological work showing that accounts are not simply representations of the world; they are part of the world they describe and are thus shaped by the contexts it which they occur (Garfinkel 1967; Sudnow 1967; Zimmerman 1969; and Wieder 1974).

Besides contributing to sociological theory, this mode of analysis also aids our assessment of the validity of the information provided by an account. The more effectively we can understand the account and its context – who produced it, for whom, and why – the better able we are to anticipate the ways in which it may suffer from biases of one kind or another as a source of information. In this sense the two ways of reading accounts – what we might call 'information' and 'perspective' analysis, respectively – are complementary. The same account can be analysed from both angles, though in asking questions of participants we may have one or other concern predominantly in mind.

Separating the question of the truth or falsity of people's beliefs, as currently assessed, from the analysis of those beliefs as social phenomena allows us to treat participant knowledge as both resource and topic. It leads us to deal with the accounts produced by others on exactly the same terms as our own, while yet avoiding relativism.

Unsolicited and solicited accounts

All human behaviour has an expressive dimension. Ecological arrangements, clothes, gesture, and manner all convey messages about people. They indicate gender, social status, occupational role, and even personality. However, the expressive power of language provides the most important resource for accounts. The most striking feature of language is its capacity to present descriptions, explanations, and evaluations of almost infinite variety about any aspect of the world, including itself. Thus, we find that in everyday life people continually provide linguistic accounts to one another: discussing one another's motives and abilities, retailing 'what happened' on some occasion, making disclaimers, and offering excuses and justifications, for example. Such talk occurs most notably when some kind of misalignment is perceived between values, rules, or normal expectations and the actual course of events (Hewitt and Stokes 1976). The resulting accounts may be concerned with remedying the discrepancy, or with finding some explanation for it, for example by categorizing someone as 'stupid', 'immoral', or whatever.

Of course accounts are not only provided by participants to one another, they are also given to ethnographers. Indeed, especially in the early stages of fieldwork, participants may be intent upon making sure that the researcher understands the situation 'correctly'. 'Telling the researcher how it is' is a recurrent feature of fieldwork. Very often the aim is to counteract what it is assumed others have told the researcher, or what are presumed to be his or her likely interpretations of what has been observed (Hammersley 1980; Hitchcock 1983).

Ethnographers also actively solicit accounts both by asking questions informally in the course of their contacts with participants, and sometimes more formally through arranging interviews. Of course in some circumstances asking questions, even informally, is difficult if not impossible, as Agar found in his research on drug addiction:

> 'In the streets, though, I learned that you don't ask questions. There are at least two reasons for that rule. One is because a person is vulnerable to arrest by the police, or to being cheated or robbed by other street people. Questions about behaviour may be asked to find out when you are vulnerable to arrest. Or they may be asked to find out when or in what way you can be parted from some money or heroin. Even if one sees no direct connection between the question and those outcomes, it might just be because one has not figured out the questioner's "game" yet.
>
> The second reason for not asking questions is that you should not have to ask. To be accepted in the streets is to be hip; to be hip is to be knowledgeable; to be knowledgeable is to be capable of understanding what is going on on the basis of minimal cues. So to ask a question is to show that you are not acceptable and this creates problems in a relationship when you have just been introduced to somebody.'
>
> (Agar 1980:456)

Similarly, while among much of the population of modern

societies the interview is a familiar phenomenon (Benney and Hughes 1956), there are groups within those societies that are unfamiliar with or hostile to it:

> 'The Gypsies' experience of direct questions is partly formed by outsiders who would harass, prosecute or convert. The Gypsies assess the needs of the questioner and give the appropriate answer, thus disposing of the intruder, his ignorance intact. Alternatively the Gypsies may be deliberately inconsistent. . . . I found the very act of questioning elicited either an evasive and incorrect answer or a glazed look. It was more informative to merge into the surroundings than alter them as inquisitor. I participated in order to observe. Towards the end of fieldwork I pushed myself to ask questions, but invariably the response was unproductive, except among a few close associates. Even then, answers dried up, once it appeared that my questions no longer arose from spontaneous puzzlement and I was making other forms of discussion impossible.'
>
> (Okely 1983:45)

While, as Okely indicates, questioning may sometimes have to be abandoned, it may sometimes be possible to overcome resistance through modification of the way in which questions are asked. Lerner (1957) reports the defensive reactions he met when he started interviewing members of French élites, and the strategy he developed to deal with them:

> 'Our first approaches to interviewing were modest, tentative, apologetic. Trial-and-error, hit-and-miss (what the French love to call "L'empiricisme anglo-saxon") finally produced a workable formula. To each prospective respondent, the interviewer explained that his Institute had undertaken a study of attitudes among the élite. As Frenchmen do not respond readily to questionnaires, he continued, we were seeking the counsel of specially qualified persons: "Would you be so kind as to review with us the questionnaire we propose to use and give us the benefit of your criticisms? In responding yourself, you could explain which questions a Frenchman would be likely to resist and why; which questions would draw ambiguous or evasive responses that could not be properly interpreted; and which questions could be altered in such a

way as to require reflective rather than merely stereotyped answers.''

By casting the interviewee in the role of expert consultant, we gave him the opportunity to indulge in a favourite indoor sport – generalising about Frenchmen.'

(Lerner 1957:27)

As we might expect, given the influence of naturalism, it is not uncommon for ethnographers to regard solicited accounts as 'less valid' than those produced among participants in 'naturally occurring situations'. Thus, for example, Becker and Geer (1960) argue that it is important to ensure that conclusions about the perspectives of participants are not entirely reliant on solicited answers, otherwise they may be vitiated through reactivity. Similarly, there is a tendency among ethnographers to favour non-directive interviewing in which the interviewee is allowed to talk at length, and in his or her own terms. The aim here is to minimize, as far as possible, the influence of the researcher on what is said, and thus to facilitate the open expression of the informant's perspective on the world.

Now it is certainly true that the influence of the researcher on the production of data is an important issue, but it is misleading to regard it simply as a source of bias that must be removed. For one thing, neither non-directive interviewing nor even reliance on unsolicited accounts avoids the problem. Hargreaves, Hester, and Mellor (1975) report the difficulties they faced in developing a non-directive way of questioning teachers about classroom events:

'Our principal method was to observe a lesson and from these observations to extract those teacher statements and/or actions which consisted of a reaction to a deviant act.

We then reported the reaction back to the teacher at a later stage, asking for his commentary upon what he did . . . we often merely quoted what the teacher had said, and the teacher was willing to make a commentary upon his action without any direct question from us. On other occasions we reported the teacher's statement back and then asked why the teacher had said or done something. Whatever method we used, the teachers always imputed some motive to us for reporting these events to them or for asking for some com-

mentary upon what had occurred. This motive, presumably, was that we were interested in understanding the events which we were investigating. More interesting, however, is the question of what we were asking for, rather than why we were asking. In reporting the teacher's statement back to him for commentary, it is clear that we are asking teachers to ''display'' to us. But often we did not actually tell the teacher precisely what we expected him to display – and we did so intentionally. In consequence the teacher always had an interpretive problem. He had to provide a commentary on his own conduct which he could assume would be seen by us as an appropriate, relevant and meaningful answer to our unspoken question. In fact, it is clear from teachers' commentaries that they imputed a wide range of implicit questions to us. Sometimes the commentary would be about the act, sometimes about the actor, sometimes about their own thinking and motives. All the commentaries have one element in common; they all take the form of teachers' attempts to explain or justify their actions. As far as possible we tried to minimize the evaluative overtones to these conversations, by suggesting that we ourselves were not making evaluative judgments on the teachers and were not interested in making personal judgments about whether or not the teacher had said or done the ''right'' thing. Nevertheless, all the teachers' commentaries consisted of explanations and justifications, which has an important bearing on their status as evidence.'
(Hargreaves, Hester, and Mellor 1975:219–20)

Even in the case of unsolicited accounts one can never be sure that the presence of the researcher was not an important influence. Even where the researcher is not a party to the interaction but simply within earshot, knowledge of his or her presence may have a significant effect. Indeed, sometimes this influence is only too obvious as the following fieldnote from a study of staffroom talk among secondary school teachers (Hammersley 1980) makes clear:

(The researcher is sitting in an armchair reading a newspaper. Two teachers, Walker and Larson, are engaged in conversation nearby, in the course of which the following exchange occurs.)

'LARSON: You ought to be official NUT (National Union
of Teachers) convenor.

WALKER: I'm only in the NUT for one reason.

LARSON: (looking significantly at the researcher) In case you
get prosecuted for hitting someone.

WALKER: That's right.'

(Hammersley 1980)

However, even if the influence of the researcher could be
eliminated through adoption of the 'complete observer' or 'complete participant' role, not only would this place serious
restrictions on the data collection process, it would also in no
sense guarantee 'valid data'. The problem of reactivity is merely
one aspect of a more general phenomenon that *cannot* be
eradicated: the effects of audience, and indeed of context generally, on what people say and do. All accounts must be interpreted
in terms of the context in which they were produced. Thus,
Dean and Whyte (1958) argue that rather than asking, for
example, 'how do I know if the informant is telling the truth?',
we should consider what the informant's statements reveal
about his or her feelings and perceptions, and what inferences
can be made from these about the actual environment or events
he or she has experienced. The aim is not to gather 'pure' data
that are free from potential bias. There is no such thing. Rather,
the goal must be to discover the correct manner of interpreting
whatever data we have.

Of course, this is not to suggest that *how* we collect data, or
what data we collect, is of no importance. The point is that
minimizing the influence of the researcher is not the only, or
always even a prime, consideration. Assuming we understand
how the presence of the researcher shaped the data, we can interpret the latter accordingly and it may provide important
insights, allowing us to develop or test elements of our theory.

Ethnographic interviewing

The main difference between the way in which ethnographers
and survey interviewers ask questions is not, as is sometimes
suggested, that one form of interviewing is 'structured' and the
other is 'unstructured'. All interviews, like any other kind of

social interaction, are structured by *both* researcher and informant. The important distinction to be made is between standardized and reflexive interviewing. Ethnographers do not decide
beforehand the questions they want to ask, though they may
enter the interview with a list of issues to be covered. Nor do
ethnographers restrict themselves to a single mode of questioning. On different occasions, or at different points in the same
interview, the approach may be non-directive or directive,
depending on the function that the questioning is intended to
serve.

Non-directive questions are designed as triggers that stimulate the interviewee into talking about a particular broad area:

> 'Ordinarily, the questions should be of this nature: "What do
> you hear from business?" (to the congressmen), "What are
> they worrying you about?" not "Do you hear from them about
> the tariff?", Even better may be, "What people do you hear
> from most?", "Does anybody pressure you?". Similarly, not
> "How about the grants your agency is supposed to get from
> such-and-such a federal department?" but "In what ways are
> you most affected in your work by national matters . . ." and
> if someone starts telling you, as an official of a racing commis-
> sion told me, about ex-FBI agents who are employed by some
> national authority, well and good, you have learned to
> redefine the impact of the federal government! A question
> which sharply defines a particular area for discussion is far
> more likely to result in omission of some vital data which
> you, the interviewer, have not even thought of.'
>
> (Dexter 1970:55)

Non-directive questions, then, are relatively open-ended, rather
than requiring the interviewee to provide a specific piece of
information or, at the extreme, simply to reply 'yes' or 'no'
(Spradley 1979).

The role of the interviewer in non-directive interviewing
appears to be passive. This is misleading though. The interviewer must be an active listener, he or she must listen to what is
being said in order to assess how it relates to the research focus
and how it may reflect the circumstances of the interview.
Moreover, this is done with a view to how the future course of

the interview might be shaped. While the aim is to minimize the influence of the researcher on what the interviewee says, some structuring is necessary in terms of what is and is not relevant. And even where what is said is highly relevant, it may be insufficiently detailed or concrete, or some clarification may be necessary if ambiguity is to be resolved. Whyte (1953) provides an illustration of the non-directive 'steering' of an interview in the questions he puts to Columbus Gary, a union official handling grievances in a steel plant:

> 'WHYTE: . . . I'm trying to catch up on things that have happened since I was last here to study this case. That was back in 1950. I think probably the best thing to start would be if you could give your own impressions as to how things are going now, compared to the past. Do you think things are getting better or worse, or staying about the same?. . . .
>
> WHYTE: That's interesting. You mean that it isn't that you don't have problems, but you take them up and talk them over before you write them up, is that it?. . . .
>
> WHYTE: That's very interesting. I wonder if you could give me an example of a problem that came up recently, or not so recently, that would illustrate how you handled it sort of informally without writing it down. . . .
>
> WHYTE: That's a good example. I wonder if you could give me a little more detail about the beginning of it. Did Mr Grosscup first tell you about it? How did you first find out?
>
> WHYTE: I see. He first explained it to you and you went to the people on the job to tell them about it, but then you saw that they didn't understand it?'
>
> (Whyte 1953:16–17)

However, as we've already indicated, interviewing in ethnography is by no means always non-directive. Often one may wish to test out hypotheses arising from the developing theory and here quite directive and specific questions may be required. Such questions may also be necessary when one suspects that informants have been lying. Nadel, a social anthropologist, reports that:

> 'the expression of doubt or disbelief on the part of the interviewer, or the arrangement of interviews with several infor-

mants, some of whom, owing to their social position, were certain to produce inaccurate information, easily induced the key informant to disregard his usual reluctance and to speak openly, if only to confound his opponents and critics.'

(Nadel 1939:323)

Confrontation of informants with what one already knows is another technique of this kind; as Perlman illustrates from his research in Uganda:

'I could not conduct formal interviews with most people or take notes in front of them; this was possible only with the relatively few educated people who understood my work. Others became suspicious when I started asking questions about their personal marital histories. Christians did not like to admit, for example, that they had at one time (or even still had) two or more wives. But in those cases where I had learned the truth from friends, neighbors, or relatives of the interviewee, I would confront him with the fact, although always in a joking manner, by mentioning, for instance, the first name of a former wife. At that point the interviewee – realizing that I knew too much already – usually told me everything for fear that his enemies would tell me even worse things about him. Although he might insist that he had lived with this woman for only six months and that he had hardly counted her as a real wife, he had at least confirmed my information. Later, I checked his story on the length of time, coming back to confront him again and again if necessary. Although I visited most people only once or twice – after first learning as much as possible about them from others – I had to go back to see some of them as many as five times until I was satisfied that all the data were accurate.'

(Perlman 1970:307)

Researchers are often warned to avoid the use of leading questions. While their dangers must be borne in mind, they can be extremely useful in testing hypotheses and trying to penetrate fronts. What is important is to assess the likely direction of bias that the question will introduce. Indeed, a useful tactic is to make the question 'lead' in a direction opposite to that in which one expects the answer to lie and thus avoid the danger of simply and misleadingly confirming one's expectations.

Clearly, directive and non-directive questioning are likely to provide different kinds of data, and thus will be useful at different stages of the inquiry. The same applies to the various strategies available for selecting informants. Sometimes it may be necessary to try to draw a representative sample of people for interview from particular categories of actor. At other times, informants will be chosen on theoretical grounds, in such a way as to get the particular information required at that stage in the research. Dean *et al.* (1967) provide an interesting example of the kind of typology of informants that might be used here:

'1. *Informants who are especially sensitive to the area of concern.*
The outsider who sees things from the vantage point of another culture, social class, community, etc.

The rookie, who is surprised by what goes on and notes the taken-for-granted things that the acclimatized miss. And, as yet, he may have no stake in the system to protect.

The nouveau statused, who is in transition from one position to another where the tensions of new experience are vivid.

The naturally reflective and objective person in the field. He can sometimes be pointed out by others of his kind.

2. *The more-willing-to-reveal informants.*
Because of their background or status, some informants are just more willing to talk than others.

The naive informant, who knows not whereof he speaks. He may be either naive as to what the fieldworker represents or naive about his own group.

The frustrated person, who may be a rebel or malcontent, especially the one who is consciously aware of his blocked drives and impulses.

The "outs", who have lost power but are "in-the-know". Some of the "ins" may be eager to reveal negative facts about their colleagues. The habitué or "old hand" or "fixture", who no longer has a stake in the venture or is so secure that he is not jeopardized by exposing what others say or do.

The needy person, who fastens onto the interviewer because he craves attention and support. As long as the interviewer satisfies this need, he will talk.

The subordinate, who must adapt to superiors. He generally develops insights to cushion the impact of authority, and he may be hostile and willing to "blow his top".'

(Dean, Eichorn, and Dean 1967:285)

Other similar strategies for selecting informants could be based on what Glaser and Strauss (1967) call 'theoretical sampling' (see Chapter 2). Who is interviewed, when, and how will be decided as the research progresses, according to one's assessment of one's current state of knowledge and one's judgement as to how it might best be developed further.

There is, of course, another important way in which ethnographic and survey interviewing differ. While in the latter interviews are the only source of data, in ethnography interview data is combined with data from other sources. As Dexter notes from his research on the United States Congress, this can have an important effect on how what people say in interviews is interpreted.

'(In my research) I sometimes appear to rely chiefly upon interviews, but in fact I was living in Washington at the time, spent much of my "free" time in a congressional office, saw a good deal of several congressional assistants and secretaries socially, worked on other matters with several persons actively engaged in relationships with Congress (lobbying and liaison), had participated in a number of congressional campaigns, had read extensively about congressional history and behaviour, and had some relevant acquaintance with local politics in several congressional districts. All these factors made my analysis of interviews somewhat credible. And, as I look back, interviews sometimes acquired meaning from the observations which I often made while waiting in congressional offices – observation of other visitors, secretarial staffs, and so forth. And, finally, most important of all, it happened that interviews with constituents, lobbyists, congressmen of different views and factions, could be and were checked and re-checked, against each other. Yet in the book we say little about all this; and in fact it is only now, in 1963 that I realize how much these other factors affected what I ''heard''.'

(Dexter 1970:15)

The effect may also work the other way. What people say in interviews can lead us to see things differently in observation, as Woods (1981) illustrates, discussing his research on secondary school pupils. The way in which pupils talked about boredom cued him into the experience of it:

'One of my outstanding memories from the enormous mass of experience at the school is that of pupils talking to me about boredom. They managed to convey, largely in a very few words, years of crushing ennui that had been ingrained into their bones. Great wealth of expression was got into ''boring'', ''boredom'', ''it's so bo-or-ring here''. The word, I realize now, is onomatopoeic. I could never view lessons in company with that group again without experiencing that boredom myself. They would occasionally glance my way in the back corner of the room with the same pained expression on their faces, and I knew exactly what they meant. This, then, provided a platform for my understanding of the school life of one group of pupils.'

(Woods 1981:22)

Interviews as participant observation

Of course it must never be forgotten that the interview represents a distinct setting and that the participant understandings that are elicited there may not be those that underlie the social interaction observed elsewhere. This problem has arisen explicitly in research on teacher typifications of pupils. Hargreaves, Hester, and Mellor (1975), using observation and formal interviews, have presented a picture of teacher typifications as elaborate and individualized. Woods (1979) challenges their account, arguing, in part, that their data is a product of the interview situation and of their own theoretical orientation. He claims that teachers would not be able to operate on the basis of such elaborate typifications in the secondary-school classroom, given the sheer number of pupils a teacher deals with each day. Whatever the merits of the arguments on each side, the fact that there is a problem about relating perspectives elicited in interviews to actions in other settings comes through clearly (Hargreaves 1977).

However, the distinctiveness of the interview setting must not be exaggerated, and it may be viewed as a resource, not simply as a problem. Interviews can be used as sites for 'experiments'. To the extent that the aim in ethnography is not simply the provision of a description of what occurred in a particular setting over a certain period of time, there may be positive advantages to be gained from subjecting people to verbal stimuli different from those prevalent in the settings in which they normally operate. In other words, the 'artificiality' of the interview when compared with 'normal' events in the setting may allow us to understand how participants would behave in other circumstances, for example when they move out of a setting or when the setting changes. Labov's (1969) work on 'the logic of non-standard English' illustrates this when he compares interviews in which the interviewer takes different roles. We might expect that the formal interview, in which the black child provides monosyllabic answers, while not an accurate indicator of his linguistic resources, does accurately reflect his behaviour in similar circumstances, such as interviews with counsellors and social workers, or lessons in school. It may be that by varying features of the interview situation in this way we can identify which aspects of the setting produce particular responses.

Of course, while it has its own roles and distribution of interactional rights, the interview is not impermeable to outside influences. How these roles are played will depend considerably upon, for example, the latent identities that the participants invoke and attribute to one another. As Dexter (1970) notes, largely from necessity the non-directive approach is much more common in interviews with 'the influential, the prominent and the well-informed' than is the standardized survey interview. Why this is so can be seen from Lazarsfeld's attempt to carry out a social survey among academics on the issue of academic freedom. As Riesman (1958:115–26) comments, 'at a number of leading universities (including my own) angry respondents had felt almost insulted to have to discuss the intangibles of academic freedom with interviewers not always or wholly acculturated to academia'. These respondents contrasted the experience of talking to Riesman, a professor from Chicago, with that of being interviewed by, as one of them said, 'a little girl who could probably check soap without any trouble'.

Platt (1981) has also noted the ways in which latent identities might affect interviews in her research on fellow sociologists. Here many of the respondents knew of Platt and her work, even if they did not know her personally. As a result, 'personal and community knowledge [were] used as part of the information available to construct a conception of what the interview [was] meant to be about and thus affected what [was] said' (Platt 1981:77). A particular problem here was the tendency of respondents to invite her to draw on her background knowledge rather than spelling out what they were saying. As a result, she sometimes gained responses lacking the explicitness and/or detail necessary to bear her interpretations.

The examples of Lazarsfeld's interviewers and of Platt are probably unusual but they highlight a more general point: the way in which latent identities of various kinds can affect interviews. Even so, as in other kinds of participant observation, here too it may be possible, by careful self-presentation, to avoid the attribution of damaging identities and to encourage ones that might facilitate rapport. What one is doing here is manipulating the audience to whom the interviewee is responding.

Frequently, the researcher him or herself is the only other person present in an interview, and the fact that the interview is confidential and that no one else will ever hear what the informant says is stressed. Under these circumstances informants may be willing to divulge information and express opinions that they would not in front of others. Of course this does not mean that this information is necessarily true or that the opinions they present are more genuine, more truly reflecting informants' perspectives than what they say on other occasions. Whether or not this is the case, and in what senses it is true, will depend on how their orientations towards others, including the researcher, are structured. But if we can discover that structure it will help us considerably in our interpretation of their responses.

However, interviews do not necessarily take one interviewee at a time; group interviews are quite common in ethnography. Apart from the fact that they allow a greater number of people to be interviewed in the same time, group interviews also have the advantage that they may make the interview situation less 'strange' for interviewees and thus less of a strain. They may thereby overcome the problem of the 'silent' or monosyllabic interviewee, as in the case of Carol, quoted by Helen Simons:

> 'INTERVIEWER: Does the lesson help the shy ones or does it make them stand out more?
>
> ANGELA: They're so quiet and then all of sudden one of them'll speak and you think ''What's come over them?'' I suppose they've got their opinion in their head and they hear everyone else talking so they think they will.
>
> PATRICIA: Carol's quiet.
>
> INTERVIEWER: You're quiet Carol?
>
> ANGELA: Not as quiet as you used to be.
>
> CAROL: I'm better than I used to be.
>
> INTERVIEWER: You didn't like speaking?
>
> CAROL: I'd only talk when I was asked a question.
>
> ANGELA: Sort of speak when you're spoken to. I noticed that when I first met her, I thought she was quiet.
>
> INTERVIEWER: But now you speak when you want to put your point of view.
>
> CAROL: Yes. When I think someone's wrong, I'll say what I think.
>
> INTERVIEWER: And how long did it take you to get to this stage?
>
> CAROL: Well, it was more friendly, we sat in a circle and we could speak to each other. That was better and it didn't take long, only a few lessons.
>
> ANGELA: I noticed after three or four lessons Carol started speaking more.
>
> PATRICIA: I spoke the first lesson.
>
> ANGELA: So did I.
>
> CAROL: It gets me mad when people say you're very quiet though. I enjoy other people's views as well.
>
> ANGELA *to Patricia*: Probably the way you shout, you probably frighten them to death.'

(Simons 1981:40)

Of course, *what* is said is also likely to be affected by whether a group or individual format is used. For example, in a group, the interviewer may find it more difficult to control a topic. On the other hand, this may be all to the good in that informants may prompt one another – 'go on tell him', 'what about when you . . .' – using information not available to the researcher and in ways which turn out to be productive for the research (Woods 1979).

Douglas used an interesting variation on this strategy in his attempts to get an informant to 'spill the beans' about massage parlours:

'we had long known that the ultimate insider in the massage parlors was a local lawyer who represented the massage parlor association and about 80 per cent of the cases. We wanted to open him up, so we tried to set him up for it. We wanted to make it manifest to the lawyer that we were on the inside and could thus be trusted. We knew it wouldn't do any good to give him verbal commitments – "Hey, man, we're on your side, you can trust us". He was used to every possible deception and double cross from all angles. It would have to be made manifest, physically real. We could have gotten ourselves arrested by starting a massage parlor, and then hired him for our defense, but that did not appeal to our sense of propriety – or practicality. We did the next best thing. We got two young masseuses to go with [us] for the interview, showing by their presence and trust in [us] what angle [we were] coming from. As [we] were ushered into the lawyer's office, two employees at the parlor where one of the girls with [us] worked came out and they had a grand reunion right there. (Researchers need luck as much as anyone else.) As the interview progressed, the two girls talked of their work. One of them, as we knew well, was under indictment for her work in a parlor. They talked about that. She was impressed by the lawyer and shifted her case to him. At the end of the interview, the lawyer told [us we] could use all his files, make xerox copies of them, use his name in doing [our] research, accompany him on cases, etc. We felt sure there were some things he wasn't telling us (and one of the girls later started

working with him to get at more and check it out), but that
seemed okay for the first hour.'

(Douglas 1976:174–75)

Of course, as far as possible, the effects of audience must be
monitored in group interviews, as they must in interviews with
individuals:

> 'For added ribaldry, the facts will probably have suffered some
> distortion, but that is a natural concomitant of laughter-
> making. Consider this example:

> TRACY: Dianne fell off a chair first and as she went to get up,
> she got 'old of me skirt, she was having a muck about,
> and there was I in me petticoat, me skirt came down
> round my ankles and Mr Bridge came in (great screams of
> laughter from girls). He'd been standing outside the
> door.

> KATE: 'E told her she'd get suspended.

> TRACY: He 'ad me mum up the school, telling her what a hor-
> rible child I was.

> KATE: "Nobody will marry you", said Miss Judge.

> TRACY: Oh yeah, Miss Judge sits there, " 'n, nobody will
> want want to marry *you*, Jones", she said. I said, "Well you
> ain't married, anyway".

> (Shrieks of laughter from girls)'

(Woods 1981:20)

Such distortion occurs in many participant accounts, since
these are often worked up for purposes where truth is not the
primary concern. On the other hand, such discussions may provide an accurate insight into participant culture: in other words,
what is lost in terms of information may be compensated for by
the insight that the accounts provide into the perspectives of
those being interviewed.

As important as who is present at an interview, often, is where
and when it is held. Skipper's and McCaghy's (1972) research on
striptease artistes illustrates this in an amusing way, as well as
the powerful effect latent identities can have. They recount how
one of their respondents asked them to come to the theatre, view

her performance, and carry out the interview backstage:

> 'On stage her act was highly sexual. It consisted primarily of fondling herself in various stages of undress while carrying on risqué banter with the audience. The act ended with the stripper squatting on the floor at the front of the stage, sans G-string, fondling her pudendum and asking a customer in the first row: "Aren't you glad you came tonight? Do you think you can come again?"

> Backstage, it was difficult for us to feign indifference over her appearance when she ushered us into her dressing room. As she sat clad only in the G-string she had worn on stage and with her legs on the dressing table, we became slightly mesmerized. We had difficulty in even remembering the questions we wanted to ask let alone getting them out of our mouths in an intelligible manner. To compound our difficulties, we felt it was obvious to the stripper what effect she was having on us. She seemed to enjoy the role. For over a half an hour she responded to our inquiries in what we perceived as a seductive voice, and her answers were often suggestive. After about forty minutes, she said very quickly, as if she had decided she had had enough, "Doesn't it seem to be getting chilly in here? I am freezing". She rose, put on a kimono, and walked out of her dressing room and started talking to another stripper. When she did not return, we knew the interview had been concluded. . . .

> When we returned to our office to record our impressions, we discovered we had not collected as much of the data as we had intended. We either had forgotten to ask many questions or had obtained inappropriate answers to those asked. In short, we had not conducted an effective interview. Our sheltered backgrounds and numerous courses in sociological methodology simply had not prepared us for this kind of research environment. . . . It was very clear to us that the nudity and perceived seductiveness of the stripper, and the general permissiveness of the setting had interfered with our role as researchers. The respondent, not we, had been in control of the interaction; we had been induced to play her game her way even to the point that she made the decision when to end the interview. . . .'

> (Skipper and McCaghy 1972:239–40)

In response to this experience the researchers arranged for future interviews with the strippers to take place in a restaurant!

Another variable that can be strategically manipulated in an effort to deal with problems posed by latent identities, then, is the place where the interviews are carried out. Whose 'territory' (Lyman and Scott 1970) is used can make a big difference to how the interview goes. However, there are no easy answers here. With many people, interviewing them on their own territory *is* the best strategy since it allows them to relax much more than they would in either a university office or a public place like a restaurant.

Of course, the question of where and when interviews are held is not simply a matter of the comfort or discomfort of interviewer and interviewee. Different settings are likely to induce and constrain talk of particular kinds. In part this will be a product of the possibility of being overheard. Or it may be that there are distractions:

> 'One mistake which I have made on a number of occasions is to try to carry on an interview in an environment unsuited for it. A legislator who is standing outside the legislative chamber, while half his attention is focused on buttonholing colleagues is not a good subject for an interview; though one might learn something from observing him. I do not know whether, if confronted with such a situation again, I would have the nerve to say in effect, "I need your full attention . . ." but I hope I would ask whether I can arrange some time when he is less preoccupied. The most common difficulty is a man who really lacks a private office; for instance, state legislators or an executive assistant whose room is used as a passageway to his chief's. In all such cases, I shall in the future ask if there is a conference room or if we can have a cup of coffee, or, if worst comes to worst, even meet for a lunch.'
> (Dexter 1970:54)

It is also important to look at how the interview fits into the interviewee's life. There is a great temptation for the researcher to see interviews purely in terms of his or her own schedule, regarding them as time-out from the everyday lives of participants. However, other people may not view them like this at all. This may well have been one source of the trouble that

Skipper and McCaghy ran into. Equally, though, there are people of whom one might say that talk is their business and indeed being interviewed may be a common experience for them. Dexter's senators and congressmen provide the obvious example.

Interviews must be viewed, then, as social, events in which the interviewer (and for that matter the interviewee) is a participant observer. In interviews the ethnographer can play a more dominant role than usual, and this can be capitalized upon, both in terms of when and where the interview takes place and who is present, as well as through the kinds of question asked. In this way different types of data can be elicited, as required by the changing demands of the research. While this feature of interviews heightens the danger of reactivity, as we saw in the previous section, this is only one aspect of a more general problem that cannot be avoided. Interview data, like any other, must be interpreted against the background of the context in which they were produced.

Conclusion

The accounts produced by the people under study must be treated in exactly the same way as those of the researcher. They must neither be dismissed as epiphenomena or ideological distortions, nor treated as 'valid in their own terms' and thus as beyond assessment and explanation. Moreover, while it may sometimes be important to distinguish between solicited and unsolicited accounts, too much must not be made of this distinction. Rather, all accounts must be examined as social phenomena occurring in, and shaped by, particular contexts. Not only will this add to sociological knowledge directly, it will also throw light on the kind of threats to validity that we may need to consider in assessing the information provided by an account.

In this chapter we have rather assumed that accounts, apart from those of the ethnographer, take oral form. While this may be true for some primitive societies, for many settings written documents are an important source of data, as we shall see in the next chapter.

6

Documents

Ethnographic research in its various guises has often been employed in the investigation of essentially oral cultures. Be they the non-literate cultures of much social anthropology, or the street cultures and the demi-monde beloved of many sociological fieldworkers, the social worlds studied by ethnographers have often been devoid of written documents, other than those produced by the fieldworkers themselves.

Although it was not the only rationale proposed for ethnographic fieldwork as a method, the fact that the 'exotic' societies studied by early anthropologists had no written history was proposed as a major justification of the method – as well as of the synchronic, functionalist analyses then associated with it. Rather than attempt to reconstruct an essentially unknowable past, one was inclined to concentrate on the construction of a working version of the present. The anthropologists thus turned their backs on conjectural history. There was, therefore, more than a coincidental relationship between ethnographic methods and the investigation of non-literate cultures.

In a rather similar way, many of the settings documented by sociologists of the Chicago School were ephemeral. It is not that they were 'outside' history or part of some timeless 'tradition' (largely a fiction even in anthropological contexts); rather, they were cultures that lacked any conscious or unconscious attempts to make a documentary record of their activities. Whether or not their members were actually illiterate, their collective actions rarely depended on the production, distribution, and preservation of written documents and records. The urban cultures of hobos, prostitutes, drug-users, and so on are mostly non-literate in that sense.

It has been repeatedly emphasized that ethnography is a method that is ideally suited to the study of such non-literate cultures. But it must not be forgotten that many of the settings in which sociologists work – and, indeed, many contemporary anthropologists as well – are literate. Not only are their members able to read and write, but also that capacity is an integral feature of their everyday lives, and particularly of their routine work. Written accounts of many sorts are regularly produced in various contexts in contemporary industrial societies. In many instances, therefore, ethnographers need to take account of documents as part of the social setting under investigation.

In recommending some attention to written sources and accounts, in appropriate social settings, we are aware of their historical place in that sociological tradition that incorporates interactionist and similar 'interpretive' perspectives. Research that emanated from the early Chicago School was sometimes based very heavily on written documents. It was indeed founded as much on such data sources as on the method of 'participant observation', which, perhaps we would now more readily associate with the Chicago School.

Thomas and Znaniecki (1927), for instance, in *The Polish Peasant in Poland and America* – generally regarded as an early classic of American sociology – relied substantially on written documents. Thomas (1967) employed the same approach in *The Unadjusted Girl*. He collected personal documentary accounts, in the belief that 'the unique value of the personal document is its revelation of the situations which have conditioned the behaviour '(1967:42). Thomas therefore proceeded by the dense accumulation of personal accounts and life histories, which were arranged thematically and juxtaposed in order to draw out the regularities and contrasts in 'definitions of the situation':

'Not only concrete acts are dependent on the definition of the situation, but gradually a whole life-policy and the personality of the individual himself follow from a series of such definitions.'

(Thomas 1967:42)

In a rather similar vein, the early use of the term 'participant observation' was to designate the generation of documents by participants, i.e. the 'subjects', who would, in contemporary common parlance, be called 'informants'. For instance, in the research that produced *The Gold Coast and the Slum*, Zorbaugh (1929) persuaded people who were inhabitants of the exclusive society of Chicago's 'gold coast' to generate such 'inside' accounts. *They* were the participant observers as much as Zorbaugh himself.

In a literate culture, then, it is possible to draw on all sorts of 'inside' written accounts – documents produced especially for the purposes of the research, and those generated for other purposes. For the most part we find ourselves dealing with the latter variety, and there are many contexts in which members of organizations and groups produce written accounts.

We shall begin with a discussion of documentary sources as 'secondary' sources for the ethnographer, and then turn our attention to a more detailed examination of the ethnography of settings where the production and use of documents is an integral feature of the everyday life under investigation.

Types of documentary source and their uses

There is, of course, a quite bewildering variety of documentary materials that might be of some relevance to the researcher. These may be ranged along a dimension from the most 'informal' to the 'formal' or 'official'. At the 'informal' end of the spectrum there are many 'lay' accounts of everyday life that the enterprising and imaginative researcher can draw on for certain purposes. These include fictional literature, diaries, autobiographies, letters, and mass media products. They all have their potential uses.

There are, for example, numerous categories of persons in contemporary society who publish versions of their own life story:

'More than ever before in history, men of affairs, including politicians, military leaders, and business executives, are intent upon recording their experiences, personal as well as public, for posterity. In recent decades a number of American governmental leaders, including those in the military, have, after resigning from their official posts, published their memories or personal accounts in which they seek public support for causes that the bureaucracy may have rejected during their period of office.'

(Sjoberg and Nett 1968:163)

There are, too, a fair number of first-hand accounts published by less eminent folk, including those drawn from the criminal underworld, and the realms of sports and entertainment. Similar personal accounts can be found in newspapers and magazines, or can be culled from radio and television documentaries, and chat-shows, for example.

Of course, such biographical and autobiographical accounts will rarely, if ever, be those of the actual people we are researching at first hand. They can nevertheless prove valuable resources for the ethnographer. They can serve as a source of 'sensitizing concepts' (Blumer 1954): they can suggest distinctive ways in which their authors, or the people reported in them, organize their experience, the sorts of imagery and 'situated vocabularies' (Mills 1940) they employ, the routine events, and the troubles and reactions they encounter. Read in this light, they can be used to suggest potential lines of inquiry, and 'foreshadowed problems'.

Documents of this sort have rather particular characteristics. Authors will have interests in presenting themselves in a (usually) favourable light; they may have axes to grind, scores to settle, or excuses and justifications to make. They are often written with the benefit of hindsight, and are thus subject to the usual problems of long-term recall. Authors have a sense of audience that will lead them to put particular glosses on their accounts.

Such considerations can be treated as sources of 'bias' in accounts of this sort. But the sources of 'bias' are, looked at from another perspective, data in themselves, as we saw in the previous chapter. As important as whether a given account is 'accurate' or 'objective' is what it tells us about the teller's perspectives and presuppositions.

Such accounts can also be used, with appropriate caution, for comparative purposes. They can furnish information (albeit partial and personal) on groups and settings that are not available for first-hand observation. As a general category of data, biographical and autobiographical sources are subject to a further sort of 'bias' in that they tend to over-represent the powerful, the famous, the extraordinary, and the articulate. But that can also be a strength since it is precisely such social categories that are often difficult to research directly. We shall comment below in more detail on the 'comparative' value of documentary sources.

In the collection and investigation of 'informal' documentary materials, the fictional – even the most popular and ephemeral – can be used profitably. The most banal ('pulp' or 'pot-boiler') fiction is often replete with images, stereotypes, and myths bearing on a vast range of social domains. Indeed, it is part of the lack of literary merit of much fiction that it does unquestioningly trade on stocks of common knowledge and conventional wisdom. Here too, then, we can become sensitized to cultural themes pertaining to sex, gender, family, work, success, failure, class, mobility, regional variations, religious beliefs, political commitments, health and illness, the law, crime, and social control. These are not necessarily to be read at face value, as accurate representations of social reality, but to suggest themes, images, or metaphors. This is no less true of more 'serious' fiction: novels can suggest different ways of organizing experience, alternative thematic models and devices. As Davis (1974) points out, ethnographers and novelists alike have to tell stories. Fictional texts are not models to be copied slavishly, but as Davis suggests here, they can be examined for parallels and perspectives. (See Chapter 9 for further discussion of parallels between ethnography and literary analysis.)

The goal of comparative analysis, referred to earlier, is also a major use for published sources of a more 'formal' nature including other published ethnographies. Glaser and Strauss propose such an employment for documentary sources in the search for grounded theory:

'Although it is quite possible for one researcher to generate

magnificent substantive theory in a relatively short time
(using field or library data) it is virtually impossible for him to
generate equally excellent formal theory through only his
own field work. Usually he also needs either the primary field
data gathered by other researchers or their published analyses
and their illustrative quotes drawn from field notes.'

(Glaser and Strauss 1967:175–76)

It is important to underline the value of comparative reading,
as advocated by Glaser and Strauss. The generation of formal
theory and generic research topics demands a broad and eclectic
reading of textual sources (formal and informal) on differing
substantive themes. Yet our own reading of much published
work suggests that a great many authors are rather bad at this.
One finds that sociologists of education refer almost exclusively
to other educational studies; sociologists of medicine confine
most of their attention to work on medical settings; specialists
in deviance are similarly restricted, and so on. This is understandable, and it is a counsel of perfection to suggest that anyone
can achieve comprehensive coverage of more than their own
specialized area. At the same time it must be acknowledged that
the interests of systematic comparison, and the generation of
formal analysis, do require attention to literary sources beyond a
given substantive field. There is every reason for the sociologist
interested in, say, hospitals or clinics to examine work on a list
of other institutional settings – schools, courts, welfare agencies, police departments, and emergency services, for example.
The precise selection of settings, and the lessons drawn from
them, will depend upon the analytic themes being pursued.
Through such comparisons one might trace the variety of
'degradation ceremonies', the conditions of information control, or the moral evaluation of 'clients' on the part of professionals in people-processing organizations. There is, in principle, no limit to such comparative work, and no prescriptions can
be offered for its conduct. The part played by serendipitous
discoveries and unpredicted insights will be considerable here,
as in all creative work. One must create the right conditions for
serendipity, however, and that includes attention to sources of
many sorts. Goffman's work on 'total institutions' illustrates
this approach, as well as providing exemplification of his own

distinctive style: a diverse collection of sources are drawn on, to turn his field work in mental hospitals into a more general treatment of institutional life, drawing on parallels with military camps, prisons, religious foundations, and so on (Goffman 1961).

As Glaser and Strauss remark, with characteristic enthusiasm:

> 'theorizing begs of comparative analysis. The library offers a *fantastic range* of comparison groups, if only the researchers have the ingenuity to discover them. Of course, if their interest lies mainly with specific groups, and they wish to explore them in great depth, they may not always find sufficient documentation bearing on them. But if they are interested in generating theory, the library can be immensely useful – especially, as we noted earlier, for generating formal theory. Regardless of which type of theory the theorist is especially interested in, if he browses intelligently through the library (even without much initial direction), he cannot help but have his theorizing impulses aroused by the happily bewildering, crazy-quilt pattern of social groups who speak to him.'
>
> (Glaser and Strauss 1967:179)

As in Goffman's work, the imaginative use of secondary documentary sources allows for the elaboration of 'perspective by incongruity' (Burke 1964; Lofland 1980; and Manning 1980). That is, the juxtaposition of instances and categories that are normally thought of as mutually exclusive. Such sources and devices are ideal for heuristic purposes: they can rejuvenate jaded imaginations, spark off novel conceptualizations, and develop theory. In his or her imagination the researcher is free to wander at large among diverse social scenes, gathering ideas, insights, hypotheses, and metaphors.

In addition to the sorts of documentary source we have referred to, in a literate culture it is possible to emulate researchers like Zorbaugh and draw on the ability of informants to generate written accounts specifically for research purposes. By such means one can gather information that complements other data sources in the field.

This strategy is advocated by Zimmerman and Wieder (1977),

who employed such a diary technique in their study of counter-culture life styles. They comment that while they were committed to participant observation, there were settings and activities that remained hard for them to observe directly. They therefore recruited insider informants who kept detailed diaries over seven-day periods. Subsequently, the researchers subjected each informant to a lengthy and detailed interview, based on the diaries, 'in which he or she was asked not only to expand the reportage, but also was questioned on the less directly observable features of the events recorded, of their meanings, their propriety, typicality, connection with other events, and so on' (1977:484).

Similarly, Robinson (1971), in the course of an investigation of the experience of illness, persuaded a series of married women in South Wales to keep a diary on the health status of themselves and the members of their households. The diaries were kept over a four-week period. These diaries enabled Robinson to gain some insight into the daily symptomatic episodes and health-related decisions characteristic of everyday life. Many of the episodes reported were minor, though not necessarily insignificant, and could easily have been overlooked in retrospective accounts from, say, interviews or questionnaires.

This sort of procedure has been drawn on widely in work on educational settings where it is often a fairly 'natural' extension of the sort of literate activities that routinely get done in schools, colleges, and universities. For example, Lacey (1970) persuaded some of the boys at 'Hightown Grammar' to keep a diary, as one of several methods that he combined in that piece of research. Ball's more recent study employs a very similar approach. Ball explicitly notes the value of combining such a data source with others:

> 'The sociometric questionnaires failed to pick up the casual friendships that existed between pupils outside school, and made it appear that they had no such contact. In addition, they failed to pick up the cross-sex friendships that were established at this time. Perhaps the notion of 'friendships' is too narrow and ill-defined to account for these other kinds of adolescent relationships. . . . The entries in the diaries that several of the pupils wrote for me did, however, refer to these contacts.
>
> (Ball 1981:100)

Research-generated personal documents of this sort embody the strengths and weaknesses of all such personal accounts. They are partial, and reflect the interests and perspectives of their authors. They are not to be privileged over other sources of information, nor are they to be discounted. Like other accounts, they should be read with regard to the context of their production, their intended audience(s), and the author's interests and motives.

Hitherto, we have discussed a range of documentary sources, but we have not yet paid a great deal of attention to the investigation of social activities that themselves directly involve the production of documents. In the following section we turn our attention explicitly to such activities and their documentary products.

Documents in context

In some settings it would be hard to conceive of anything approaching an ethnographic account without some attention to documentary material. For instance, Gamst, in his study of locomotive engineers, drew on a wide range of documents:

'Some documents are published, for example: rule books; timetables; technical manuals for use of equipment; and instructional, regulating, and investigating publications of many kinds issued by railroads, trade unions, government, and other firms. Unpublished documents include: official correspondence; reports in mimeographed and other forms; railroad operating bulletins and circulars, train orders and operating messages, and sundry other items.'

(Gamst 1980:viii)

Whether or not one would draw on all such sources, one would certainly expect an ethnography of work on the railway to make full reference to such features as operating schedules and timetables (whatever disgruntled passengers might feel). A similar instance is provided by Zerubavel (1979) in his formal analysis of time in hospitals; he necessarily draws on such sources as timetables, work rosters, and clinical rotations, as embodied in organizational documents. In many organizational settings the use and production of such documents is an integral part of everyday life.

Douglas, writing in 1967, commented on the importance of 'official' data and enumerations in contemporary society, while simultaneously drawing attention to the relative neglect of such topics by sociological commentators:

'Throughout the Western world today there exists a general belief that one knows something only when it has been counted . . . . Considering the importance of such statistics for the formation and testing of all kinds of common-sense and scientific theories of human action, it is a remarkable fact that there is at present very little systematic knowledge of the functioning of official statistics-keeping organizations.'

(Douglas 1967:163)

Since Douglas made those observations there has been some work along the lines suggested. However, in comparison with the sheer volume of 'literate' record-keeping and so on in modern society, the empirical investigation of such socially organized activity has been relatively slight. Rees, for instance, writing on medical records, remarks:

'A common feature of many people-processing organizations is the presence of 'client' records. In the medical setting, the patient record has considerable implications for both the organization of medical work and the treatment received by patients. Few studies, however, have explored the way in which the record may be used as a lever on many of the prac- tical accomplishments of medical staff, and on the organiza- tion of ward routines. Both medicine and medical sociology have to a large extent neglected the record. Indeed, so rarely is it mentioned that one could be forgiven for thinking that medicine is a purely oral discipline.'

(Rees 1981:55)

Medical sociology is not alone; similar comments could be made about most, if not all, areas of sociological work.

Because of the recent critique of 'official statistics' stemming largely from the ethnomethodological movement, some con- temporary ethnographers may feel reluctant to engage in the systematic investigation or use of documentary data. We would argue that they are right to treat seriously the objections used against 'official' data in that context, but they would be wrong to ignore such materials for that reason.

The point of departure for the critics of 'data from official sources' was the contention that, traditionally, the tendency had been for sociologists to adopt an uncritical attitude towards such material. That is, they had been content to treat such information at face value, and had not paid adequate attention to its character as a social product.

It is, of course, a long-standing concern of sociologists that data derived from official sources may be inadequate in some way, that they may be subject to bias or distortion, or that bureaucracies' practical concerns may mean that the data they collect are not formulated in accordance with sociologists' interests. The ethnomethodologists, on the other hand, have proposed more radical problems. Cicourel remarks, for instance:

> 'For years sociologists have complained about ''bad statistics and distorted bureaucratic record-keeping'' but have not made the procedures producing the ''bad'' materials we label ''data'' a subject of study. The basic assumption of conventional research on crime, delinquency, and law is to view compliance and deviance as having their own ontological significance, and the measuring rod is some set of presumably ''clear'' rules whose meaning is also ''ontological and epistemologically clear''.'
>
> (Cicourel 1976:331)

The argument is that rather than being viewed as a (more or less biased) source of data, official documents and statistics should be treated as social products; they must be *examined* not simply used as a resource. To treat them as a resource and not a topic is to trade on the interpretive and interactional work that went into their production, to treat as a reflection or document of the world phenomena that are actually produced by it.

In this way attention is diverted towards the investigation of the socially organized practices whereby 'rates' and categorizations are produced by those whose job it is to evaluate such matters. An early example of such work was that of Sudnow (1965) on the production of 'normal crimes' in a Public

Defender's office. Sudnow details the practical reasoning that informs how particular crimes or misdemeanours become categorized in accordance with typifications of 'normal' crimes, in the course of 'plea bargaining' for example. Thus, Sudnow looks 'behind' the classification of 'official' rates, based on convictions, to the socially organized work of interpretation and negotiation that generates such statistics.

In addition to Sudnow's ethnographic study of crime rates, we have a relatively small number of studies that have addressed this issue directly. Prominent among these is the work of Cicourel (1976) on juvenile justice, and of Cicourel and Kitsuse (1963) on the organization of educational decision making and the categorization of students' abilities and biographies.

The great value of the ethnomethodological critique is that it points up the importance of official documents and statistics as social phenomena that must be subjected to sociological analysis, not merely treated as sources of data. A whole new area for investigation is thus opened up: the socially organized practices whereby documents are written and read, and 'facts' produced.

At the same time, however, the ethnomethodological critique is seriously misleading. It applies just as much to accounts produced by the researcher, or by other participants, as to statistics produced by officials. Taken to its logical conclusion, this critique denies the very possibility of knowledge of the social world since any account, including those of ethnomethodologists themselves, can be shown to be a product of interpretive and interactional work.

The whole 'official statistics' debate has tended to polarize issues unnecessarily. The reflexive ethnographer will be aware that *all* classes of data have their problems, and none can be treated as unquestionably valid representations of 'reality'. There is no logical reason to regard documents as especially problematic or totally vitiated. As Bulmer remarks in this context:

'Firstly, there is no logical reason why awareness of possible serious sources of error in official data should lead to their rejection for research purposes. It could as well point to the need for methodological work to secure their improvement. Secondly, a great many of the more thorough-going critiques of official statistics relate to statistics of suicide, crime, and delinquency, areas in which there are special problems of reliable and valid measurement, notoriously so. The specific problems encountered in these fields are not, *ipso facto*, generalizable to all official statistics whatever their content. Thirdly, cases of the extensive use of official data – for example, by demographers – do not suggest that those who use them are unaware of the possible pitfalls in doing so. The world is not made up just of knowledgeable sceptics and naive hard-line positivists.'

(Bulmer 1980:508)

In other words, then, while drawing some inspiration from the ethnomethodological critique of 'official statistics' and similar documentary sources, we by no means endorse a radical view that suggests that such sources are totally vitiated. Data of this sort raise problems, to be sure, but they provide information as well as opening up a range of analytic problems. The ethnographer, like any other social scientist, may well draw on such documents. Furthermore, he or she may be particularly well placed to engage in principled and systematic research bearing on their validity and reliability as data, through the first-hand investigation of their contexts of production and use.

Woods (1979) provides a good example of such an approach in his analysis of school reports. In the construction of school reports, Woods suggests, teachers draw on 'professional', 'educationalist' conceptions of their task, rather than on the negotiated, 'survival' ethos of everyday classroom life. Here models of the ideal pupil are reproduced, and teachers voice their 'expert' valuations of students' activities, motivation, behaviour, and so on. The writing of such apparently authoritative accounts helps to 'cultivate the impression of detachment and omniscience, such as is attributed to the professions' (1979:185).

Woods cites a number of striking examples, where ideals of behaviour are announced in reports. For instance, the following clearly illustrates the teacher's appeal to norms of appropriate conduct for girls:

'Apart from French and music, Sara's report is below standard for a 3rd year, 2nd term, pupil. Her slovenly ways, moodiness and inelegant speech are reflected in her work.

She is a cheerful girl who is rather boisterous, at times too much so. We must in this final year try to turn her into a quieter young lady.

Tends to make her presence heard forcibly and often uses rather strong language. I feel that if she can be made to see that this is not the behaviour we expect from young ladies, it will be to her advantage.'

(Woods 1979:188)

Woods abstracts a number of typical categories that were used by teachers in formulating such normative characterizations:

Desirable	*Undesirable*
Concentration	Easily distracted, lacks concentration
Quiet	Chatterbox
Industrious (works well)	Lazy
Willing/Co-operative	Unco-operative
Responsible, mature	Immature
Courteous	Bad-mannered
Cheerful	Sullen
Obedient	Disobedient

(Woods 1979:173)

In many ways, as Woods points out, such typifications resemble those used by teachers in other contexts (such as staffroom conversations) as reported by other authors. It is important, however, to resist any temptation to condense all these different usages into a single category of 'teacher stereotypes'. In their differing social contexts, they may be formulated in different ways, with different practical purposes. The audiences for such statements differ, and the rhetoric may vary correspondingly.

Woods also touches on the fact that record making can provide for the concrete display of 'professional' competence; such documents vouch for the fact that work that should be done, has indeed been done, and renders it accountable to superiors. Rees, whose work on medical records we have already referred to, makes this point:

'What the House Officer writes, and the way in which he goes about constructing the history and examination, is one way his seniors can make inferences about the standard of his other activities. The supposition others make is that a House Officer who writes an organized and clearly thought out account of his work will be well organized in the way he carries out those activities. By paying attention to the construction of the account, and by ensuring that it conforms to the accepted model, the House Officer is able to influence one of the ways in which he will be judged by his seniors.'

(Rees 1981:58–9)

This reflects Garfinkel's remarks on records, where he suggests that they should be thought of as 'contractual' rather than 'actuarial'. That is, they are not literal accounts of 'what happened' but are tokens of the fact that the relevant personnel went about their business competently and reasonably. This is something taken up by Dingwall (1977b) in his study of the education of health visitors. Dingwall writes about the students' production of records of their visits to clients, and notes that since the actual conduct of the work is invisible to the supervisor, the record was the main focus of administrative control. Likewise, the record constitutes a major means of self-defence for the 'face-workers'.

In various ways, then, records have considerable importance in certain sorts of social setting. In some, the production of 'paperwork' is a major preoccupation. Even in organizations that have 'people-processing' tasks, this usually involves the translation of events into *records* of those events, which can be filed, stored, and manipulated. Such files are a primary resource for members of the organization in getting through their everyday work. Often, the exigencies of record making can play an important part in organizing the work that gets done, and the routines used to accomplish it. Records of previous encounters with clients can be used to formulate appropriate objectives and activities for a current consultation. As Dingwall says of his student health visitors:

'The good health visitor can derive sufficient data from the face sheet to identify the relevant areas of her knowledge about clients and the tasks she should be accomplishing in a visit. Unusual events are flagged in various ways. Thus, a child who is at risk may be marked by a red star on the card. Particular social problems may be pencilled on the cover.'

(Dingwall 1977b:112)

Heath (1981) has recently commented on this sort of use of medical records in the context of doctor-patient encounters. He explains how general practitioners use their record cards to open the encounter with a patient: 'It is often through the elaboration of the appropriate record's contents prior to thc initiation of first topic, that the doctor is able to render the relevant characteristics of the patient, and thereby design a 'successful' first topic initiator' (1981:85).

Records, then, are used to establish actors as 'cases' with situated identities, which conform to 'normal' categories or deviate in certain identifiable and recordable ways. Records are made and used in accordance with organizational routines, and depend for their intelligibility on shared cultural assumptions. Records construct a 'documentary reality' that, by virtue of its very documentation, is often granted a sort of privilege. Although their production is a socially organized activity, official records usually have a sort of anonymity, which warrants their treatment as 'objective', 'factual' statements rather than mere personal 'belief', 'opinion', or 'guesswork' (although it is the case that some records may contain specific entries, such as differential medical or psychiatric diagnoses, that are explicitly flagged as tentative).

It should be apparent from what we have outlined already that there are many locales where literate social activity is of some social significance, and may indeed be of major importance. Modern industrial and administrative bureaucracies, professional or educational settings are obvious cases in point, and it requires little reflection to remind oneself of how pervasive the activity of writing and reading written documents is. It should be equally apparent, therefore, that it would be quite inappropriate to treat such settings as if they were illiterate, oral cultures. And even in the case of settings where documents are not a central feature there is often an enormous amount of biographical, autobiographical, and fictional material published that can be an invaluable resource; and, of course, the ethnographer can also elicit written accounts in the form of diaries, letters, and essays from participants.

The presence and significance of documentary products provides the ethnographer with a rich vein of analytic topics, as well as a valuable source of information. Such topics include: How are documents written? How are they read? Who writes them? Who reads them? For what purposes? On what occasions? With what outcomes? What is recorded? What is omitted? What is taken for granted? What does the writer seem to take for granted about the reader(s)? What do readers need to know in order to make sense of them? The list can readily be extended, and the exploration of such questions would lead the ethnographer inexorably towards a systematic examination of each and every aspect of everyday life in the setting in question.

The ethnographer who takes no account of such matters, on the other hand, ignores at his or her peril such features of a literate culture. There is nothing to be gained, and much to be lost, by representing such a culture as if it were an essentially oral tradition. In the scrutiny of documentary sources, the ethnographer thus recognizes and builds on his or her socialized competence as a member of a literate culture. Not only does the researcher read and write, but he or she also reflects on the very activities of reading and writing in given social settings. Thus, such everyday activities are incorporated into the ethnographer's topics of inquiry as well as furnishing analytic and interpretative resources.

7

Recording and

organizing data

There is a sense in which it is impossible ever to record all the data acquired in the course of fieldwork. As Radcliffe-Brown notes:

'However exact and detailed the description of a primitive people may be, there remains much that cannot be put into such a description. Living, as he must, in daily contact with the people he is studying, the field ethnologist comes gradually to "understand" them, if we may use the term. He acquires a series of multitudinous impressions, each slight and often vague, that guide him in his dealings with them. The better the observer the more accurate will be his general impression of the mental peculiarities of the race. This general impression it is impossible to analyse, and so to record and convey to others. Yet it may be of the greatest service when it comes to interpreting the beliefs and practices of a primitive society. If it does not give any positive aid towards a correct interpretation, it at least prevents errors into which it is only too easy for those to fall who have not the same immediate knowledge of the people and their ways.'

(Radcliffe-Brown 1948b:230)

In fact, such tacit knowledge is a ubiquitous phenomenon, extending even to physical science, as Michael Polanyi (1958) has shown. The existence of an inevitable residue of 'multitudinous impressions' or 'tacit knowledge' cannot be ignored. However, it does not negate the responsibility of the social scientist to be as explicit as possible about the data by means of which his or her theories have been generated, developed, and tested.

While it is possible to rely on memory to preserve this data over the course of the research, and some reliance on memory is unavoidable, there are limits to the amount of data that can be retained in this way. There is also a serious danger of distortion. We all know how memory can play tricks. A particular danger is that the data will be subconsciously transformed in line with emerging theory. In order to prevent this, it is essential to employ some system of recording data as, or soon after, they are collected.

There are several methods ethnographers use for recording their data, most notably fieldnotes, audio-taping, video-taping, and filming. Which of these is the most appropriate depends very much on one's purposes, the nature of the setting, and the financial resources available, though these techniques are not mutually exclusive. Their usefulness also varies according to the type of data to be recorded.

Observational data

Fieldnotes are the traditional means in ethnography for recording observational data. In accordance with ethnography's commitment to discovery, fieldnotes consist of relatively concrete descriptions of social processes and their contexts. The aim is to capture these in their integrity, noting their various features and properties, though clearly what is recorded will depend on some general sense of what is relevant to the foreshadowed problems of the research. As we noted in Chapter 1, while it is impossible to provide any description without some principle of selecting what is and is not important, there are advantages (as well as disadvantages) in adopting a wide focus. At least prior to the closing stages of data collection, then, there is no attempt to code systematically what is observed in terms of existing theoretical categories. Indeed, the main purpose is to identify and develop what seem to be the most appropriate theoretical categories.

The construction and collection of fieldnotes is not something that is (or should be) shrouded in mystery: it is not an especially esoteric activity. On the other hand, it does constitute a central research activity, and it should be carried out with as much care and self-conscious awareness as possible. A research project can be as well organized and theoretically well informed as you like, but with inadequate note taking, the exercise will be like using an expensive camera with poor quality film. In both cases, the resolution will prove unsatisfactory, and the results will be poor. Only foggy pictures result.

The compilation of fieldnotes may appear to be a straight-forward matter. However, like most aspects of intellectual craftsmanship, some care and attention to detail are prerequi-sites, and satisfactory note taking needs to be worked at. It is a skill demanding continual reassessment of purposes and prior-ities and of the costs and benefits of different strategies. Thus, the standard injunction, 'write down what you see and hear', glosses over a number of important issues. Among other things, the fieldworker will have to ask *what* to write down, *how* to write it down, and *when* to write it down.

Let us deal with this last point first: when to write notes? In principle, one should aim to make notes as soon as possible after the observed action that is to be noted. Most fieldworkers report that while they can train themselves to improve recall, the qual-ity of their notes diminishes rapidly with the passage of time: the detail is quickly lost, and whole episodes can be forgotten or irreparably muddled.

The ideal would be to make notes during actual participant observation. But this is not always possible, and even when it is possible, the opportunities may be very limited. There may be restrictions arising from the social characteristics of the research setting, as well as from the nature of the ethnographer's social position(s) *vis-à-vis* the hosts.

If the research is covert, then note taking in the course of par-ticipation will often be practically impossible. In most settings, participants are not visibly engaged in a continual process of jot-ting down notes, seizing notebooks during conversations, and similar activities. In many circumstances, such activity would prove totally disruptive to any 'natural' participation. It is hard to think of Laud Humphreys (1970), for example, taking copious notes while acting as 'watchqueen' in public lavatories and observing casual homosexual encounters. In a few contexts, of course, writing may be such an unremarkable activity that covert note taking is feasible. In a covert study of students' time-wasting strategies in a university library, spasmodic writing on the part of the ethnographer would be possible, though care would have to be taken not to appear too diligent!

However, overt research does not solve the problem of note taking. To some extent our comments concerning covert partic-ipation apply here as well. The conduct of note taking must be broadly congruent with the context of the setting under scru-tiny. In some contexts, however well 'socialized' the hosts, open and continuous note taking will be perceived as threat-ening or inappropriate, and will prove disruptive to the action. In other contexts, fairly extensive notes can be recorded without undue disruption. Thus, for example, Whyte (1981) reports how he took on the role of secretary to the Italian Community Club because it enabled him to take notes unobtrusively in their meetings.

The possibility of on-the-spot note taking may vary across situations even within a single setting, as the case of studying a medical school illustrates:

'The quantity and type of on-the-spot recording varied across recurrent types of situation. During "tutorials", when one of the doctors taught the group in a more or less formal manner, or when there was some group discussion, and conducted in one of the teaching rooms, then it seemed entirely natural and appropriate that I should sit among the students with my notebook on my knee and take notes almost continuously. At the other extreme I did not sit with my notebook and pen whilst I was engaged in casual conversations with students over a cup of coffee. Whereas taking notes during a University class is a normal thing to do, taking notes during a coffee-break chat is not a normal practice. To have done so openly in the latter context would have been to strain the day-to-day relationships that I had negotiated with the students. Whilst I never pretended that everything I saw and heard was not ''data'', it would not have been feasible to make continuous notes. . . . Less clear-cut was my approach to the observation and recording of bedside teaching. On the whole I tried to position myself at the back of the student group and make occasional jottings: main items of information on the patients, key technical terms, and brief notes indicating the 'shape' of the session (e.g. the sequence of topics covered, the students who were called on to perform and so on). As I did this over a period I discovered that a substantial amount of the interaction could be recalled and summarised from such brief and scrappy jottings.'

(Atkinson 1976:24–5)

Even in situations where note taking is 'normal', however, such as in tutorials, care must be taken if disruption is to be avoided:

'I feel it much easier to write when the students write, and listen when they do; I have noticed that when I attempt to write when the students are not, I attract (the tutor's) attention and on a few such occasions she seems to falter in what she is saying. . . . Similarly when all the students are writing and I am not, but rather looking at her, I again seem to ''put her off''. And so it is that I've become a student, sometimes slightly at the loss of my self-esteem when I find myself lazily inserting a pencil in my mouth. (Fieldnotes: February, third year.)'

(Olesen and Whittaker 1968:28)

Many of the initial fieldnotes that ethnographers take, then, are jottings, snatched in the course of the observed interaction. A common joke about ethnographers relates to their frequent trips to the lavatory where such hasty notes can be scribbled in private soon after the action. Even the briefest of notes can be valuable aids in the construction of an account. As Schatzman and Strauss suggest:

'A single word, even one merely descriptive of the dress of a person, or a particular word uttered by someone usually is enough to ''trip off'' a string of images that afford substantial reconstruction of the observed scene.'

(Schatzman and Strauss 1973:95)

Moreover, it is important to record even things that one does not immediately understand because these might turn out to be important later. Even if it proves possible to make fairly extended notes in the field, they, like brief jottings, will need to be worked up, expanded upon, and developed.

Many social activities have a timetable of their own, and it may prove possible to match phases of observation with periods of writing up fieldnotes in accordance with such timetables. For instance, in the medical-school study referred to earlier, most of the clinical teaching that formed the main focus of the observation took place during the morning; the afternoon was devoted to laboratory work in the various medical sciences. Thus, it proved possible to undertake three or four hours of sustained observation before lunch, and to spend the afternoon and/or evening in writing up full notes. (The afternoon was also available for other forms of data collection such as interviewing and analysis.)

In other settings, the phasing of observation and writing will be much less straightforward to organize, but there are usually times when participants are engaged in activities that are not relevant to the research. At the very least, they sleep at regular times and at the risk of fatigue notes can be written up then. Carey (1972) reports a rare exception, that of 'speed freaks' (those addicted to amphetamines), who, under heavy doses, stay awake for several days in a hyperactive state:

'The peculiar round of life wherein people stay up for three, four, or five days at a time and then sleep for several days posed enormous practical difficulties for the research. Our conventional commitments (family, friends, teaching responsibilities) had to be put aside for a time so that we could adapt ourselves more realistically to this youthful scene. As we became more familiar with this particular universe, we developed a crude sampling plan that called for observations at a number of different gathering spots, and this relieved us somewhat from a very exacting round of life. If we were interested, however, in what happened during the course of a run when a small group of people started shooting speed intravenously, it meant that one or two fieldworkers had to be present at the beginning and be relieved periodically by other members of the team until the run was over. Fatigue was a constant problem and suggests that more than one field-worker is required in this type of research.'

(Carey 1972:82)

Clearly, in such cases, finding time to write up fieldnotes poses particularly severe problems. The problem remains serious, however, even with less exhausting schedules. But some time for writing up fieldnotes must always be set aside. There is no advantage in observing social action over extended periods if inadequate time is allowed for the preparation of notes. The information will quickly trickle away, and the effort will be wasted. There is always the temptation to try to observe everything, and the consequent fear that in withdrawing from the field, one will miss some vital incident. Understandable though such feelings are, they must, in most circumstances, be suppressed in the interests of producing good-quality notes. Nevertheless, the trade-off between data collection and data recording must be recognized and resolved continually in the manner that seems most appropriate given the purposes of the research. Thus, for example, the organization of periods of observation, with alternating periods of writing and other work, must be done with a view to the systematic sampling of action and actors (Chapter 2).

It is difficult to overemphasize the importance of meticulous note taking. The memory should never be relied on, and a good maxim is 'If in doubt, *write it down*'. It is absolutely essential that one keep up to date in processing notes. Without the discipline of daily writing, the observations will fade from memory, and the ethnography will all too easily become incoherent and muddled. The overall picture will become fuzzy.

What of the *form* and *content* of fieldnotes? One can never record everything; social scenes are truly inexhaustible in this sense. Some selection has to be made. However, the nature of this is likely to change over time. During the early days of a research project, the scope of the notes is likely to be fairly general, and one will probably be reluctant to emphasize any particular aspects; indeed, one will probably not be in a position to make such a selection of topics. As the research progresses, and emergent issues are identified, then the notes will become more restricted in subject matter. Moreover, features that previously seemed insignificant may come to take on new meaning, a point that Johnson illustrates from his research on social workers:

> 'Gradually I began to ''hear different things said'' in the setting. This happened through a shift in attention from *what* was said or done to *how* it was said or done. The following excerpts from the fieldnotes illustrate several instances of my changing awareness. From the notes near the end of the sixth month of the observations:
>
>> ''Another thing that happened today. I was standing by Bill's desk when Art passed by and asked Bill to cover the phone for a couple of minutes while he walked through a request for County Supp over to Bess Lanston, an EW supervisor. Now I don't know how many times I've heard a comment like that; so many times that it's not even problematic any more. In fact, it's so routine that I'm surprised that I even made any note to remember it. The striking feature about this is that in my first days at Metro [the social work agency] I would have wanted to know all about what kind of form he was taking over there, what County Supp was, why and how one used it, got it, didn't get it, or whatever, who and where Bess Lanston was, what she did and so on. But all the time I've missed what was crucial about such a comment, the fact that he was *walking* it through. Before I would have only heard what he was doing or why, but today, instead, I began to hear the how.'' '
>>
>> (Johnson 1975:197)

As theoretical ideas develop and change, what is 'significant' and what must be included in the fieldnotes also changes. Over time, notes may also change in *character*, in particular becoming more concrete and detailed. Indeed the preservation of concreteness is an important consideration in fieldnote writing. For most analytic purposes, compressed summary accounts will prove inadequate for the detailed and systematic comparison or aggregation of information across context or across occasions. As far as possible, therefore, speech should be rendered in a manner that approximates to a verbatim report and non-verbal behaviour in relatively concrete terms; this minimizes the level

of inference and thus facilitates the construction and reconstruction of theory.

Below we reproduce two extracts from notes that purport to
recapture the same interaction. They are recognizably 'about'
the same people and the same events. By the same token, neither
lays any claim to completeness. The first obviously compresses
things to an extreme extent, and the second summarizes some
things, and explicitly acknowledges that some parts of the conversation are missing altogether:

'1. The teacher told his colleagues in the staffroom about the
wonders of a progressive school he had been to visit the day
before. He was attacked from all sides. As I walked up with
him to his classroom he continued talking of how the
behaviour of the pupils at X had been marvellous. We
reached his room. I waited outside, having decided to
watch what happened in the hall in the build up to the
morning assembly. He went into his classroom and
immediately began shouting at his class. He was taking it
out on them for not being like the pupils at X.

2. (Walker gives an enthusiastic account of X to his colleagues in the staffroom. There is an aggressive reaction.)

GREAVES: Projects are not education, just cutting out
things.

WALKER: Oh no, they don't allow that, there's a strict
check on progress.

HOLTON: The more I hear of this the more wishy washy it
sounds.

(. . .)

WALKER: There's a craft resources area and pupils go and
do some dress-making or woodwork when they want to,
when it fits into their project.

HOLTON: You need six week's basic teaching in woodwork or metalwork.

(. . .)

HOLTON: How can an immature child of that age do a
project?

WALKER: Those children were self-controlled and well-
behaved.

(. . .)

HOLTON: Sounds like utopia.

DIXON: Gimmicky.

(. . .)

WALKER: There's no vandalism. They've had the books four years and they've been used a lot and I could see the pupils were using them, but they looked new, the teacher had told them that if they damaged the books she would have to replace them herself.

(. . .)

HOLTON: Sounds like those kids don't need teaching.

((Walker and I go up to his room: he continues his praise for X. When we reach his room I wait outside to watch the hall as the build up for the morning assembly begins. He enters his room and immediately begins shouting. The thought crosses my mind that the contrast between the pupils at X he has been describing and defending to his colleagues and the ''behaviour'' of his own pupils may be a reason for his shouting at the class, but, of course, I don't know what was going on the classroom.))

(( )) = observer descriptions.

(. . .) = omission of parts of conversation in record.'

(Hammersley 1980)

The second version is much more concrete in its treatment of the events; indeed, much of the time the speech of the actors themselves is preserved. We can inspect the notes with a fair assurance that we are gaining information on how the participants themselves described things, who said what to whom, and so on. When we compress and summarize we do not simply lose 'interesting' detail and 'local colour', we lose vital information.

The actual words people use can be of considerable analytic importance. The 'situated vocabularies' employed provide us with valuable information about the way in which members of a particular culture organize their perceptions of the world, and so engage in the 'social construction of reality'. Situated vocabularies and folk taxonomies incorporate the typifications and recipes for action that constitute the stock-of-knowledge and practical reasoning of the members of any given culture. Arensberg and Kimball provide an example from their study of interpersonal relations among family members in rural Ireland:

'The relations of the members of the farm family are best described in terms of the patterns which uniformity of habit and association build up. They are built up within the life of the farm household and its daily and yearly work. The relations of the fathers to sons and mothers to sons fall repeatedly into regular and expectable patterns of this kind that differ very little from farm to farm.

If we are to understand them, then, we must trace them out of this setting and see in what manner they offer us explanation of Irish rural behaviour. In terms of a formal sociology, such as Simmel might give us, the position of the parents is one of extreme superordination, that of the children of extreme subordination. The retention of the names "boy" and "girl" reflects the latter position. Sociological adulthood has little to do with physiological adulthood. Age brings little change of modes of address and ways of treating and regarding one another in the relationships within the farm family.'

(Arensberg and Kimball 1968:59)

Recently, there has been increased attention to the significance of the terminologies used by participants. A number of classic ethnographic studies have included lexicons of local terms. Examples include the studies of prison inmates by Sykes (1958) and Giallombardo (1966), and Davis's (1959) account of cab-drivers' evaluations of their clients (their 'fares').

The potential richness and detail of the connotations of such members' terms can perhaps be illustrated by reference to just one term from one such collection. American hospital speech includes the term 'gomer', which is part of the rich and colourful situated vocabulary characteristic of most medical settings. George and Dundes summarize its use:

'What precisely is a "gomer"? He is typically an older man who is both dirty and debilitated. He has extremely poor personal hygiene and he is often a chronic alcoholic. A derelict or down-and-outer, the gomer is normally on welfare. He has an extensive listing of multiple admissions to the hospital. From the gomer's standpoint, life inside the hospital is so much better than the miserable existence he endures outside that he exerts every effort to gain admission, or rather readmission to the hospital. Moreover, once admitted, the gomer attempts to remain there as long as possible. Because of the gomer's desire to stay in the hospital he frequently pretends to be ill or he lacks interest in getting well on those occasions when he is really sick.'

(George and Dundes 1978:570)

Of course, this brief account glosses over a wide range of uses and connotations associated with this one folk term. In practice, the research worker will not be content simply to generate such a composite or summary definition, important though that may be in summing up one's understanding and cultural competence. The important task is to be able to document and retrieve the actual contexts of use for such folk terms.

In a study of tramps, Spradley (1970) identified a number of categories of actors who seemed to have their own languages: tramps themselves, social workers, police officers, counsellors, judges, court clerks, lawyers, guards, not to mention the ethnographer. Such languages are not, of course, totally self-contained and mutually unintelligible. However, they are major markers of cultural difference constitutive of differing, and differentially distributed, definitions of the situation. They include the specialized languages of occupational groups, underworld argot, local sayings, and regionally and class-based dialects.

Making fieldnotes as concrete and descriptive as possible is not without its cost, however. Generally the more closely this ideal is approximated, the more restricted the scope of the notes. Unless the focus of the research is extremely narrow, some concreteness and detail will have to be sacrificed for increased scope. Even in the relatively detailed fieldnotes on an incident in a school staffroom quoted earlier, the level of concreteness and detail varied somewhat within the account. Such variations will follow, among other things, current assessments of the relative importance for subsequent analysis of the various features of the scene. There is no neutral observation language in which any scene can be described completely and definitively. Even in the case of recording language 'word for word', interpretation plays its part. Not only is it usually impossible to record everything that is said, and indeed we generally 'tidy up' speech when we write it down, omitting repetitions, hesitations, false starts, and so on, but accompanying non-verbal behaviour cannot usually be recorded unless its significance is of obvious importance. To one degree or another, then, selection, summary, and interpretation are always involved. That this involves dangers is clear, but so is the neglect of the wider context in which the events occurred. Some trade-off between detail and scope in note taking is inevitable and must be determined according to the priorities of the research.

Whatever the level of concreteness of fieldnotes, it is essential that direct quotations are clearly distinguished from summaries provided by the researcher, and that gaps or uncertainties in the quotations are clearly indicated. When we refer back to notes, there must be no ambiguity on that score. One should not have to puzzle 'Is that what they themselves said?' Even when only isolated or fragmented sequences can be recalled and noted, they should be kept typographically distinct from the observer's own descriptive glosses.

Equally important is that records of speech and action should be located in relation to *who* was present, *where*, at what *time*, and under what *circumstances*. When we come to the stage of analysis, when one will be gathering together, categorizing, comparing, and contrasting instances, then it may become crucial that one can distinguish the circumstances surrounding an activity, such as the audience, and the main participants (see Chapter 8).

Spradley suggests one elementary checklist that can be used to guide the making of field records, and adherence to which would normally allow one to approximate to the provision of context we have referred to:

'1. Space: the physical place or places.
2. Actor: the people involved.
3. Activity: a set of related acts people do.
4. Object: the physical things that are present.
5. Act: single actions that people do.
6. Event: a set of related activities that people carry out.
7. Time: the sequencing that takes place over time.
8. Goal: the things people are trying to accomplish.
9. Feeling: the emotions felt and expressed.'

(Spradley 1980:78ff)

Such lists are very crude and rest on arbitrary classifications such as that between acts, activities, and events. Nevertheless, they indicate a range of relevant features of context that might need to be noted.

We have seen, then, how the process of fieldnote writing is shot through with decisions about when and what to record. Indeed, very often these decisions take on the form of dilemmas: higher quality notes can often only be bought at the risk of missing important data; concreteness may sometimes have to be sacrificed to gain the necessary descriptive scope. However, there is one way in which it may seem that some of these dilemmas can be avoided: by the use of a tape recorder. The tension between note writing and observation can be eased, for example, by taping fieldnotes rather than writing them up. As Schatzman and Strauss (1973:97) note, this saves time. However, they also point to some problems, not the least of which is the temptation to generate a huge backlog of under-analysed tapes.

Even more tempting as a solution to the dilemmas involved in fieldnote writing is to resort to electronic recording techniques, audio or audio/visual, in the actual course of observation. While neither provides a complete record – selection is still involved in the placing of the cameras and/or microphones – clearly they provide a much more accurate and detailed account of events than can be provided in notes. And, indeed, these techniques are a very important resource especially where the research focuses on the details of social interaction. The work of McDermott (1976) provides an example. McDermott video-taped two reading groups in a first-grade classroom, looking at the detail of interpersonal interaction, verbal and non-verbal. He was able to show that while interaction in one group looked orderly and in the other disorderly, and was viewed as such by the teacher, what occurred was simply a different kind of order, in part sustained by the teacher's attitude, and that this had dire consequences for the achievement levels of the pupils. There has been similar detailed work on interactional processes by conversational analysts using audio-taping.

Where research is concerned with this level of detail, electronic recording is probably essential. Where the focus is wider, where every word spoken and gesture made is not relevant, such techniques are still useful because of the accuracy and concreteness they provide. However, their advantages must be weighed against some important disadvantages.

Of course, permission will not always be given for their use and this may restrict the range of settings from which an appropriate site for the research can be chosen, or restrict the parts of a setting that can be studied. For example, while teachers will often permit their lessons, and even their staff meetings (Hargreaves 1981) to be tape-recorded or even video-taped, these techniques are unlikely to be allowed in staffrooms. Moreover, even where permission is given, awareness that proceedings are being recorded may significantly affect what occurs. This is particularly true where recorders are carried around and switched on and off to capture particular events, as Altheide illustrates from his research in a TV newsroom:

'I used a tape recorder mainly for debriefing, although I also used it for recording in the setting. In this way, data collection and data recording were combined. However, I found that, with some exceptions, the recorder disrupted the naturalness of the conversation. This occurred during a talk I was having with an anchorman who was making a documentary about alcoholism. His fascinating comments about using actors to play alcoholics because "real alcoholics talk too much", prompted me to ask him if he would mind if I got my recorder. When I turned it on, he cleared his throat and began lecturing me on the magnitude of alcoholism in Western City, never returning to the original topic.

In other situations the recorder did not disrupt the event. One reporter's explanation about how he 'reduced' an interview was recorded without distortion. I know this to be true since I had watched him reduce other interviews in the same way. A few cameramen and reporters permitted me to routinely record their work and assessments of the news scene, while others, like the cameraman who threatened to throw me out of the car, did not approve. However, the recorder did have a situated significance for all workers.'

(Altheide 1976:213)

The effects of audio- and audio-visual recording vary considerably across people and settings. We would expect TV workers to be particularly sensitive, for example, and recording may be easier and less obtrusive where interaction is confined to a single, small setting, as in the case of school lessons or college tutorials. Moreover, the effects of the presence of recording equipment often dissipate over time.

The development of the cheap portable cassette recorder has made audio-recording relatively easy. Moreover, the small size of these machines makes them relatively unobtrusive. There are, of course, technical limitations on what can be recorded in this manner. It is an obvious point, but one of some significance, that only the soundtrack of a setting is recorded in this way, non-verbal behaviour and the physical environment of activities must still be recorded by fieldnotes. Indeed, sometimes this may have to be recorded in considerable detail if the audio-tape is to be comprehensible, as Walker and Adelman indicate in reporting their research on 'open' classrooms:

'Initially we experimented with sound tape recordings – keeping records over several weeks. These proved interesting in this context because, to a surprising extent they were incomprehensible. We do not mean this in the strictly technical sense of noise and distortion; we could hear the words but for much of the time we simply could not make complete sense of what was being said. We had previously made similar recordings in more orthodox classrooms and found them quite self-explanatory, even when reduced to transcript, but in this situation we were unable to apply any of the usual techniques of analysis. . . . For the most part transcripts prepared from tape recordings made of the teacher in this class revealed talk that was, for much of the time, fragmented, truncated, interrupted, unclear and cluttered with curious hesitations and pauses. Yet we knew from extensive observation that this class was one where a complex division of labour and considerable differentiation of tasks were in operation. From observation our impression was that talk in these classrooms was articulate and fluent, moreover, in all the time we had observed we could not recall any complaint that a child had been unable to understand the teacher, or misunderstood what she was saying. The transcripts came to us as something of a surprise.'

(Walker and Adelman 1972:8–9)

It was in response to this experience that Walker and Adelman synchronized film records with sound recordings. They often discovered then that identifying who was being addressed allowed them to make sense of what was being talked about: 'The talk we found strangely frustrating in transcript because it seemed fragmented, awkward and illogical, often came alive when seen in context, seeming economical, vivid and apt' (1972:10).

There are also, of course, technical limits to the scope of the interactions that can be recorded. Walker and Adelman's example of school classrooms provides a striking example of this too. Where lessons are very formal and predominantly oral, the whole lesson can be captured on tape with high fidelity. As we move towards the progressive end of the specturm, however, not only does the quality and so the intelligibility of the recording decline, because of higher background noise produced by increased movement of pupils about the room, but the scope of the recording becomes more restricted. It is no longer possible to capture the whole lesson; one can only record fragments of it since the teacher and the pupils move about the room and the very organization of the lesson is decentralized. And there are many more social occasions that are like informal than formal teaching. Moreover, even in the case of recordings of traditional teaching, it is a mistake to assume that the whole event has been captured on tape. Not only is non-verbal behaviour – such as reading and written work – missing, but some talk may escape the recording, such as that between the teacher and individual pupils, or among pupils themselves. Similarly, in audio recordings of court proceedings, the public talk will be preserved, but not usually the private talk, between judge and counsel at the bench, among lawyers, and between them and their clients. How significant this is depends on the purpose of the research, of course, but the selectivity involved must not be forgotten since it may have implications for what conclusions can be legitimately drawn from the data.

While video-recording and filming avoid some of these problems, they are, of course, more expensive and likely to be more intrusive. Moreover, they share another somewhat ironic feature with audio-recording: they produce too much data. Schatzman and Strauss's remarks about taping field-notes – that transcription still remains to be done and that keeping in touch with the data so that theoretical sampling can proceed becomes more difficult – are even more true where events in settings are recorded themselves. While transcription is not always essential – one can simply treat the tape as a document, indexing, summarizing, and/or copying sections of it (see p. 163) – even then a considerable amount of time is required, probably more than is involved in writing up extended field-notes. When using audio- and video-recording techniques, it is very easy to record more data than one can ever actually use. One may also find that one's purpose and findings are constrained by the very techniques used. The use of audio- and video-recording devices does not avoid the dilemma of detail versus scope, though it may obscure it. While they provide data of great concreteness and detail, precisely because of this they may obscure longer term patterns; detailed pictures of individual trees are provided but no sense gained of the shape of the forest.

We noted in Chapter 1 that in ethnography the ethno-grapher is the research instrument. What we have said about audio- and video-recording techniques should make clear that they are no replacement for the participant observer and his or her fieldnotes. They may, however, be a useful supplement, depending on the nature of the setting and the purposes of the research. Used selectively, to provide detailed data on partic-ularly important events or a sample of events, or used as a check on fieldnotes, they can be very helpful.

Interview data

In the case of the highly structured interviews typical of sur-vey research, the problem of recording responses is minimized because they are usually brief and generally fall into one or other pre-coded category. The interviewer simply rings one or other code, or at most writes in a few words in the space provided. With ethnographic interviews, on the other hand, generating lengthy responses not structured to fit a pre-given set of categories, the problem of recording looms large. It is, of course, possible to take notes and here much the same considerations – what is to be noted, when, and how – arise as in the case of observational fieldnotes. Once again reliance will most likely have to be placed on jotted notes, and the dilemma of summarizing versus verbatim reporting is just as acute. Similarly, note taking can prove disruptive, much as in the tutorial cited by Olesen and Whittaker (1968), with the interviewee becoming self-conscious about what is being written down; though the effects are probably lessened because note taking is a standard feature of interviews. However, the need to take notes makes the kind of reflexive interviewing we advocated in Chapter 5 very difficult, if not impossible, since much of the interviewer's attention is taken up with recording what has been said; especially since not just the informant's responses, but also the interviewer's questions should be recorded.

Given these problems, the advantages of audio-recording are considerable. While interviewees will sometimes not give permission (because, for example, 'you can't argue with a tape'), agreement is generally forthcoming once it is explained that the purpose is simply to aid note taking and that confidentiality will be maintained. Moreover, tape-recording, particularly using a portable cassette recorder, may actually reduce reactivity rather than increase it. When the recorder is not in the informant's immediate line of sight, he or she is more likely to forget that the recording is being made than when the interviewer is hastily scribbling throughout the conversations. The tape recorder provides a more complete, concrete, and detailed record than fieldnotes, though once again non-verbal aspects and features of the physical surroundings are omitted. For this reason it is usually advisable to supplement the tape recording with jotted notes covering these matters.

Problems of processing the tapes arise, of course. Once again transcription may be necessary, though sometimes taking notes from the tape will prove adequate. Either way, rather more time is involved than simply filling out jotted notes, though the product is far more effective as a record of the interview.

Documents

Some documents are freely available and can be retained for later use. This is often true, for example, of such items as promotional material, guides of one kind or another, and circulars. Other documents can be bought relatively cheaply. Even where documentary sources are not produced in large numbers, the researcher may be able to produce copies for retention. Photocopiers are available in some settings, of course, and the ethnographer may be allowed access to them. Alternatively, it may sometimes be possible to borrow documents for short periods in order to copy them. Of course, there are constraints of time and finance here. Even if the copying can be done at no cost, time spent photocopying is time that otherwise might have been spent reading the documents, or in participant observation, or interviewing. For this reason, copying documents *in toto* is not necessarily the most effective recording strategy. While it avoids the dangers of omitting something important or losing the context of what is recorded, this has to be balanced against costs in time and money.

Frequently, because multiple copies are not available and photocopying is not possible, or is too costly, there is no alternative to note taking. Here too, though, there are different strategies available. One can index a document so that the relevant sections of it can be consulted as appropriate at later stages of the research. This can be done relatively quickly, but it requires easy and repeated access to the documentary sources. Alternatively, one may summarize relevant sections of material or copy them out by hand. The choice between summarizing and copying revolves around a dilemma that we have already met in recording observational and interview data. By summarizing one can cover much more material in the same time, thus releasing scarce time for work of other kinds. On the other hand, summarizing involves some loss of information and introduces interpretation. In producing a summary one must not only decide on the important points that require mentioning, but also translate these into general categories.

These three modes of note taking – indexing, copying, and summarizing – are not mutually exclusive, of course, and each should be used according to the accessibility of the documents and the anticipated nature of the use to which the notes will be put. Both these considerations may vary across different documents or even sections of documents. Where access to the documents is difficult and the precise wording used is likely to be important, there is little alternative to making painstaking copies. Where the need is for background information, summaries might be sufficient. Incidentally, it should be noted that notes need not necessarily be written on the spot; where access to documents is restricted it may be more efficient to read the indexes, summaries, or relevant sections into a portable tape-recorder. In general, these will need to be written or typed out later and similar considerations arise as in the case of tape-recording fieldnotes.

Analytic notes and memos

While reading documents, making fieldnotes, or transcribing audio or video tapes, promising theoretical ideas often arise. It is important to make note of these because they may prove useful when analysing the data. At that stage any contributions should be gratefully accepted! It is important though, to distinguish analytic notes from accounts provided by participants and from observer descriptions. This can be done typographically by encasing them in square or double brackets, for example, or by labelling them in some way.

Equally important is regular review and development of analytic ideas in the form of analytic memos. These are not fully developed working papers, but periodic written notes whereby progress is assessed, emergent ideas are identified, research strategy is sketched out, and so on. It is all too easy to let one's fieldnotes, and other types of data, pile up day by day and week by week. The very accumulation of material usually imparts a very satisfactory sense of progress, which can be measured in physical terms, as notebooks are filled, interviews completed, periods of observation ticked off, or different research settings investigated. But it is a grave error to let this work pile up without regular reflection and review: under such circumstances that sense of progress may prove illusory, and a good deal of the data collection could be unnecessarily aimless.

As we have emphasized, the formulation of precise problems,

hypotheses, and an appropriate research strategy, is an emergent feature of the research programme itself. This process of progressive focusing means that the collection of data must be guided by the unfolding but explicit identification of topics for inquiry. The regular production of research memoranda will force the ethnographer to go through such a process of explication, and prevent any aimless drifting through the collection of data. Ideally, every period of observation should result in both processed notes, and reflexive monitoring of the research process. As such memoranda accumulate, they will constitute preliminary analyses, providing the researcher with guidelines through the corpus of data. If this is done there is no danger of being confronted at the end of the day with a more or less undifferentiated collection of material, with only one's memory to guide analysis.

The construction of such notes therefore constitutes precisely that sort of internal dialogue, or thinking aloud, that is the essence of reflexive ethnography. Such activity should help one avoid lapsing into the 'natural attitude', and 'thinking as usual' in the field. Rather than coming to take one's understanding on trust, one is forced to question *what* one knows, *how* such knowledge has been acquired, the *degree of certainty* of such knowledge, and what further lines of inquiry are implied.

These analytic notes may be appended to the daily fieldnotes, or they may be incorporated into yet a fourth variety of written account, the fieldwork journal. Such a journal or diary provides a running account of the conduct of the research. This includes not only a record of the fieldwork, but also of the ethnographer's own personal feelings and involvement. The latter is not simply a matter of gratuitous introspection or narcissistic self-absorption. As we point out elsewhere in this book, feelings of personal comfort, anxiety, surprise, shock, or revulsion are of analytic significance. In the first place, our feelings enter into and colour the social relationships we engage in during fieldwork. Second, such personal and subjective responses will inevitably influence one's choice of what may be noteworthy, what is regarded as problematic and strange, and what appears to be mundane or obvious. One often relies implicitly on such feelings, and their existence and possible influence must be acknowledged and, if possible, explicated in written form.

Similarly, feelings of anxiety can pose limitations on data collection, leading to a highly restricted sort of tunnel vision.
Although some commentators have drawn attention to the
importance of recording one's feelings (e.g. Johnson 1975),
the following remark from Olesen and Whittaker remains
broadly true: 'The reading of most fieldwork studies leaves the
impression that fieldworkers glide silkily and gracefully through
the process without a twinge of anxiety or a single *faux pas*'
(1968:44). Yet it seems unlikely that the intense personal
involvement and commitment called for by ethnography
commonly proceeds in such a smooth and 'silky' manner.

One of us (Atkinson) found some explicit reference to personal
feelings of some value, for instance, in studying the Edinburgh
medical school. One's own personal reactions to clinical
encounters – fascination, revulsion, and embarrassment for
example – cannot simply be used to extrapolate to the feelings of
others such as doctors and medical students. However, they can
be used to alert one to possible issues, such as the process of
socialization that has been referred to as 'training for detached
concern', or the 'cloak of competence', whereby medical
practitioners' most extreme feelings may be masked or
neutralized. Participation can be used to simulate the experience
of other participants, and thus the researcher's own feelings can
be an important form of data in their own right:

> '(O.C. I feel quite bored and depressed on the ward tonight. I
> wonder if this has anything to do with the fact that there are
> only two attendants working now. With only two attendants
> on, there are fewer diversions and less bantering. Perhaps this
> is why the attendants always complain about there not being
> enough of them. After all, there is never more work here than
> enough to occupy two attendants' time so it's not the fact that
> they can't get their work done that bothers them.)

> (O.C. Although I don't show it, I tense up when the residents
> approach me when they are covered with food or excrement.
> Maybe this is what the attendants feel and why they often
> treat the residents as lepers.)'
>
> (Bogdan and Taylor 1975:67)

There is, then, a constant interplay between the personal and emotional on the one hand, and the intellectual on the other. Private response is thus transformed, by reflexive analysis, into potential public knowledge. The fieldwork journal is the vehicle for such transformation. At a more mundane level, perhaps, the carefully made fieldwork journal will enable the conscientious ethnographer painstakingly to retrace and explicate the development of the research design, the emergence of analytic themes, and the systematic collection of data. The provision of such a 'natural history' of the research is a crucial component of the final report.

Storing and retrieving data records

It is usual to organize written data records chronologically as a running record in which the data is stored by time of collection. Once analysis begins, however, reorganization of the data in terms of topics and themes generally becomes necessary. The first step here is to segment the data. Often there are 'natural' breaks in the material that can be used to break it up into chunks that can then be allocated to particular categories. This is usually the case with participant observation fieldnotes that often consist of notes on a sequence of incidents, each of which can be treated as a separate segment. Sometimes, particularly in the case of transcripts, 'natural' breaks are so few and far between that, simply for practical purposes, the data must be broken up in a more artificial way. Little seems to be lost by this.

The first categories in terms of which the data is normally reorganized are usually relatively descriptive, relating to particular people or types of people, places, activities, and topics of concern. The reorganization of the data in this way provides an important infrastructure for later data retrieval. However, it can also play an active role in the process of discovery, as the Webbs note:

'It enables the scientific worker to break up his subject-matter, so as to isolate and examine at his leisure its various component parts, and to recombine the facts when they have been thus released from all accustomed categories, in new and experimental groupings. . . .'

(Webb and Webb 1932:83)

Moreover the selection of categories is of some significance:

'As I gathered my early research data, I had to decide how I was to organize the written notes. In the very early stage of exploration, I simply put all the notes, in chronological order, in a single folder. As I was to go on to study a number of different groups and problems, it was obvious that this was no solution at all.

I had to subdivide the notes. There seemed to be two main possibilities. I could organize the notes topically, with folders for politics, rackets, the church, the family, and so on. Or I could organize the notes in terms of the groups on which they were based, which would mean having folders on the Nortons, the Italian Community Club, and so on. Without really thinking the problem through, I began filing material on the group basis, reasoning that I could later redivide it on a topical basis when I had a better knowledge of what the relevant topics should be.

As the material in the folders piled up, I came to realize that the organization of notes by social groups fitted in with the way in which my study was developing. For example, we have a college-boy member of the Italian Community Club saying: ''These racketeers give our district a bad name. They should really be cleaned out of here''. And we have a member of the Nortons saying: ''These racketeers are really all right. When you need help, they'll give it to you. The legitimate business-man – he won't even give you the time of day''. Should these quotes be filed under ''Racketeers, attitudes toward?''. If so, they would only show that there are conflicting attitudes toward racketeers in Cornerville. Only a questionnaire (which is hardly feasible for such a topic) would show the distribution of attitudes in the district. Furthermore, how important would it be to know how many people felt one way or another on this topic? It seemed to me of much greater scientific interest to be able to relate the attitude to the group in which the individual participated. This shows why two individuals could be expected to have quite different attitudes on a given topic.'

(Whyte 1981:308)

The allocation of data to categories in ethnography differs

from the kind of coding typical in quantitative research and even some other qualitative research (Goode and Hatt 1952). Here there is no requirement that items be assigned to one and only one category, or that there be explicit rules for assigning them:

> 'We code (the fieldnotes) inclusively; that is to say if we have any reason to think that anything might go under the heading, we will put it in. We do not lose anything. We also code them in multiple categories, under anything that might be felt to be cogent. As a general rule, we want to get back anything that could conceivably bear on a given interest. . . . It is a search procedure for getting all of the material that is pertinent.'
>
> (Becker 1968:245)

Indeed, Lofland (1971) argues that in the case of analytic categories it pays to be 'wild', to include anything, however long a shot.

The identification of categories is a central element of the process of analysis. As a result, the list of categories in terms of which the data is organized generally undergoes considerable change over the course of the research. In particular, there is typically a shift towards more analytic categories as theory develops. In some research on staffroom talk in an inner-city secondary school (Hammersley 1980), the exchanges recorded in the fieldnotes were initially categorized according to whether they related to the teachers' views of pupils on the one hand, or to other aspects of teaching and the life of teachers on the other. As the analysis progressed, however, more refined and theoretically relevant categories were developed, concerning, for example, the 'crisis' that the teachers saw facing them, the way in which teachers traded 'news' about pupils, and how they sought to explain why pupil performances were so 'bad' despite their best efforts.

Organizing and reorganizing the data in terms of categories can be done in a number of different ways. The simplest is 'coding the record'. Here data is coded, that is assigned to a category, on the running record itself, or a copy of it. Comments relating the data to descriptive or analytic categories are written in the margin or on the back of each page. (Clearly, provision has to be made for this in the format employed for writing up notes and transcribing tapes.) The advantage of this procedure is that it can be done relatively quickly and it allows analysis of an item in the immediate context in which it is recorded. On the other hand, the amount of time subsequently taken up with reading through the running record finding items relevant to a particular category may be prohibitive with anything but the smallest data sets.

In more sophisticated versions of 'coding the record', an analytic index is produced. Here each data segment is assigned an identifying mark: a number, or letter, or combination of the two. (It is often useful, where different types of data have been collected – for example, observational and interview fieldnotes – to distinguish between them so that the status of any data segment can be identified at a glance.) A list of categories is prepared, and constantly up-dated as new categories emerge, with the codes for the segments of data relevant to each category listed under it, these too being up-dated as new data comes in. This requires a little more time and effort than simply coding the record. However, it greatly facilitates the speed and rigour of data retrieval. Indeed, analytic memos can be combined with an index, a file card being prepared for each category, providing a definition, relevant further information, and discussion of the relationship of the concept to others, etc. At the same time, the items of data relevant to that category can be listed by number on the card. The cards would need to be kept in some kind of order, perhaps alphabetical, to facilitate ready access.

An alternative method of data organization, used by Whyte, the Webbs, and many other ethnographers, is physical sorting. Here, multiple copies need to be made of each segment of data and a copy is filed under all of the categories to which it is relevant. With this system, when it is time for detailed analysis of a particular category all the relevant data is readily available, there is no need to sift through the running record to find the relevant data segments. An additional advantage is that all the items relevant to the same category can be put side by side and compared. On the other hand, considerable time and expense may be involved in producing the number of copies of the data necessary (this number depends on the number of categories any particular segment is relevant to). Furthermore, a large number of file folders and perhaps several filing cabinets may be required to store the data.

More recently, more sophisticated systems of data filing and retrieval have been developed. For example, punched cards have been used (Becker 1968:245–46). This is a development of physical sorting, but here only one copy of the data additional to the running record is required. Each segment of data is written on, or affixed to, a punched card. The holes around the edge of the card are used to represent the categories and an index noting which numbered hole relates to which category is maintained. Where a data segment is relevant to a particular category, the hole is clipped; the holes representing categories to which the item is not relevant are left intact, or vice versa.

With this system all the data can be kept together in the form of cards, in no particular order. When the materials relevant to a particular category are required a long needle pushed through the appropriate hole and lifted brings out or leaves the relevant cards (depending on whether the holes representing relevant categories have been clipped or left intact). Moreover, as with physical sorting, all the relevant data can be scanned simultaneously, but without the need for multiple copies and at a considerable saving in storage space. Furthermore, with this system sub-sorts identifying data relevant to two or more categories can be carried out. On the other hand, however, punched cards, needle, and clippers are fairly expensive and some time is taken in putting the data on the cards and punching them, though once this is done retrieval is easier than with any other system with the exception of physical sorting.

As one might expect, computers have also started to be used in data filing. Some ethnographers have used main frame computers to prepare analytic indexes. The advantage over manually prepared indexes is that the computer is able to carry out sub-sorts, listing items of data relevant to two or more categories. Of course, this requires computer time and an appropriate program. Alternatively, the data can be typed directly into the computer. Each segment is given an identifying number and an index is prepared on the computer listing the categories and the items relevant to each. With an appropriate program the computer is able to present all the material relevant to a particular category, sequentially on a video screen or to print it out. In principle this system is the one that gives most ready access to the data, especially given the declining cost of microcomputers. It combines the advantages of all the other systems. The disadvantages lie in the problems of expense and possible system breakdown, and in the fact that this strategy for handling data is still largely unproven. At the moment programs for filing, sorting, and retrieving ethnographic data are not easily available, but it is likely that they soon will be. An example of such a program is discussed in Drass (1980).

As with most other aspects of ethnographic technique, there is no ideal storage and retrieval system; the advantages and disadvantages of each strategy will take on varying importance according to the purposes of the research, the nature of the data, and the resources available to the researcher. Indeed, different methods may be appropriate for different data sets within the same research project. As a general guide, where the amount of data is relatively small, coding the record and analytic indexing are strong options. Where there is a large amount of data but each item is relevant to only one or two categories, physical sorting is probably the best technique. Where the amount of data is large and many items are likely to be relevant to a large number of categories (this depends on the categories as much as the data), punched cards have great advantages. With cheap and ready access to a microcomputer, and available back-up maintenance, computer filing is probably the best method all round, though as yet this possibility remains largely unexplored.

Conclusion

While it is probably impossible to render explicit all the data acquired in fieldwork, every effort must be made to record it. Memory is an inadequate basis for analysis. Of course, data recording is necessarily selective and always involves some interpretation, however minimal. There is no set of basic, indubitable data available from which all else can be deduced. What is recorded, and how, will depend in large part on the purposes and priorities of the research, and the conditions in which it is carried out. Moreover, in using various recording techniques we must remain aware of the effects their use may be having on participants and be prepared to modify the strategy accordingly. Similarly, there is no single correct way of retrieving the data for analysis. The various systems differ in appropriateness according to one's purposes, the nature of the data collected, the facilities and finance available, as well as personal convenience. And here, too, their use must be monitored in terms of changing purposes and conditions.

As with other aspects of ethnographic research, then, recording, storing, and retrieving the data must be reflexive processes in which decisions are made, monitored, and, if necessary, re-made in light of methodological and ethical considerations. At the same time, however, these techniques play an important role in facilitating reflexivity. They provide a crucial resource in assessing typicality of examples, checking construct-indicator linkages, searching for negative cases, triangulating across different data sources and stages of the fieldwork, and assessing the role of the researcher in shaping the nature of the data and findings. In short, they facilitate the process of analysis, a topic to which we turn in the next chapter.

8

The process
of analysis

In ethnography the analysis of data is not a distinct stage of the research. It begins in the pre-fieldwork phase, in the formulation and clarification of research problems, and continues into the process of writing up. Formally, it starts to take shape in analytic notes and memoranda; informally, it is embodied in the ethnographer's ideas, hunches, and emergent concepts. In this way the analysis of data feeds into the process of research design. This is the core idea of 'grounded theorizing' (Glaser and Strauss 1967): the collection of data is guided strategically by the developing theory. Theory building and data collection are dialectically linked.

Much ethnographic research, however, suffers from a lack of reflexivity in the relationship between analysis, data collection, and research design. The data required to check a particular interpretation are often missing, or the typicality of crucial items of data cannot be checked, or some of the comparative cases necessary for developing and testing the emergent theory have not been investigated.

One reason for this is the influence of naturalism, with its emphasis on 'capturing' the social world in description. Naturalism reinforces what Lacey (1976) calls 'the it's all happening elsewhere syndrome', a common ailment in fieldwork where the researcher feels it necessary to try to be everywhere at once and to stay in the setting for as long as possible. As a result of this, little time is left for theoretical reflection. Likewise, the naturalistic commitment to 'tell it like it is' tends to force the process of analysis to remain implicit and underdeveloped.

Ethnographic research has a characteristic 'funnel' structure, being progressively focused over its course. Progressive focusing has two analytically distinct components. First, over time the research problem is developed or transformed, and eventually its scope is clarified and delimited and its internal structure explored. In this sense, it is frequently only over the course of the research that one discovers what the research is really 'about', and it is not uncommon for it to turn out to be about something quite remote from the initial foreshadowed problems. This processual, developing nature of the work is very well illustrated by Bohannon (1981). He identifies the various stages of a research project on poor residents of inner-city hotels, illustrating the importance of preliminary analysis, and the nature of 'progressive focusing'. Bohannon also describes how the 'problem' was progressively redefined:

> 'We did indeed begin this project with the "notion" (it was actually more formal than that – it was a hypothesis that proved wrong) that elderly individuals living in run-down hotels in the center city have established support networks. By and large they have not. Their networks are shallow and transient. It is, by and large, part of the life adjustment of these people to run from the commitment that a support network implies.'
>
> (P. Bohannon 1981:45)

Starting from a view based on 'disorganization' or 'dislocation', Bohannon and his research team came to reformulate their research in terms of 'adaptation'. In the course of this they were able to demonstrate that welfare policies predicated on the former were not soundly based.

Progressive focusing may also involve a gradual shift from a concern with describing social events and processes to developing and testing explanations. However, different studies vary considerably in the distance they travel along this road. Some are heavily descriptive, ranging from narrative life histories of an individual, group, or organization to accounts of the way of life to be found in particular settings. Of course, these are in no sense pure descriptions, they are constructions involving selection and interpretation, not mere unedited recordings of sounds and movements. But they involve little attempt to derive any general theoretical lesson. The 'theory' remains implicit and largely unorganized. Of course, such accounts can be of great value. They may provide us with knowledge of ways of life hitherto unknown and thereby shake our assumptions about the parameters of human life or challenge our stereotypes. Herein lies the interest of much anthropological work and of sociological accounts revealing the ways of life of low-status and deviant groups.

A variation on this theme is to show the familiar in the apparently strange (Turnbull 1973; Goffman 1961) or the strange in the familiar (Garfinkel 1967). Alternatively, descriptive accounts may contrast present conditions with an ideal, pointing up a discrepancy. Decision-making procedures among staff within schools may be compared with an ideal type of democracy, for example; or curricular practices in classrooms using nationally produced curriculum materials may be compared with the goals of the project team that produced those materials. Such comparisons are common in ethnographic work, though they are not always explicit.

By no means all ethnography remains at this descriptive level, however. Often, there is an attempt to draw out theoretical models of one kind or another. Here, features of the history or nature of the phenomenon under study start to be collected under more general categories. They are presented as examples of, for example, particular kinds of cognitive perspective or interactional strategy. Going further, a typology of perspectives or strategies may be developed (Lofland 1971 and 1976). Finally, a whole range of analytic categories may be integrated into a model of some aspect of the social process to be found in the history or character of the people or settings studied (Glaser and Strauss 1967; Glaser 1978).

This is a long road to travel and there are many way-stations along its course. Moreover, as with all journeys, something is left behind. Concrete descriptions cover many different facets of the phenomena they describe, they give a rounded picture, and open up all manner of theoretical possibilities. Theory development involves a narrowing of focus and a process of abstraction. Theorized accounts give a much poorer representation of the phenomena with which they deal. On the other hand, assuming the theoretical ideas are well founded, they begin to give us much more knowledge about how a particular aspect of social process is organized and perhaps even why events occur in the patterned ways they do.

Generating concepts

In Chapter 1 we noted the complementary failings of positivism and naturalism. For example, where one tends to identify the process of scientific inquiry with the rigorous testing of hypotheses, the other emphasizes the discovery of facts and the development of theories, underplaying the assessment of rival accounts. From our point of view, both the development and testing of theory are important. Indeed, as we shall see later, these two aspects of scientific inquiry are closely interrelated.

The development of theoretical categories and models has often been treated as a mysterious process about which little can be said and no guidance given. One must simply wait on the theoretical muse, it is implied. While we would certainly not wish to deny or downplay the role of creative imagination in science, we would point out that it is not restricted to the development of theory, but is equally important in devising ways of testing it. Moreover, in neither case does recognition of the role of imagination negate the fact that there are general strategies available.

Besides obscuring the importance of strategies for generating concepts and models, overemphasis on the role of creative imagination in the development of theories also leads us to forget the function that our existing knowledge of the social world performs in this process. It is only when we begin to understand that imagination works via analogies and metaphors that this becomes plain. An important feature of ethnography is that it allows us to feed the process of theory generation with new material, rather than relying on our previous knowledge of cases relevant to the theoretical ideas we wish to pursue. In this way the fertility of the theoretical imagination can be enhanced.

The first step in the process of analysis, then, is a careful reading of the data collected up to that point, in order to gain a thorough familiarity with it. At this stage the aim is to use the data to think with. One looks to see whether any interesting patterns can be identified; whether anything stands out as surprising or puzzling; how the data relate to what one might have expected on the basis of common-sense knowledge, official accounts, or previous theory; and whether there are any apparent inconsistencies or contradictions among the views of different groups or individuals, or between people's expressed beliefs or attitudes and what they do. Some such features and patterns may already have been noted in previous fieldnotes and analytic memos, perhaps even along with some ideas about how they might be explained.

Concepts sometimes arise 'spontaneously', being used by participants themselves. And, indeed, unusual participant terms are always worth following up since they may mark theoretically important or interesting phenomena (Becker and Geer 1975; Wieder 1974). Some forms of ethnography, especially those based on or influenced by 'ethnoscience', are devoted almost exclusively to the listing, sorting, and interpretation of such 'folk' terms. They are concerned with the more-or-less formal semantics of such inventories. However many ethnographies, while using such types, attempt to do more than simply document their meaning. Their use will be examined as evidence of knowledge, beliefs, and actions that are located within more general analytic frameworks.

Alternatively, types and cases may be 'observer-identified' (Lofland 1971): they represent classes that are construed as such by the ethnographer rather than the members themselves. In the development of such classifications, the analyst may draw together a diverse range of different phenomena under the aegis of one type. Such types may derive from general, common-sense knowledge or from personal experience. Spencer and Dale provide an example:

'Initially, we were concerned with failures to adapt, blocked change . . . that we had observed both in our professional and social lives. . . . These concerns became focused around the idea of a *locked situation* or social *deadlock.'*

(in Spencer and Dale 1979:669)

Such terminologies, of course, find their way into the disciplinary literature, and, in due course, become treated as 'technical' terms. Very often the robust concepts of middle-range theory consist of happily chosen typings of this sort.

Such types can also be generated by borrowing or adapting existing concepts from other disciplines. For instance, in their research on the transition of pupils from middle to high schools, Measor and Woods (1982) found that a number of stories about life at the high school circulated among middle-school pupils. These stories had a standard form and seemed to reappear each year. Measor and Woods came to regard such stories as myths, and drew upon anthropological literature to understand the role they played in pupils' lives.

Sometimes, one may find it necessary to develop new terms to capture and characterize observer-identified types. Hargreaves (1981) provides an example with his development of the notion of 'contrastive rhetoric', which

'refers to that interactional strategy whereby the boundaries of normal and acceptable practice are defined by institutionally and/or interactionally dominant individuals or groups through the introduction into discussion of alternative practices and social forms in stylized, trivialized and generally pejorative terms which connote their unacceptability.'

(A. Hargreaves 1982:309)

Hargreaves uses the notion to analyse talk in a school staff meeting, though he notes that many parallels are to be found in the sociology of mass media and of deviance. It is, incidentally, interesting to compare Hargreaves's formulation with the notion of 'atrocity stories', used by Stimson and Webb (1975), and Dingwall (1977a), to refer to accounts produced by actors in subordinate positions in medical settings.

At this stage in their development, the concepts will not be well-defined elements of an explicit theory. Rather, they will take the form of 'sensitizing concepts' (Blumer 1954). These contrast with what Blumer refers to as 'definitive concepts', which 'refer precisely to what is common to a class of objects, by the aid of the clear definition of attributes or fixed bench-marks'. A sensitizing concept, on the other hand, lacks such specificity, and

> 'it gives the user a general sense of reference and guidelines in approaching empirical instances. Where definitive concepts provide prescriptions of what to see, sensitizing concepts merely suggest directions along which to look.'
>
> (Blumer 1954:7)

Sensitizing concepts are an important starting point, they are the germ of the emerging theory, and they provide the focus for further data collection.

Having acquired one or two analytic categories, whether members' or observers' types, the next task is to begin to develop these into a theoretical scheme: finding links between the concepts and adding new ones. One strategy here is what Glaser and Strauss (1967) call the 'constant comparative method'. Each segment of data is taken in turn, and, its relevance to one or more categories having been noted, it is compared with other segments of data similarly categorized. In this way, the range and variation of any given category can be mapped in the data, and such patterns plotted in relation to other categories.

As this process of systematic sifting and comparison develops, so the emerging model will be clarified. The mutual relationships and internal structures of categories will be more clearly displayed. However, the development of theory rarely takes the purely inductive form implied by Glaser and Strauss (heuristically useful though their approach is). Theoretical ideas, common-sense expectations, and stereotypes often play a key role. Indeed, it is these that allow the analyst to pick out surprising, interesting, and important features in the first place. Blanche Geer's (1964) famous account of her 'first days in the field' is a classic exemplification of the place of assumptions and stereotypes – and their disconfirmation in the fieldwork – in the development of analytic themes.

Where a category forms part of an existing theory, however loosely constructed, the theory provides other categories and hypothetical relations among them that can be tentatively applied to the data. Where the fit is good and the theory is well developed, it may even be possible to set about rigorously testing the theory. However, only rarely are sociological theories sufficiently well developed for hypotheses to be derived and tested in this way. Generally, the process of testing requires considerable further development of the theory as a precondition, and in particular, specification of what would be appropriate indicators for its concepts.

Of course, the ethnographer need not limit him or herself to a single theory as a framework within which to analyse the data. Indeed, there are great advantages to be gained from what Denzin (1978) terms 'theoretical triangulation', approaching data with multiple perspectives and hypotheses in mind. Bensman and Vidich (1960) provide an interesting example of this from their community study of Springdale. They report that they subjected their data to theoretical perspectives derived from Redfield, Weber, Tönnies, Veblen, Merton, Lynd, Warner, Mills, Sapir, and Tumin. In each case they asked themselves 'What in [these] theories would permit us to comprehend our data?' Theories were not simply taken as off-the-peg solutions to research problems, but were used to provide focus for analysis and further fieldwork. They go on to note that:

> 'When one set of theories does not exhaust the potentialities of the data, other sets can be employed to point to and explain the facts which remain unexplained. Thus, for any initial statement of the field problem a whole series of theories may be successively applied, each yielding different orders of data and each perhaps being limited by the special perspectives and dimensions on which it is predicated.'
>
> (Bensman and Vidich 1960:165–66)

Developing typologies

One of the major way-stations on the road to theoretical models in ethnographic work is the development of typologies. Here, a set of phenomena is identified that represents sub-types of some more general category. Taking Hargreaves's concept of 'contrastive rhetoric' mentioned earlier, for example, one may wish to examine it as one type of talk to be contrasted with another – Hargreaves counterposes it to 'extremist talk'. Alternatively, one might treat it as one type of strategy that can be used to maintain the hegemony of a certain conception of 'reality' or a particular 'ideology'. Then again, contrastive rhetoric might itself be taken as a general category and different types of it identified.

Typologies in ethnographic accounts vary considerably in the degree to which they have been systematically developed. Lofland (1970) has complained that in this respect much ethnographic research suffers from 'analytic interruptus'. In their development of categories, Lofland suggests, many analysts fail 'to follow through to the implied logical . . . conclusion . . . to reach (the) initially implied climax' (1970:42). Taking the example of typologies of strategies, Lofland argues that the investigator must take the time and trouble

'1. to assemble self-consciously all his materials on how a (problem) is dealt with by the persons under study
2. to tease out the variations among his assembled range of instances of strategies
3. to classify them into an articulate set of . . . types of strategies, and
4. to present them to the reader in some orderly and preferably named and numbered manner.'

(Lofland 1970:42–3)

Elsewhere, Lofland has provided an extended discussion of the varieties of typology and how they might be developed (Lofland 1971).

Lazarsfeld and Barton (1951) go even further in their recommendations for the systematic development of typologies. An initial set of categories differentiating a particular range of phenomena can be developed into a systematic typology, they argue, by specifying the dimensions underlying the discrimination it makes. Not only does this force clarification and perhaps modification of the categories already identified, it throws up other categories that may also be of importance. As an example, we can take Glaser and Strauss's typology of 'awareness contexts'.

The concept of 'awareness contexts' was developed by Glaser and Strauss to characterize the different kinds of social situation found among terminally ill hospital patients, their families, and medical personnel. The idea refers to the differential distribution of knowledge and understanding of the dying person's condition, from conditions of 'closed awareness' when the diagnosis and prognosis are kept secret from the patient, to 'open awareness', where the knowledge is shared openly by all parties. Here, then, the idea of an awareness context is closely linked to the dynamics of information control characteristic of many medical encounters. In the following extract the notion is treated as a more general formal category. In such a formulation it is clearly applicable to a much wider range of social settings approximating to the general type of 'information games' (cf Scott 1968). It is, for instance, directly applicable to the substantive issue of 'coming out' among homosexuals, and the management of the revelation or concealment of such an identity (Plummer 1975:177–96).

> 'We have singled out four types of awareness context for special consideration since they have proved useful in accounting for different types of interaction. An open awareness context obtains when each interactant is aware of the other's true identity and his own identity in the eyes of the other. A closed awareness context obtains when one interactant does not know either the other's identity or the other's view of his identity. A suspicion awareness context is a modification of the closed one: one interactant suspects the true identity of the other or the other's view of his own identity, or both. A pretense awareness context is a modification of the open one: both interactants are fully aware but pretend not to be.'
>
> (Glaser and Strauss 1964:669)

By identifying the dimensions underlying this typology along the lines suggested by Barton and Lazarsfeld, we find that there are rather more possibilities than Glaser and Strauss's initial typology allows (see *Figure 2*). Furthermore, some of them look fruitful, such as for example when one party pretends while the other knows, or when one suspects while the other does not know; others seem of less significance. Glaser (1978) warns us against what he calls the 'logical elaboration' of categories, and he is right to do so. Typologies should not be extended beyond the limits of the data, nor stretched beyond

Figure 2   Typology of awareness contexts

	Party A			
	Know	Pretend	Suspect	Don't know
Party B Know	Open		Suspicion	Closed
Pretend		Pretence		
Suspect	Suspicion			
Don't know	Closed			

their analytic value. Nonetheless, specification of the dimensions underlying a typology encourages us to think seriously and systematically about the nature of each category and its relationships with others. It may help us to spot previously unconsidered possibilities, or unsuspected interactions between categories. (For a further general discussion of the value of systematizing typologies, see Lazarsfeld and Barton 1951.)

Concepts, types, and indicators

There is little point in developing highly systematized typologies and models if they provide little purchase on the data. The development of an effective typology is not a purely logical or conceptual exercise: there must be constant recourse to the data. As the categories of analysis are being clarified and developed in relation to one another, so also must the links between concepts and indicators be specified and refined. In Blumer's (1954) terms, sensitizing concepts must be turned into something more like definitive concepts.

The problem of construct validity – of the validity of the lines of inference running between data and concepts – has been given much more explicit attention by conventional methodologists than by ethnographers. And much can be learned from discussions of this issue in the methodological literature. Some, notably McCall (1969) and Evans (1983), have indeed recommended that ethnography take over the methods of assessing construct validity used in quantitative research. In our view, however, any wholesale adoption of the conventional approach to construct validity would be misconceived. There are at least two important ways in which the problem of construct validity takes on a different form in ethnography.

First, what is involved is not simply a matter of finding indicators for a concept. Rather, there is an interplay between finding indicators and conceptualizing the analytic categories. This derives from the inductive, reflexive character of ethnography where the process of analysis involves the simultaneous development of constructs and indicators to produce a 'fit' between the two. It is only when the analysis is written up that the relationship between concept and indicator becomes an asymmetrical one, with the latter serving as evidence that the claims made by means of the concept are valid.

The second difference between ethnography and quantitative research over construct validity stems in large part from the rather different theoretical perspectives that have influenced each. Despite its decline in influence as a psychological theory, behaviourism nevertheless continues to shape the methodological procedures employed by quantitative researchers. One area in which this influence can be found is in the desire to identify standard indicators for concepts. As we noted in Chapter 1, this concern with standardization is based on the idea that if people are responding to 'the same stimulus' their responses will be commensurable, so that inferences can be drawn that ignore the effects of the research process itself. This is the traditional concern with reliability. However, such an approach relies on some very questionable assumptions. Reliability tests give us very weak ground for conclusions about construct validity. They show that the relations between construct and indicator hold up under certain conditions, but there may well be other conditions in which the link is not sound, and indeed the relation may yet be an artefact of the research process itself.

Once we drop the behaviouristic assumptions involved here, and replace them with the principle of reflexivity, the very possibility of identifying standard indicators appears doubtful. However, the search for standard indicators also becomes unnecessary. The presentation of a standard set of indicators is not an essential feature of a theory. Indeed, if it is a valid theory of wide scope it will be able to predict phenomena quite different from those in relation to which it was originally developed. Dependence on a single set of standard indicators would be highly suspect. What is required is that the theory be explicit in its predictions of what will occur under given conditions. The question of whether and when those conditions hold can, and indeed must, be a matter for subsequent investigation.

In moving between data and concepts we must take great care to note plausible alternative links to those made in the emerging theory. While in no sense is it necessary, or even possible, to lay bare all the assumptions involved in concept-indicator linkages, it is important to make explicit and to examine those assumptions to which strong challenges can be made.

We can illustrate this by reference to Willis's (1977) research on the adaptations of working class pupils to school. Willis argues that the 'lads' he studied displayed a counter-culture, an 'entrenched, general and personalized opposition to ''authority'' '. In supporting this claim he uses descriptions of the 'lads' ' behaviour as well as quotations from group interviews such as the following comments about teachers:

> 'JOEY: (. . .) they're able to punish us. They're bigger than us, they stand for a bigger establishment than we do, like, we're just little and they stand for bigger things, and you try to get your own back. It's, uh, resenting authority I suppose.
>
> EDDIE: The teachers think they're high and mighty 'cos they're teachers, but they're nobody really, they're just ordinary people ain't they?
>
> BILL: Teachers think they're everybody. They are more, they're higher than us, but they think they're a lot higher and they're not.
>
> SPANKSY: Wish we could call them first names and that . . . think they're God.
>
> PETE: That would be a lot better.
>
> PW: I mean you say they're higher. Do you accept at all that they know better about things?
>
> JOEY: Yes, but that doesn't rank them above us, just because they are slightly more intelligent.

BILL: They ought to treat us how they'd like us to treat them.
(. . .)
JOEY: (. . .) the way we're subject to their every whim like.
They want something doing and we have to sort of do it,
'cos, er, er, we're just, we're under them like. We were with
a woman teacher in here, and 'cos we all wear rings and one
or two of them bangles, like he's got one on, and out of the
blue, like, for no special reason, she says, 'take all that off'.
PW: Really?
JOEY: Yeah, we says, 'One won't come off', she says, 'Take
yours off as well'. I said, 'You'll have to chop my finger off
first'.
PW: Why did she want you to take your rings off?
JOEY: Just a sort of show like. Teachers do this, like, all of a
sudden they'll make you do your ties up and things like
this. You're subject to their every whim like. If they want
something done, if you don't think it's right, and you
object against it, you're down to Simmondsy [the head], or
you get the cane, you get some extra work tonight.
PW: You think of most staff as kind of enemies (. . .)?
- Yeah.
- Yeah.
- Most of them.
JOEY: It adds a bit of spice to yer life, if you're trying to get him
for something he's done to you.'

(Willis 1977:11–12)

In assessing the way in which Willis links the concept of
counter-culture with the various indicators he uses, we need to
consider whether, for example, pupils' expressions of opposition to teachers reflect a more general opposition to 'authority'
as such, or only to particular types of authority. And, indeed, in
the course of doing this, we may need to clarify the concept of
authority itself. Would it make any sense, for example, to argue
that Joey, who seems to be the leader of the 'lads', has authority
among them? Whether or not we use the concept of authority in a
broad or narrow sense, we need to be clear about exactly what it
is that the theory claims the 'lads' are rejecting.

Another question we might ask is whether the 'lads' are opposed to all aspects of teachers' authority or only to those teacher

demands that they regard as overstepping its legitimate bound-aries. For example, the 'lads' complain about rules relating to their personal appearance, a complaint also reported in a similar study by Werthman (1963). However, whereas Willis takes such complaints as an indicator of a general antipathy to 'authority', Werthman interprets them as signifying the boundaries of what the boys he studied regarded as a teacher's legitimate area of control. Clearly, such alternative interpreta-tions have serious implications for the character and validity of the theory produced.

While the nature of the alternative interpretations that must be considered will vary between studies, we can point to a num-ber of general issues that must be borne in mind when examining concept-indicator links. These correspond to the dimensions we discussed in Chapter 2 in relation to sampling within cases.

SOCIAL CONTEXT

The issue of context is at the heart of the conflicting inter-pretations of pupil behaviour to be found in the work of Willis and Werthman. For Willis, opposition characterized the 'lads' ' contacts with all forms of authority. For Werthman, on the other hand, the behaviour of gang members towards teachers varied across contexts according to the actions of the teacher and how these were interpreted.

We shall focus our discussion here on one of the most impor-tant elements of context, the audience to which the actions or accounts being used as data were directed. One important pos-sible audience is, of course, the ethnographer. This is most obvi-ous in the case of interviewing, an interactional format in which the researcher plays a key role through the questions he or she asks, however non-directive the interview is. In interviews the very structure of the interaction forces participants to be aware of the ethnographer as audience. Their conceptions of the nature and purposes of social research, and of the particular research project, may, therefore, act as a strong influence on what they say.

This can be both a help and a hindrance in the production of relevant data and valid interpretations of it. 'Well-trained' infor-mants and respondents can act as highly effective research assis-tants in reporting relevant data, data of which the ethnographer might not otherwise become aware. They will also make the data collection process much more efficient since they can select out what is relevant from the mass of irrelevant data that is available to them.

There are some dangers here too, though. The more 'sophisticated' the interviewee the greater the tendency for him or her to move away from description into analysis. While there is no such thing as 'pure' description, it is essential to minimize the inference involved in description in order to provide for the possibility of checking and rechecking, constructing and reconstructing theoretical interpretations. If the interviewee provides heavily theorized accounts of the events or experiences he or she is describing, however interesting or fruitful the theoretical ideas are, the data base has been eroded.

Spradley (1979) provides a particularly good example, that of Bob, an informant he worked with in the course of his study of tramps. Bob had spent four years on skid row; he was also a Harvard graduate, and had gone on to do postgraduate work in anthropology. Spradley recounts:

> 'On my next visit to the treatment center I invited Bob into my office. We chatted casually for a few minutes, then I started asking him some ethnographic questions. "What kind of men go through the Seattle City Jail and end up at this alcoholism treatment center?" I asked. "I've been thinking about the men who are here" Bob said thoughtfully. "I would divide them up first in terms of race. There are Negroes, Indians, Caucasians, and a few Eskimo. Next I think I would divide them on the basis of their education. Some have almost none, a few have some college. Then some of the men are married and some are single". For the next fifteen minutes he proceeded to give me the standard analytic categories that many social scientists use.'
>
> (Spradley 1979:53)

We must be careful, then, in analysing our material, to be alert for the effects of audience in terms of actors' views of the researcher's interests.

Even when the ethnographer is acting as observer, he or she may be an important audience for the participants, or at least for some of them. Informal questioning often forms part of participant observation, and Becker and Geer (1960) have pointed to the importance of distinguishing between solicited and unsolicited statements when we are assessing the evidence supporting theoretical claims. However, as we found in discussing insider accounts, such a distinction is too crude. We cannot assume that unsolicited statements are uninfluenced by the researcher's presence. The same applies to other actions. In recent years we have become increasingly aware of the way in which people seek to manage impressions of themselves and of the settings and groups with which they are associated (Goffman 1959). In a study of an Indian village community, Berreman (1962) only discovered the extent to which his data were the product of impression management by the villagers when he was forced to change his interpreter. This change modified his relationships with them, and produced different kinds of data.

Sometimes participants will actually tell an ethnographer that they have been presenting a front. Bogdan and Taylor quote the comment of an attendant in a state institution for the mentally retarded made to an ethnographer at the end of the first day of fieldwork: 'Yeah, we didn't do a lot of things today that we usually do. Like if you wasn't here we woulda snitched some food at dinner and maybe hit a couple of 'em around. See before we didn't know you was an ok guy' (Bogdan and Taylor 1975:89).

Of course, such admissions do not necessarily indicate that full access has finally been granted. They may be a piece of impression management themselves. While over the course of an extended stay in a setting participants generally acquire increasing trust of the ethnographer and find it more and more difficult to control the information available to him or her, members' creation and management of their personal fronts can prove a persistent problem for the ethnographer. (See Douglas 1976 for an extended discussion of the problem and some remedies.) In the case of observational data too, then, one must be aware of the possible effects of the ethnographer as audience.

However, this concern with reactivity, with the effects of the researcher on the nature of the data he or she collects, can be somewhat misleading. Much as quantitative researchers seek to minimize reactivity through standardization, under the influence of naturalism, ethnographers sometimes regard any effects of their presence or actions on the data simply as a source of bias. And, of course, from the point of view of ecological validity it is indeed a threat to validity. However, participants' responses to ethnographers may nevertheless be an important source of information. Data in themselves cannot be valid or invalid; what is at issue are the inferences drawn from them. And, indeed, similar considerations regarding the effects of audience arise even where the effects of the research on events studied are minimized or avoided.

In interpreting documents and data produced through secret research, we must still bear in mind the ways in which audience considerations may have shaped the actions and accounts produced. Documents are always written for some audience, perhaps for several different ones simultaneously. This will shape the nature of the document through what is taken as relevant, what can be assumed as background knowledge, what cannot or should not be said, and what must be said even if it is untrue.

In secret participant observation, assuming the cover has not been 'blown', the ethnographer, as such, cannot be an audience. However, he or she may be an important audience in one or another participant identity. In the same way, in open participant observation and interviewing, considerations of audience must be extended beyond the role of the ethnographer. Indeed, one of the strengths of even open participant observation as regards ecological validity is that in 'natural' settings other audiences are generally much more powerful and significant for participants than the ethnographer, and their effects are likely to swamp those of the research.

The significance of audience is heightened by the fact that the participants in a setting are rarely a homogeneous audience for one another. Different categories, groups, or factions are often clearly demarcated. And even within these divisions there will be more informal networks of communication that include some participants and exclude others, as Hitchcock shows in the case of a primary school staff:

'On many occasions throughout the fieldwork, staff's comments would be prefaced by such statements as "I know it's unprofessional of me talking like this". . . . "I don't suppose I should really be telling you this". . . . "don't tell him I said this for goodness sake". On other occasions when staff told me things these prefaces were not present, it was rather *assumed* that I wouldn't ''blow the scene'' by telling someone else what had been said about them. That is I was ''trusted'' to keep things quiet or to keep what was said to myself.'

(Hitchcock 1982:30)

Different things will be said and done in different company. In particular we must interpret differently what is done 'in public' and what is done 'in private' since the category to which an action belongs may have important consequences for how it relates to actions and attitudes in other contexts. Of course, whether something is 'private' or 'public' is not always obvious, and there is a subtle shading between the two. One may have to know a setting very well in order to be able to recognize the public or private status of actions and even then it is easy to be mistaken.

Even in the case of interviews, the ethnographer may not be the most significant audience. To one degree or another, and whatever assurances of confidentiality the ethnographer may give, interviewees may regard what they say as 'public' rather than 'private'; they may expect it to be communicated to others, or recorded for posterity. Krieger (1979a) provides an example from her research on a radio station. Reflecting on interviewees' confidence or trust, she remarks:

'I came to think it reflected an expectation that this telling in the interview situation was more than to one person, it was a telling to the world at large, and not only a bid for recognition by that world, but also perhaps for forgiveness.'

(Krieger 1979a:170–71)

Analysing data for the effects of audience is not, then, simply a matter of assessing the impact of the researcher, but also that of any other audience the actor might be addressing, consciously or subconsciously. This applies to all forms of data and it is a crucial consideration if invalid inferences are to be avoided.

TIME

Discussing the problem of understanding in Chapter 1, we noted how it is necessary to use the temporal context of actions to make sense of them. What people say and do is produced in the context of a developing sequence of interaction. If we ignore what has already occurred or what follows we are in danger of drawing the wrong conclusions.

By temporal context we mean not only the host of events that occur before and after the action or event under study, but also the temporal framework in terms of which the people involved locate that action or event. Glaser and Strauss (1968) provide a striking example in their study of how dying patients are dealt with by hospital staff. They note how staff construct and reconstruct conceptions of the dying trajectories of patients and how these play a key role in shaping their attitudes to the treatment of patients. Moreover, deviations from expected patterns can cause problems.

How hospital staff react to signs of improvement in a patient, then, is dependent on the temporal context in terms of which they read those signs. Relevant here is not only what has happened in the past, but also estimates of what is likely to happen in the future. Nor is this restricted to the staff; patients' families may also not welcome signs of improvement in the patients' condition, not only because of the inconvenience it may cause them but also because they perhaps see these as part of a painful, lingering death (Wright 1981).

Time is also an important consideration in the interpretation of interview data. Not only may what is said at one point in an interview be influenced by the interviewee's interpretation of what has been said earlier and what might be said later, but it is also affected by what has happened in the field prior to the interview and what is anticipated in the near future.

Ball (1982a) has pointed out that many organizations are characterized by short- and long-term temporal cycles. Most universities and schools, for example, have terms whose beginnings and endings are important benchmarks for staff and students. Moreover, the different terms are not equivalent, they form part of a longer term cycle based on the year – the autumn term is very different in many ways from the spring term, for example. For students, the years form part of an even larger cycle, their first year as freshers being very different in status from their final year as seniors. Data, of whatever kind, recorded at different times need to be examined in light of their place within the temporal patterns, short or long term, that structure the lives of those being studied. (For more on such patterns see Roth 1963.)

From this point of view there are considerable advantages to be gained from combining interviews with participant observation. Each may provide information about temporal contexts whose implications for interpreting data can be assessed. The dangers of neglecting the effects of time are particularly great where reliance is placed upon a single data source, especially interviews or documents. Where interviews are used alone it is wise to give over some interview space to casual conversation about current events in the interviewee's life. Indeed, this may be a useful way of opening the interview to build rapport.

Once again, it is not a matter of accepting or rejecting data, but rather of knowing how to interpret it; there is a great temptation to assume that actions, statements, or interview responses represent stable features of the person or of settings. This may be correct, but it cannot be assumed. Actions are embedded in temporal contexts and these may shape them in ways that are important for the analysis.

PERSONNEL

People's identities or social locations (that is, the patterns of social relationships in which they are enmeshed) can have two kinds of effects on the nature of the accounts or actions they produce. First, social locations determine the kind of information available to people. They clearly affect what it is possible for people to see and hear 'at first hand'; they also determine what people will get to know about, and how they will get to know things 'second hand'. The second way in which identities affect actions and accounts is through the particular perspectives that people in various social locations tend to generate and that will filter their understanding and knowledge of the world. In particular, the interpretation of information available to a person is likely to be selected and slanted in line with his or her prevailing interests and concerns. There may even be a strong element of wish-fulfilment involved. One must be aware of the effects of social location with all kinds of data, including ethnographers' observational reports. They too occupy particular social locations and what they observe, what they record, and how they interpret it will be influenced by these.

The implications of identity vary somewhat between information and perspective analysis. In the first, one is concerned with what an account or action tells one about the setting. Here social location may be an important cause of ignorance or source of bias, it is a threat to validity that must be monitored. This kind of consideration must underlie the selection of informants and the interpretation of the data they provide as well as the treatment of data from other sources, where it is being analysed for information. In perspective analysis, on the other hand, social location is no longer a source of bias, it is a key element in the analysis. Here the aim is precisely to document the perspectives of those in different social locations.

Of course, as we saw in Chapter 5, the two forms of analysis are complementary, the one provides facts in terms of which the other should be interpreted. In the case of observational data produced by the ethnographer, this is the essence of reflexivity.

Respondent validation

A recognition of the importance of actors' social locations leads directly to the issue of 'respondent validation', a notion that has an uncertain and sometimes contested place in ethnographic analysis. Some ethnographers have argued that a crucial test for their accounts is whether the actors whose beliefs and behaviour they purport to describe recognize the validity of those accounts. The aim is therefore to 'establish a correspondence between the sociologist's and the member's view of the member's social world by exploring the extent to which members recognize, give assent to, the judgments of the sociologist' (Bloor 1978:548–49).

In his own research on the decision rules employed by ENT (ear, nose, and throat) specialists, Bloor sent each specialist a report describing that specialist's assessment practices. This was accompanied by a letter that asked each specialist to 'read through the report to see how far it corresponded with his own impressions of his clinic practice'. Bloor then discussed the reports in interviews with doctors. Bloor reports that for the most part the exercise was successful: 'some respondents endorsed my description of their practices, and where they did not the nature of the exercise was such as to enable me to correct the analysis so that this assent was no longer withheld' (1978:549). Using a different strategy, Ball (1982), in his study of Beachside comprehensive school, held two seminars for the school's staff at which he presented some of his findings. Ball's experience was rather less happy and fruitful, and suggests that while there is merit in the strategy, it is far from being problem-free.

The value of respondent validation lies in the fact that participants involved in the events documented in the data may have access to additional knowledge of the context – of other relevant events, of thoughts they had or decisions they made at the time, for example – that is not available to the ethnographer. They may also be part of information networks that are more powerful than those accessible to the ethnographer. In addition, they have access to their own experience of events, which may be of considerable importance. Such additional evidence may materially alter the plausibility of different possible interpretations of the data.

At the same time, it is important to recognize the limitations of respondent validation. Thus, we cannot assume that any actor is a privileged commentator on his or her own actions, in the sense that an account of the intentions, motives, or beliefs involved are accompanied by a guarantee of their truth. As Schutz (1964) and others have noted, we can only grasp the meanings of our actions retrospectively. Moreover, these meanings must be reconstructed on the basis of memory; they are not given in any immediate sense. Nor will the evidence for them necessarily be preserved in memory. Much social action operates at a subconscious level, leaving no memory traces. Thus, in the case of Bloor's specialists, we cannot assume that they are consciously aware of the decision rules they use, or even that, infallibly, they can recognize them when someone documents them. In short, while actors are well-placed informants on their own actions, they are no more than that; and their accounts must be analysed in the same way as any other data, with close consideration being given to possible threats to validity.

This is reinforced once we recognize that it may be in a person's interests to misinterpret or misdescribe his or her own actions, or to counter the interpretations of the ethnographer. Both Bloor and Ball point out that participants generally interpret data in the light of different concerns and sometimes by criteria at odds with those of the ethnographer. Bloor acknowledges, for instance that:

'I had expected the specialists to respond to the reports in a manner similar to that of an academic colleague when one asks him to criticize a draft paper one has written. I became aware of having made this assumption when it was violated – I suspected that some of the specialists had not read the report in the expected critical spirit. They had read the report, I felt, in the way that we today might read a nineteenth century religious tract – with a modicum of detached, superficial interest, with a feeling that it displayed a certain peculiar charm perhaps, but without being so moved by its content as to feel the necessity to define one's own beliefs and practices in accordance with it or in contrast to it. They were unversed in the conventions of academic sociological criticism and they were perhaps only marginally interested in the content of the reports.'

(Bloor 1978:550)

As with all data collection and analysis, then, respondents' reactions to the ethnographer's account will be coloured by their social position and their perceptions of the research act. As with Bloor's doctors, they may have only a marginal interest. Ball's school teachers, on the other hand, displayed a keener commitment. But this, too, was directly related to their social locations:

'many of the staff had apparently read my chapter solely in terms of what it had to say about them or their subject. There was little or no discussion of the general issues I was trying to raise or the overall arguments of the chapter. . . . I had taken as my task as ethnographer the description and analysis of large scale trends which extended as I saw them across the whole school, an overview. The staff responded from their particular view of the school, from the vantage point of the position they held.'

(Ball 1982:18–19)

Ball's teachers interpreted his work as critical, and queried the validity of his findings.

Such feedback, then, can be highly problematic. Whether

respondents are enthusiastic, indifferent or hostile, their reactions cannot be taken as direct validation or refutation of the observer's inferences. Rather, such processes of so-called 'validation' should be treated as yet another valuable source of data and insight.

Triangulation

Respondent validation represents one kind of triangulation. What it amounts to is checking inferences drawn from one set of data sources by collecting data from others. More generally, data-source triangulation involves the comparison of data relating to the same phenomenon but deriving from different phases of the fieldwork, different points in the temporal cycles occurring in the setting, or, as in respondent validation, the accounts of different participants (including the ethnographer) involved in the setting. This last form of data-source triangulation can be extended indefinitely by showing each participant the others' accounts and recording his or her comments on them (Adelman 1977). This is very time consuming but, besides providing a validity check, it also gives added depth to the description of the social meanings involved in a setting.

The term 'triangulation' derives from a loose analogy with navigation and surveying. For someone wanting to locate their position on a map, a single landmark can only provide the information that they are situated somewhere along a line in a particular direction from that landmark. With two landmarks, however, their exact position can be pinpointed by taking bearings on both landmarks; they are at the point where the two lines cross. In social research, if one relies on a single piece of data there is the danger that undetected error in the data-production process may render the analysis incorrect. If, on the other hand, diverse kinds of data lead to the same conclusion, one can be a little more confident in that conclusion. This confidence is well founded to the degree that the different kinds of data have different types of error built into them.

There are a number of other kinds of triangulation besides that relating to data sources. First, there is the possibility of triangulating between different researchers. While team research has sometimes been used by ethnographers, often the data generated by different observers have been designed to be complementary, relating to different aspects of a setting or different settings, rather than intended to facilitate triangulation. Nevertheless, team research offers the opportunity for researcher triangulation. Of course, to maximize its potentialities the observers should be as different as possible, for example adopting very different roles in the field. Second, there is technique triangulation. Here, data produced by different techniques are compared. To the extent that these techniques involve different kinds of validity threat, they provide a basis for triangulation. Ethnography often involves a combination of techniques and thus it may be possible to check construct validity by examining data relating to the same construct from participant observation, interviewing, and documents.

In triangulation, then, links between concepts and indicators are checked by recourse to other indicators. For example, we might check inferences from teachers' staffroom talk to a common staff perspective by examining interview data and reports from classroom observation. However, triangulation is not a simple test. Even if the results tally, this provides no guarantee that the inferences involved are correct. It may be that all the inferences are invalid, that as a result of systematic or even random error they lead to the same, incorrect, conclusion. What is involved in triangulation is not the combination of different kinds of data *per se*, but rather an attempt to relate different sorts of data in such a way as to counteract various possible threats to the validity of our analysis.

One should not, therefore, adopt a naively 'optimistic' view that the aggregation of data from different sources will unproblematically add up to produce a more complete picture. Although few writers have commented on it, *differences* between sets or types of data may be just as important and illuminating. Lever (1981) provides a valuable commentary on this. Researching sex differences in children's play, she collected data by means of questionnaires and diaries. The former suggested greater sex differences than the latter. Lever argues that this reflects varying effects of stereotyping according to 'the nature of the method or the posing of the question'. She claims that this is why the children's statements of what they 'usually do' collected in her questionnaire show stronger sex differences than the information about what they 'actually do' collected in diaries. In short, Lever suggests that 'abstract or unconditional inquiries yield responses that more closely correspond to a person's perceptions of social norms than inquiries of a concrete or detailed nature' (1981:205).

The lesson to be learned here, once again, is that data must never be taken at face value. It is misleading to regard some as true and some as false. Rather, as Lever's research indicates, what is involved in triangulation is not just a matter of checking whether inferences are valid, but of discovering which inferences are valid. Incidentally, it is worth noting that the sort of remarks offered by Zelditch (1962) on the suitability of different methods for field research, and by Becker and Geer (1957) on participant observation and interviewing, can be read in this light. These papers and others like them are normally cited either to advocate one method against another, or to commend the combination of different methods, but even more they lend weight to the idea of reflexive triangulation.

Theories and the comparative method

Ethnographers have sometimes been reluctant to admit that one of their concerns is the production of causal models. This stems in part, no doubt, from the positivist connotations of the term 'causality', and perhaps also from a recognition of the extreme difficulty of assessing the validity of claims about causal relations. Nevertheless, such models, not always explicit or well developed, are common in ethnographic accounts. It is important that the presence and significance of such models are recognized and explicated as fully as possible, and, indeed, that they are systematically developed and tested.

There is only one general method for testing causal relations – the comparative method – though there are different ways of using it. By assessing the patterning of social events under different circumstances, we can test the scope and the strength of the relationships posited by a theory. One version of the comparative method is the experiment. Here, at its simplest, a particular factor is introduced into one situation but not into another that is identical in all respects considered relevant. By holding constant factors relevant to plausible rival explanations, and manipulating the explanatory factor, the existence of the presumed causal relation can be checked. Experiments are the most powerful means of assessing the validity of claims about causal relations, though one can never be certain that all relevant variables have been controlled. There are, of course, some serious disadvantages to the experimental method, notably its tendency to low ecological validity, as well as political and ethical limits on its use.

The positivist emphasis on the experiment as the model of scientific inquiry goes hand in hand with what Becker (1970) has called the 'single study model'. While, as we argued in Chapter 1, ethnography can certainly be used to subject theories to rigorous test, by no means all ethnographies are, or need to be, of this kind. Often they simply provide relatively concrete descriptions or rather more developed typologies and models. While the fact that these are way-stations on the road to theory must not be forgotten, there is no obligation on the part of an ethnographer to travel all the way in any particular study. It can be left to later studies, or other researchers, to test the model. However, it should be said that many models are still waiting in vain for such treatment. In this respect, ethnographic research as a whole suffers from an even more serious form of 'analytic interruptus' than that which Lofland (1970) diagnoses.

There has been some ethnographic work that has grappled with the problems of testing theories. The procedural model usually adopted here is that of analytic induction. Denzin outlines the steps in analytic induction as follows:

'1. A rough definition of the phenomenon to be explained is formulated.
2. An hypothetical explanation of that phenomenon is formulated.
3. One case is studied in the light of the hypothesis with the object of determining whether the hypothesis fits the facts in that case.
4. If the hypothesis does not fit the facts, either the hypothesis is reformulated or the phenomenon to be explained is redefined, so that the case is excluded.
5. Practical certainty may be attained after a small number of cases has been examined, but the discovery of negative

cases disproves the explanation and requires a reformulation.

6. This procedure of examining cases, redefining the phenomenon, and reformulating the hypothesis is continued until a universal relationship is established, each negative case calling for a redefinition or a reformulation.'

(Denzin 1978:192)

There are relatively few accounts of this method in use. Cressey's (1950) work on 'trust violation' provides a good example, as does that of Lindesmith (1947) on drug addiction.

Analytic induction was originally developed by Znaniecki (1934) in explicit opposition to the statistical method. Znaniecki claimed that it was the true method of the physical and biological sciences, and asserted its superiority on the grounds that it produces universal not probability statements. However, Znaniecki's argument is not convincing. As Robinson (1969) has pointed out, he drew too sharp a distinction between analytic induction and statistical method, and in fact the capacity of analytic induction to produce universal statements derives from the fact that it concerns itself only with necessary, and ignores the question of sufficient conditions.

However, analytic induction can be developed to deal with both necessary and sufficient conditions, as Bloor's (1978) study of ENT specialists shows. Bloor's interest was the puzzling variations in the use of adeno-tonsillectomy, the surgical removal of the tonsils and adenoids. In order to throw light on this he set about investigating the decision-making processes employed by a sample of ENT specialists in deciding whether or not to recommend adeno-tonsillectomy. Bloor's procedure was as follows:

1. For each doctor all the cases were provisionally classified according to the clinical decision arrived at (e.g. removal of the tonsils, a course of treatment with antibiotics etc.); these categories of clinical decision and intervention were referred to as 'disposal categories'.

2. The data on all a specialist's cases in a particular 'disposal category' were examined in an attempt to produce a provisional list of features common to that category (e.g. features of the history of the patient's complaint, the findings on clinical examination etc.).

3. Some cases were identified as 'deviant'. That is, they lacked features in common with other cases of the same disposal category. These deviant cases were examined with a view to (a) modifying the list of common case-features so as to accommodate the otherwise 'deviant' case, or (b) modifying the scheme for classifying cases. Either way, the analytic framework was gradually developed in order to incorporate all the observed cases.

4. Bloor then compared the 'disposal categories', looking for those case features which were shared by more than one category, and those which uniquely defined categories. Bloor decided that the shared features were 'necessary', and the differentiating features 'sufficient' in generating one or another clinical intervention.

5. On the basis of these necessary and sufficient conditions, associated with the various clinical outcomes, Bloor derived decision-making rules for each of the clinicians.

6. The cases to which the rules had been applied were then re-examined in an attempt to derive the criteria or 'search procedures' used by the clinician in applying the rule to the case.

7. To complete the analysis, Bloor repeated the above analytic steps for all the disposal categories of each consultant in turn.

In this way it was possible to build up a comprehensive picture of the decision-making processes and criteria used by each of the doctors Bloor studied. Amongst other things, therefore, he was able to document the extent to which doctors relied on idiosyncratic rules and routines in managing their cases. While one consultant might start from the assumption that the presence of a child in the clinic was *prima facie* evidence of the need for an operation, another consultant might place very different emphasis on the medical history. On examining the patient, each would approach the interpretation of clinical signs rather differently. These rules and search procedures are, as Bloor showed, embedded in routines of consultation management, but could be inferred inductively from the observed consultations.

Besides the inclusion of sufficient as well as necessary conditions, there is another element we might add to analytic induction. Gregory Bateson's father, the geneticist William Bateson, is reported to have advised his students: 'Treasure your exceptions! . . . (they are) like the rough brickwork of a growing building which tells that there is more to come and shows where the next construction is to be' (quoted in Lipset 1980:54). Both Cressey and Bloor do this, but they do not seem actively to have searched for exceptions, a strategy rightly recommended by Popper (1972). As we saw in Chapter 2, while no number of confirming instances can ever guarantee the validity of a theory, we can increase the chances of our acceptance of it being well founded if we specifically choose to study those cases where, because of the strength of rival explanatory factors, it seems least likely to be proved correct. Here again we refer to the notion of 'critical cases'.

Analytic induction, developed to cover both necessary and sufficient conditions, and to include the search for negative evidence, seems a plausible reconstruction of the logic of science, not just of ethnography. In this sense Znaniecki was almost certainly correct in the claims he made for it. In many respects it corresponds to the hypothetico-deductive method. Where it differs, and most importantly, is in making clear that the testing of theoretical ideas is not the end point of the process of scientific inquiry but is generally only one step leading to further development and refinement of the theory.

Types of theory

We have emphasized that by no means all ethnographic work is, or need be, concerned explicitly with the refinement and testing of theories. Equally, we should note the range of different types of theory with which ethnographers may be concerned. In sociology there is a well-established, though often by no means clearly expressed, distinction between macro and micro levels of analysis.

'Macro' refers to theories that apply to large-scale systems of social relations linking many different settings to one another through causal networks. This may involve tracing linkages across the structure of a national society or even relations among different societies. Micro research, by contrast, is concerned with analysing more local forms of social organization, whether that of particular institutions (for example occupations and organizations of various kinds) or of particular types of face-to-face encounter. What we have here, then, is a dimension along which the scale of phenomena under study varies.

While in many respects ethnography is better suited to research on micro theory, it can play an important role in developing and testing macro theories (see, for example, Willis 1977 and 1981). Macro theories make claims about processes occurring in particular types of place and time that can be tested and developed through ethnographic research. It should be noted, however, that this is very different from the misguided project of seeking to link macro and micro levels in a grand synthesis (Hammersley 1984).

Cross-cutting the macro-micro dimension is the distinction that Glaser and Strauss (1967) make between substantive and formal theory. While macro-micro relates to variation in the scope of the cases under study, the substantive–formal dimension concerns the generality of the categories under which cases are subsumed. Formal categories subsume substantive categories. Thus, for example, the substantive study of taxi-drivers and their 'fares' can be placed under more formal categories such as 'service encounters' or 'fleeting relationships' (Davis 1959). Similarly, the study of a particular society can be used as an initial basis for theory about a general type of society.

Given these two dimensions, we can identify four broad types of theory, and, indeed, examples of all of these can be found in the work of ethnographers. Analysis of the structure, functioning, and development of societies in general, such as that of Radcliffe-Brown (1948), Sahlins and Service (1960), and Harris (1979), is macro-formal. Studies of particular societies, for instance Malinowski (1922), Beattie (1965), or Chagnon (1968), fall into the macro-substantive category. Micro-formal work consists of studies of more local forms of social organization. Examples would be Goffman on the 'presentation of self' (1959), 'total institutions' (1961) and 'interaction ritual' (1972); Glaser and Strauss (1971) on 'status passage'; and Sacks on the organization of conversation (Sacks, Schegloff, and Jefferson 1974). Finally, there is micro-substantive research on particular types of organization or situation: Becker (1953) on 'becoming a marijuana user'; Strong (1979) on 'doctor-patient interaction';

Piliavin and Briar (1964) on 'police encounters with juveniles'; or Werthman (1963) on 'delinquents in schools'. All these types of theory are worthwhile, but it is important to keep clearly in mind the kind of theory one is dealing with since each would require the research to be pursued in a different direction. (See Glaser and Strauss 1967 and Glaser 1978 for a discussion of the development of formal as opposed to substantive theory.)

Conclusion

In this chapter we have looked at the process of analysis in ethnography, as well as at the different kinds of product that may result: from descriptions of sequences of events or typical patterns of interaction in a setting to various types of theory. Nevertheless, we have given particular emphasis to theory, in part because it has often been neglected by ethnographers, but also because we take it to be the primary goal of social research. This is a view we share with positivists. However, our conception of the process of theoretical research is rather different to theirs. For us, the development and testing of theory are not separate activities, nor is priority given to one over the other. Analytic induction seems to us to capture the nature of scientific inquiry much better than the hypothetico-deductive method. Moreover, the research process itself must not be left out of the theorizing. It is only through understanding the effects of our research procedures on the data produced that we can learn how to interpret it correctly. This, rather than following some method reified as scientific, or naively attempting to get into direct contact with social reality, is the essence of social science, and thus of ethnography.

We must not forget, however, that all the various products of ethnographic work, from descriptions to theories, take on the form of texts: ethnographic analysis is not just a cognitive activity but a form of writing. This has some important implications, as we shall see in the next chapter.

9

Writing ethnography

Ethnography as text

When it comes to writing up, the principle of reflexivity implies a number of things. The construction of the researcher's account is, in principle, no different from other varieties of account: just as there is no available neutral language of description, so there is no neutral mode of report. The reflexive researcher, then, must remain self-conscious as an author, and the chosen modes of writing should not be taken for granted. There can be no question, then, of viewing writing as a purely technical matter to be addressed only in the final phase of a research project. In some contexts writing a thesis, report, research paper, or monograph might be seen (for better or worse) as a more or less straight-forward affair: after the research is 'completed' then the 'results' are presented through the 'neutral' medium of conventionally organized reports. This is doubly problematic for the reflexive observer. In the first place, the logic of ethnography, and the data so produced, do not readily lend themselves to such conventions. Second, the reflexive observer will be acutely aware of their very conventionality.

Newby (1977a) throws some personal light on the problem of

moulding and integrating ethnographic data with sociology of a more 'traditional' or 'straightforward' format:

> 'when it came to writing up the research, the survey data in general dominated the monograph and the style of authorship. . . . Apart from anything else survey and participant observation require two very different styles of authorship: the former is impersonal, formal and hence usually written in the third person; the latter is more informal and impressionistic and thus written in the first person. Academic convention frowns upon a mixing of the two styles, and even literary consistency makes it difficult to switch suddenly into a first person anecdotal style in the middle of the measured presentation of hard data. Thus much to my surprise, the final monograph . . . contains little of the material gathered through participant observation, despite my voluminous fieldwork notes, which I faithfully wrote up every evening.'
>
> (Newby 1977a:127)

Whether or not Newby is right in his diagnosis of the problem, it is remarkable that the construction of his major monograph (Newby 1977b) was apparently largely determined by considerations of writing and style. Indeed, this seems to have governed even the selection of data to be reported.

In the course of fieldwork, the ethnographer will normally be doing a great deal of writing in any case. Fieldnotes, journals, and diaries are, in one sense, the 'data' that are collected; in another sense, they are written up, in ways that constitute preliminary analyses and presentations. Glaser and Strauss (1967), for instance, comment on the production of memoranda as preliminary analyses. In that sense, there can be no hard-and-fast distinction between 'writing' and 'analysis'. The same is true when we come to the preparation of the 'final product'. The 'analyses' that ethnographies embody are often embedded in, and constituted by, their very organization as texts, their 'style', the choice of language, and so on. The writing of an ethnography is, then, a major part of any such research project. This is a fact that is reflected in the most basic advice research supervisors are forever passing on to their students: 'Allow plenty of time for your writing, and then at least double it – it takes longer than you think.'

Surprisingly, since it is so important, little has been written on this subject. One of the noticeable features about textbooks on field methods, is that, by and large, the further one progresses through the research process, the less explicit commentary and advice they have to offer. They usually have a good deal to say about pre-fieldwork stages, and the initial phases of data collection: finding and 'casing' a research setting, negotiating access, first days in the field, establishing a 'field role', and similar topics are usually generously covered. Later stages of fieldwork are much less visible (where are the discussions of 'last days in the field', for instance?). With one or two exceptions (e.g. Spradley 1979 and Lofland 1974), most authors are all but silent on the activity of writing an ethnography.

It is not altogether fanciful to suggest that the act of 'interpretation' in interpretative sociology is as much an act of writing, of the organization of sociological texts, as it is a matter of cognitive processes of understanding. It is certainly the case that ethnographers need to cultivate skills of writing, and to become self-conscious about their written products. It is no good being reflexive in the course of planning and executing a piece of research if one is only to abandon that reflexivity when it comes to writing about it. Likewise, one is guilty of a dangerous double standard if research is conducted under the auspices of an interest in meaning and language, and the language and meaning of one's own products are not also scrutinized.

This is not intended to imply that ethnography should aspire to becoming 'literature', or that ethnographers should try to turn themselves into literary critics, or compete with literary writers. Rather, we wish to urge a rather more modest awareness of the mechanics of writing, the organization of literary texts, and so on. There is much to be gained by some degree of 'literary' awareness. After all, as Davis points out, the ethnographer is engaged in 'telling a story': 'I do think it is essential that you try somehow to find some kind of story which will give you an opening, a beginning working stratagem with respect to the data' (1974:311). Davis goes on to commend the use of literary parallels which may present themselves to the sociologist as storyteller:

'For example, the equivalent of the anomie story of Durkheim is, perhaps, *The Great Gatsby*. A good piece of work in family sociology dealing with the kind of interaction which underlies a phenomenon like Bateson's double-bind is Eugene O'Neill's *Long Day's Journey into Night*. Certainly a fine story on the meaning of a vocation, as Max Weber would have analyzed it, is the Thomas Mann short story Tonio Kroger.'

(Davis 1974:311)

Of course, Davis's remarks here beg many questions: he has little or nothing to say about what counts as a story, or how different types of story are constructed, or how one is to select one story rather than another. Further, what is normally thought of as 'story-telling' is only part of the ethnographer's task. He or she is, to one degree or another, also engaged in the explication of theory, the development of causal models, and the construction of typologies. Nevertheless, Davis's remarks are useful in alerting us to the general importance of textual organization.

Consideration of textual strategies draws ethnography towards aspects of contemporary literary studies, particularly those associated with structuralism and poststructuralism. In recent years literary critics have increasingly turned their attention to the organization of texts. (See, for instance, Belsey 1980; Culler 1975 and 1981a; Hawkes 1977 for introductory texts on various aspects of this movement.) The work of critics such as David Lodge has concentrated attention on the literary modes and conventions available to writers for the representation of 'reality' in modern fiction (e.g. Lodge 1977 and 1981). While such critical theory has been concerned primarily with literary texts, its analytic machinery is not confined to such works, and part of the thrust of much recent critical writing has been to question the very distinction between the literary and other forms of writing, analytically speaking. In this vein there has been a growing realization that the lessons learned from literary studies can usefully be applied to other contexts. For instance:

'The study of basic narrative structures is one example of the way in which models and categories that are initially drawn from the study of literary works turn out to have wider implications, and make possible productive investigations of the relationship between literature and other modes of ordering and representing experience.'

(Culler 1981b:11)

The ethnographer is frequently engaged in something closely akin to narrative writing, pregnant with theme and argument. The threads of the text parallel what Diesing (1972) refers to as the 'pattern' model of understanding, which characterizes a good deal of ethnographic work. These patterns are as much inscribed in the narrative organization as they are conveyed in explicit argument.

This is not the place for us to enter into a detailed discussion of the relevance of critical theory and poetics to sociological reading and writing. It requires separate treatment of monograph length itself. A preliminary exploration of some aspects is provided by Brown, who suggests:

> 'With the verbal arts the physical qualities – that is, the immediate auditory or visual surface – are largely irrelevant. It is meaning and structure that count. Sociology, like the verbal arts, also lacks this surface quality, but it can, like them, be judged in terms of its formal and mimetic power. For these reasons the critical concepts associated with the novel, poetry and drama – that is, "poetics" – provide a privileged vocabulary for the aesthetic consideration of sociological theory.'
>
> (Brown 1977:7)

Brown's commentary on metaphor and irony are particularly apposite foundations for a reflexive awareness of ethnographic writing. The use of *irony* is a particularly important feature of ethnographic writing, which frequently rests on the juxtaposition and comparison of opposites, or of classes and categories that are commonsensically treated as mutually exclusive.

Hymes (1978:16) is one of the rare commentators on ethnography to have drawn attention to such matters explicitly. He reflects on the fundamental significance of a narrative mode of understanding: 'Instead of thinking of narrative accounts as an early stage that in principle will be replaced, we may need to think of them as a permanent stage, whose principles are little understood, and whose role may increase.' The issue, Hymes goes on to suggest, is never to replace narrative presentations, but rather 'to discover how to assess them'. Hitherto we have not progressed very far in this particular direction.

A detailed discussion of this area of interest could eventually lead us to consider many aspects of the poetics of sociology. We shall not attempt to do so here. Rather, we shall go on to consider some of the available strategies for ordering and organizing ethnographic texts, in the production of an overall narrative structure. We shall not try to be prescriptive in our comments. There is no single correct method for the construction of texts. Different methods have different implications, however, and we shall try to draw attention to these, as an aid to the reflexive formulation of ethnographic writing.

Organizing texts

One of the difficulties most commonly encountered in writing ethnographies is this: the re-ordering of one's data, and one's achieved competence as participant observer into a linear arrangement. Somehow or other one has to arrange the text into a sequence of chapters, themes, topics, arguments, and so forth. It goes without saying that a text has to start at the beginning, and continue until the end, and then stop. The everyday life under investigation is not itself organized in such a neat linear array. Presentation of aspects of it in this way is something that has to be achieved, and worked at in preparing the text. It is also something that many people find singularly difficult. So often one finds that one wants to write 'everything' first; that before one can discuss some particular analytic point, one has to acquaint the reader with every possible aspect of the relevant setting.

Often, the would-be writer has to work hard at establishing a new degree of distance or estrangement from the data. During the first days in the field, the participant observer must make the effort of sociological imagination to make everyday life anthropologically strange. As the fieldwork progresses, however, the researcher becomes inescapably familiar with the setting, and the accumulated fieldnotes and transcripts represent a physical record of that familiarity. Before embarking on any major writing up, therefore, one has to undertake a further task of estrangement. If one does not distance oneself from them, then there is a danger of being unable to dismantle the data, select from them, and re-order the material. One is left in the position of someone who, when asked to comment on and criticize a film or novel, can do no more than rehearse the plot. The ethnographer who fails to achieve distance will easily fall into the trap of recounting 'what happened' without imposing a coherent thematic or analytic framework.

Such recounting is admittedly integral to the writing. As we have already remarked, the narrative organization is fundamental to our modes of reality construction in the text. Hymes exemplifies this in a brief commentary on Geertz's description of Balinese cock-fighting:

'Through his narrative skill, he is able to convey a sense (mediated by his personal involvement) of the quality and texture of Balinese fascination with cock fighting. Evidence of the fascination is important. It supports taking the activity as a key to something essential about the Balinese, it helps us understand the analytic statements. A film might help too, but it would need something verbal from Geertz to teach us what we should learn from it. The narrative part of Geertz's article in effect points, as the narrator of a film might do, and, also, in the absence of a film, shows. It does so through texture and proportion.'

(Hymes 1978:16)

Without detailed cultural descriptions and narratives, the substantive or formal theoretical statements would be empty. For instance, it would be hard to conceive of such work as Krieger's (1979b) study of the KMPX strike without detailed narrative presentations that chronicle a particular event or sequence of events.

Indeed, Krieger (1979a) is one of the very few authors to have reflected on the production of her own research text. Krieger comments on the process whereby she constructed a narrative account of the development of a radio station, a narrative that ultimately formed her doctoral dissertation. She draws explicit parallels with literary forms; of the available models she looked to the novel as a strategy:

'The one I pursued was, in some respects, a novelistic style in that it used people of the station as characters to tell a story of its changes. Developing a text which did that was in part a process of devising a set of narrative and stylistic rules.'

(Krieger 1979a:175)

Unfortunately Krieger's self-analysis is somewhat limited: she has rather little to say on how the narrative is constructed as such, nor how her characters are portrayed. Finally, the stylistic rules that she derives are rather less important than the general insight she offers: 'What theory there was lay embedded in the text in the pattern of its use of concrete detail' (1979a:185).

Although relatively little has been written relating directly to the organization of an ethnographic text, Lofland (1974) provides us with a valuable 'sideways look' at the topic, from the point of view of readers' receptions of such texts. Lofland's perspective derives from an analysis of referees' evaluations of papers submitted for journal publication. At the outset he notes, as we have, that in comparison with other traditions, there is a lack of consensus over the appropriate form for such writing:

> 'At least in its sociological version, qualitative field research seems distinct in the degree to which its practitioners lack a public, shared, and codified conception of how what they do is done, and how what they report should be formulated.'
>
> (Lofland 1974:101)

On the other hand, members of the academic community who are called on to do so seem to evaluate ethnographic writing in terms of its overall structure. Lofland derives a number of styles that seem to be preferred by evaluators.

Lofland's typology consists of the following: the 'generic frame'; the 'novel frame'; the elaborated frame'; the 'eventful frame'; and the 'interpenetrated frame'. Each of these is subdivided into various further varieties. The main types are summarized as:

> '1. The report was organized by means of a *generic* conceptual framework;
> 2. The generic framework employed was *novel*;
> 3. The framework was *elaborated* or developed in and through the report;
> 4. The framework was *eventful* in the sense of abundantly documented with qualitative data;
> 5. The framework was *interpenetrated* with the empirical materials.'
>
> (Lofland 1974:102)

While not seeking to reproduce the detail of how these various styles are manifested or recognized, we can note here how such considerations reinforce our contention that textual organization is implicative. There certainly appear to be conventions for reading and evaluating ethnography, even though we lack explicit conventions for the construction of such texts.

Some of the readers' strategies that Lofland outlines are related to those that we identify in the textual strategies described below. Ours are: the natural history; the chronology; narrowing and expanding the focus; separating narration and analysis; and thematic organizations. This list is not intended to be definitive or exhaustive, and the characterization of textual strategies remains at a gross level. It is intended as a very preliminary survey of the topic.

The natural history

One possible way of ordering the text might be to parallel the unfolding of the text to the process of discovery and exploration that characterized the 'natural history' of the fieldwork itself. In this way the linear organization of the text would correspond to the passage of time in the field, and to the process whereby the research itself developed. Such an account would have to be highly selective, of course; otherwise, the written-up text would be virtually indistinguishable from the fieldnotes or the researcher's field journal.

This device may be a useful one to use for particular purposes in a written account. One might find it a relatively 'natural' way to present a methodological account of the conduct of the research. Or it might furnish a telling method to elucidate how a particular theme or problem was identified and progressively focused upon in the course of the fieldwork. On the other hand, this device poses considerable difficulties when it comes to a sustained ethnographic account on any scale, which deals with a number of themes. Although there is always a process of 'progressive focusing' in an ethnographic project, it does not offer a very manageable way of organizing a comprehensive analysis. Topics, themes, and data do not unfold in a neat sequential fashion, and cannot normally be presented in such a simple way.

There is yet a further difficulty in using this strategy for any sustained presentation. Not only do topics and problems emerge in different ways and at different rates, but also one's theoretical understandings and conceptual sophistication change. Ideas are retrospectively formulated and redefined in the light of such changes. It is therefore difficult to do justice to the 'natural history' as well as presenting an adequate portrayal of one's current or best available theoretical position. These latter considerations, indeed, throw some doubt on the general validity of the notion of 'natural history' in this context. The development of research projects and of theory is almost certainly a good deal less smooth, and certainly a good deal less 'natural' than such a notion would seem to imply.

In general, then, this is an unwieldy and unsatisfactory way in which to approach the production of a major piece of writing, such as a complete monograph or thesis. It is much more manageable if this device is used to provide some sort of 'way in' or introduction to major themes in the research, which may subsequently be dealt with *seriatim*. Indeed, this organization may be used to link a discussion of fieldwork strategy with a preliminary presentation of substantive topics. The latter can be taken up and developed subsequently. To some extent this is the logic outlined in the classic 'first days' paper by Blanche Geer (1964), where she reproduces her early fieldnotes and reflections in which potential lines of further enquiry were identified and noted.

It is, perhaps, particularly apt to adopt such a strategy of presentation if the researcher's problems in 'discovery' or 'focusing' can be shown to parallel the members' problems in finding their own way. One of us (Atkinson) was able to use this strategy in part in writing up the ethnography of the Edinburgh Medical School. The school was a complex organization where the clinical training was divided up into a large number of different 'firms', each with a distinctive and unique style. The ethnographer's task in understanding the study included the task of 'theoretical sampling' by selecting from among all those 'firms' for periods of observation. It became apparent at an early stage in the fieldwork that the ethnographer's problem here, in selecting research sites in the organization, was a member's problem too. The medical students were faced with very similar issues: they had to choose which units they wished to attend for their clinical training over the course of the year. They also faced the problem of sampling within a complex organization. Needless to say, the criteria employed by the ethnographer and the students were not identical, and their interests differed. Nevertheless, the homology between the two sets of concerns meant that it was possible to intertwine the two in introducing the setting, the research, and one of the main substantive themes (how students manage such career-relevant choices).

In this last instance, the 'progressive focusing' approach was relevant in so far as the members concerned (the students) were novices or recruits, facing a similar problem to that of the ethnographer. The following strategy relies upon a similar chronological parallel between members' experiences, the data collection, and the presentation of the finished ethnography.

The chronology

Like the 'natural history', this strategy also uses the passage of time for the linear organization of the final text. Here the author does not necessarily follow the chronology of the study (although it may be similar). Rather, the pattern follows some 'developmental cycle', 'moral career', or 'timetable' characteristic of the setting or actors under investigation. This is clearly an appropriate strategy for the presentation of ethnographic material where the passage of time is of considerable analytic importance, usually where some process of social change is central to the topical or thematic organization. (The passage of time is of potential relevance in all social contexts, but may have particular significance in some.)

One can instance the study of young polio victims and their families reported by Fred Davis (1963). Its very title, *Passage Through Crisis*, highlights the temporal significance of the analysis and presentation. For the most part the text is organized in terms of the stages of the 'passage' through the illness and subsequent rehabilitation. Hence, the analysis progresses from the onset of polio, through the child's stay in hospital, on to the child's return home, and recovery or rehabilitation. Further stages are identified within these main temporal divisions. For instance, in discussing the early stages of the polio episode,

Davis talks of 'the prelude stage', 'the warning stage', 'the impact stage', and 'the inventory stage'. Davis explicitly canvasses the merits of such 'stage analysis':

> 'The advantages of a sequential-stage analysis of this type are obvious. It allows the investigator to break down his subject matter into more manageable parts, to relate those parts to one another in a relatively systematic way, and, in general, to bestow a semblance of analytic order on the chaos of contradictory reports and observations. . . .'
>
> (Davis 1963:19)

We might add, as Davis is implying here, that such analytic devices also translate fairly straightforwardly into linear textual organizations with an apparently 'natural' logic. At the same time, Davis acknowledges that this has some dangers: 'the segmented description of the crisis experience tends to suggest that more order and coherence exist than is usually the case in such situations' (1963:19).

This chronological approach is particularly well suited to the presentation of analysis of life in institutions that are themselves organized on the basis of some seasonal cycle or rhythm, or in which the temporal transformation of members' identities is accomplished. Socialization processes and agencies, for example, may well lend themselves to this mode of presentation. Here, the passage of time is an issue of primary significance, and the analysis may be ordered in terms of a chronological sequence. Here again the linear unfolding of the text can be made to parallel the passage of time as experienced by the actors and the main phases of a socialization process. The segmentation of the analysis, and of the text, may follow organizationally given stages (such as academic years, terms, or occupational grades) or observer-identified phases, or a mixture of both.

To some extent, the very obviousness of this mode of textual organization makes it an appealing one. But for the very same reason, it must be treated with some caution. It would, after all, be counter-productive if one had worked hard at rendering institutions and interactions 'strange' only to lapse back into presenting them in ways that do not capitalize on that hard-won 'strangeness'. This can only be a caution, however, as it must be recognized that this way of organizing one's material is in

accordance with many of the theoretical commitments of interpretative or interactionist sociology. Such perspectives stress
the processual, developmental nature of social life, and of social
selves or identities. Process, with its twin themes of continuity
and change, rests on a temporal dimension. The processual or
temporal emergence of social identities is, for instance, a prominent theme in many texts based on ethnographic work. It is thus
highly appropriate that such arguments should, at least in part,
be presented through a temporal unfolding that follows and recounts such a process of 'becoming'.

It is in this vein, then, that the theme of 'career' or 'moral
career' provides a highly appropriate (and frequently used) conceptual scheme, or formal concept, which readily implies some
sequential organization for the data and analysis. Becker's
famous paper Becoming a Marihuana User (1953) is a *locus
classicus* in this style, although it does not present an extended
ethnography based on extensive fieldwork. No less famous is
Goffman's (1961) presentation of the moral career of the asylum
inmate. In a much more recent British example, Ditton (1977)
offers us the moral career of the bread roundsman: this theme
does not furnish an over-arching organization for Ditton's entire
monograph, but is the topic for just one section.

The developmental 'career' perspective shows very clearly
how the very organization of the text and the analysis are mutually interdependent. Any phase analysis, or one that attempts to
chart some *rite de passage*, decision-making process, passage
through crisis, or socialization experience, may lend itself to
this sort of presentation. Nanette Davis's (1974) analysis of
women's passage through a network of referral and decision
making in the search for abortion is organized in such a fashion.
Davis's account is organized in terms of five stages: defining the
problem; constructing alternatives; contacting help; ter-
minating the pregnancy; and evaluating the experience. This is
closely paralleled by Macintyre's (1977) account of stages in the
pregnancy of single women.

Paul Rock's (1973) monograph on debt collection is another
example that follows the temporal sequence of events reported.
The chapters are: Entering the Career; The Debt-Collector;
The Solicitor; The County Court; Execution; The Judgment
Summons Hearing and Committal Orders; The Bailiff's

Working Personality; The Prison; The Debtor as Inmate; and Typifications of Debtors.

This chronological-developmental approach to writing the ethnography is thus a highly engaging one. It is, to a considerable extent, faithful to the spirit of much interpretative sociology. It has its dangers, however. It is dangerously easy, for example, to use it to suggest implicitly that processes of 'becoming' are matters of straightforward socialization, and a more or less smooth set of transitions from one stage to another. The presentation of a chronological unfolding may thus seductively substitute for adequate sociological analysis. Like any other mode of presentation it demands careful treatment and one must avoid unreflecting reliance upon it. It is, however, highly suited to the elaboration of such basic themes as 'moral career', 'status passage', and 'labelling'.

Narrowing and expanding the focus

An equally valuable and appealing way of organizing a text is to move the presentation through different levels of generality or inclusiveness. This can be done in either direction – from the particular to the general, or vice versa. A metaphor for such a textual arrangement might be that of the 'zoom lens', by means of which the field of vision and corresponding degree of magnification may be progressively varied. One might wish to think of the progressively detailed analytic or institutional levels as corresponding, metaphorically, to a Chinese box, or a Russian doll; they are nested inside one another.

One might, therefore, present a text, the organization of which corresponded to the different layers or analytic levels, moving from macro to micro analyses, or from concrete details up and out towards more inclusive and general frames of analysis. Observational data gathered in, say, legal, medical, or educational settings (courts, clinics, or classrooms) might thus be embedded in textual settings that progressively located them in wider occupational, local, bureaucratic, or national frameworks.

Lacey's (1970) account of 'Hightown Grammar' is a complex realization of a text of this sort. He moves backwards and forwards through the analytic levels of society, education system, school, and classroom. It is important to note that this method of organization has (or may have) important implications for the mode of analysis. Whether or not such implications are regarded as valid depends upon the desired effect, and cannot be established a priori. It does imply some theory of the existence of such levels, and of their analytic value.

This method of presentation may, therefore, satisfy a legitimate analytic goal, if such distinctive levels, and their interrelationships, are recognized. On the other hand, it may easily pander to a vague desire to place data of an interactional sort within some social context. It may therefore be used in an almost ritualistic manner, to satisfy a felt need to generalize one's findings without actually doing so.

In other words, we are suggesting that it is not enough simply to present a series of Chinese boxes, unless an adequate theoretical and analytic rationale can be provided for doing so. Otherwise, the *appearance* of such analytic presentation may be conveyed by the arrangement of the text, without actually being achieved by explicit argument. Of course, the textual arrangement must carry the argument, but it is dangerous if the arrangement of sections or chapters comes to substitute for sociological analysis, so that the appearance of coherence is achieved only by means of a sort of stylistic sleight of hand. (As we repeatedly point out, this applies to all forms of arrangement and presentation.)

Separating narration and analysis

As we have already remarked, a common problem faced by ethnographers is how to translate their knowledge and descriptions of a given culture into a serial order while simultaneously imposing some sort of analytic and thematic order upon the material. There is, therefore, one fairly attractive expedient, that of separating the ethnography (the data, the cultural description) from the analysis. This is a device that has been used recently by Paul Willis (1977) in his study of young working-class men and their transition from school to work.

This textual recourse has some notable attractions. It (apparently) allows the author to present an engaging and accessible account of the data, relatively unencumbered. The reader is, or can be, given considerable information about and 'feel for' the culture in question. This narrative need not be held up by too much discussion or clouded by too many analytic problems. Once the reader is fully acquainted with the culture, then the author may feel free to embark on a discussion of themes and problems, now relatively unimpeded by any need to clutter such discussion with data.

In some ways this arrangement does work. The success of Willis's work bears witness to this (though we do not wish to imply that it is attributable to this one characteristic alone). There are, however, some inherent dangers and pitfalls in this approach. The separation between the ethnography and the analysis can allow the author to develop flights of sociological fancy that are not in fact grounded in and systematically related to the data. The reader encounters what purports to be the analysis of the culture that he or she has already assimilated in the first half of the account. The textual separation means that the relationship may be more apparent than real. The relationship may be achieved by the reader supplying the link, reading the analysis in a sympathetic light on the basis of a sympathetic appreciation of the culture gained in the first part.

This sort of problem is certainly apparent in the case of Willis's work. Commentators have in fact found Willis's presentation highly contentious, and the link between his portrayal of the culture and the analytic superstructure he builds upon it tenuous at best, while many other readers appear to have been persuaded by his presentation and his argument.

In fact, the separation of the ethnography and the analysis masks a further problem. It is clear that any orderly presentation of the ethnography/cultural description is itself analytic. Willis's ethnographic account is certainly no less analytic than others. In presenting it in the way he does, Willis has already performed a great deal of analytic work. But the separation between ethnography and analysis may *appear* to imply that the ethnographic account is somehow innocent or pre-analytic: this may seduce the reader into placing greater credence in the ethnography, and hence, as we have suggested, in the following analysis. However, it masks the analytic work that has informed its production.

As with all other methods, therefore, this strategy demands

careful treatment. Any use of this approach must be informed by an explicit awareness of its analytic implications.

Thematic organizations

There are various methods of thematic or topical organization. These imply not so much a single linear order to the text, as a typology of concepts such that the precise order of their presentation is not necessarily of prime importance. One such tried and tested method is the format whereby the culture or social structure is presented in terms of a limited number of major components or social institutions. One might refer to such textual formats as corresponding to the 'Notes and Queries' model, referring to the classic vade-mecum of social anthropologists, which incorporates a set of standard topics for investigation in field studies. This list of research topics was designed to aid in the collection of data by people not themselves trained anthropologists. Many of the classic anthropological monographs are arranged in this manner. They may go through such components as kinship and marriage, political institutions, economic institutions, witchcraft and religion, or some such similar collection. Sociological community studies often follow very similar lines.

Whyte (1981), in his appendix to *Street Corner Society*, notes the powerful influence exercised by early community studies such as the Lynds's Middletown studies. Whyte records how he started to think of his own Cornerville Study in such terms:

'My early outline of the study pointed to special researches in the history of the district, in economics (living standards, housing, marketing, distribution, and employment), politics (the structure of the political organization and its relation to the rackets and the police), patterns of education and recreation, the church, public health, and – of all things – social attitudes.'

(Whyte 1981:284)

Whyte soon abandoned this approach. As he describes it, it would probably have required a team of some ten research workers anyway. As it is, his own text reveals how he adopted an approach to the fieldwork that reflects his more selective view and his commitment to progressive discovery, starting from his relationship with 'Doc', his sponsor in Cornerville: Doc and his Boys; Chick and his Club; The Social Structure and Social Mobility; The Social Structure of Racketeering; The Racketeer in the Cornerville S. and A. Club; and Politics and the Social Structure. We can see here, in the chapter titles, Whyte organizing the text by means of mixture of themes of different sorts, some of which remain close to the local issues, others of which derive more directly from sociological categories and concerns.

Nevertheless, the 'Notes and Queries' format provides a potentially convenient way of organizing a great deal of cultural information into a relatively coherent ordering of a few categories. In some contexts (such as the community study or anthropology monograph) there may be well established and commonly used categories available for such purposes. In other contexts the categories may not be so traditionally defined, but may still be derived by essentially similar processes of abstraction and reasoning. One might, for instance, think of ordering an ethnography in terms of a division into the main different groups of actors involved, or into the main institutions or different settings that actors come into contact with. This general approach tends to proceed as if the general substantive area or topic can best be analysed in terms of such a division into institutions or domains. There is a danger here of adopting such analytic categories uncritically, and deriving them from accepted lay or sociological ways of conceptualizing a given culture, setting, or activity.

That is not to say that the strategy is without merit. Far from it: it can be an excellent way of encapsulating a great deal of information, drawn from a range of settings, in terms that may be broadly comparable with other published accounts. In one form or another it has been used in many texts, and no doubt reflects the way in which many ethnographers have thought about their data, or at least *one* way they think about them. On the other hand, it does have the potential drawback of leading one towards orthodox or obvious themes. If, for instance, one were always to write up a community study in terms of separate sections for, say, family and kinship on the one hand, and economics or work on the other, then one could well produce a traditional analysis, and miss the analytic potential for treating 'the family' as a place of productive work: one might thus find oneself treating the distinction between work and domestic life as unproblematic, rather than making it a potentially fruitful sociological problem.

Of course, this does not have to be the case. One's choice of textual organization does not determine totally the nature of the sociological argument, nor vice versa. We are not proposing some version of a Sapir-Whorf argument whereby the entire thrust of a work of sociology is inexorably driven by its formal arrangement. Nevertheless, as we point out repeatedly in this chapter, there are important affinities between the two. It may be more difficult to put an argument across if its stated analytic purpose is apparently at odds with the implicit message of its textual form. Such implicit themes are often more potent than explicit messages.

It is worth remembering, for instance, how the 'Notes and Queries' style of presentation reflected the theoretical and analytic interest of essentially functionalist ethnographies. The culture or social structure is portrayed in terms of its institutional components in such a way that the coherence of the text parallels the organic model of society, in that the text hangs together in precisely the same way as do the various institutional or cultural components. The arrangement of the text thus pictures the functional interdependencies that it proclaims.

An alternative textual arrangement would be to organize the ethnography in terms of members' categories (folk categories), rather than the institutional components we have referred to as the 'Notes and Queries' approach. Under this latter arrangement, the main analytic and textual themes are provided by, say, the situated vocabulary of the culture. In such formulations, what is stressed as the thematic coherence is less how the sociologist or anthropologist itemizes the culture, but rather how the members themselves set about doing so.

This is rarely used to provide the entire framework for a complete ethnography, for observers' analytic categories and members' categories are normally interwoven. Agar's (1973) account of urban heroin addicts provides one example where members' terms are used to carry a good deal of the text's themes, embedded within observer-identified categories and typologies.

For instance, the chapter Events in Process is subdivided into sections, including Copping; Getting-Off; The Bust; The Burn; and The Rip-Off. These are all terms employed by the addicts, and their use is in accordance with Agar's general methodological position, which implies the elucidation of emic categories in members' identifications of behaviour and events.

This mode of organizing the ethnographic account is, then, in keeping with an analytic approach that stresses the heuristic importance of members' own categories, taxonomies, and vocabularies. One makes sense of the culture via such culturally defined constructs, and the culture is portrayed through their reproduction. (Of course, irrespective of whether they are used as major organizational themes, one will expect the analysis to include the documentation of such categories and their use.) The relative prominence and importance of such folk terms in organizing the account will vary from ethnography to ethnography, although they will feature in all to some extent.

A third type of thematic organization may be generated by the use of formal analytic concepts. These differ somewhat from those already discussed. They are normally identifications of the analyst, rather than folk terms, but are not normally equivalent to the 'Notes and Queries' reliance upon given institutional, social, or cultural boundaries. In this third case, the themes drawn on by the ethnographer represent formal, or ideal-typical notions by which key processes and forms of a given cultural setting may be represented.

In his recent monograph on paediatric encounters, Strong (1979) draws on a series of such formal analytic themes to order his material. The main chapters in which the ethnographic data are presented are entitled Natural Parenthood; Collegial Authority; A Joint Venture; Medical Control; and Ease and Tension in the Alliance. This overall organization in Strong's book is thus a direct reflection of his stated analytic purpose, in which he aims to deal in 'forms':

> 'There is . . . scope for a detailed study of the social forms of medical consultations. Such forms I shall call "role formats", although I will not stick unswervingly to this terminology. . . . In the consultations reported on here, there were four types of role format in use, which I have named the

''bureaucratic'', '' charity'', ''clinical'' and ''private'' modes respectively.'

(Strong 1979:8)

Here, then, Strong clearly outlines a formal approach to his subject matter, and his textual organization clearly reflects this commitment (though he does not simply arrange his chapters in terms of his four ideal-typical formats).

In terms of the sorts of categories employed, this textual-cum-analytic framework is very different from the 'Notes and Queries' sort of approach we outlined above. And, indeed, it can be a very effective presentational strategy. Like all such such styles, however, it brings with it its own pitfalls for the careless or unwary. It, too, may become ossified into another sort of taken-for-granted orthodoxy.

Audiences and texts

A reflexive awareness of ethnographic writing should also take account of the potential audience for the finished product. Ethnographers are, after all, enjoined to pay close attention to the social contexts in which actors construct their everyday accounts (see Chapter 5). We note whether accounts are solicited or unsolicited, to whom they are made, with what effect (intended or unintended), and so on. Ethnographers do not, however, always carry over such an attitude towards the published accounts of their own devising. There are potentially many types of audience for social research: fellow research workers, hosts, students and teachers in the social sciences; professionals and policy-makers; and publishers, journal editors and referees. There is, too, that amorphous audience 'the general public'. By the same token, audiences may require different forms and styles of writing: an academic monograph, a learned journal article, a popular magazine article, a polemical essay, or a methodological or theoretical paper (Schatzman and Strauss 1973).

Audiences differ in the background assumptions, knowledge, and expectations they bring to the ethnographic text. Some will be well versed in the particularities of the setting and may have particular interests deriving from that. Others will be more thoroughly familiar with sociological perspectives, but have little or no knowledge of the field. Some readers will use methodological and theoretical perspectives that are in sympathy with the ethnographer's; some will start from a position of incomprehension or hostility and will need to be won over by the author. Some readers address themselves directly to practical and evaluative considerations. Some will prove impatient with the details of the 'story' while others will read precisely for the details and the vignettes, skipping over the explicitly sociological commentary and theorizing.

We can never tailor our ethnographies to match the interests of all our potential audiences simultaneously. No single text can accomplish all things for all readers. A sense of audience and a sense of style will guide the author towards multiple written and spoken accounts. And, indeed, such awareness may lead towards analytic insights. As Schatzman and Strauss put it:

> 'In preparing for any telling or writing, and in imagining the perspective of his specific audience, the researcher is apt to see his data in new ways: finding new analytic possibilities, or implications he has never before sensed. This process of late discovery is full of surprises, sometimes even major ones, which lead to serious reflection on what one has 'really' discovered. Thus, it is not simply a matter of the researcher writing down what is in his notes or head; writing or telling as activities exhibit their own properties which provide conditions for discovery.'
>
> (Schatzman and Strauss 1973:132)

Just as the ethnographer has grappled with problems of strangeness, familiarity, and discovery *vis-à-vis* the hosts and their knowledge, so a consideration of possible audiences may lead to parallel insights.

However, this should not be taken to imply that we should forever be trying to match the substance and form of an account to the expectations of a given audience. This runs the risk of simply reproducing and reinforcing existing perspectives, rather than challenging and changing them. The point is that unless we pay some attention to these matters, we shall never be in a position to take them into account in a principled and systematic fashion. The relationship between the ethnographer, the ethnography, and the reader will go by default, rather than being constituted as part of the general process of reflexivity.

One of the potential pitfalls consequent on the expectations and capacities of audiences relates to the 'tidying up' of accounts. The average reader of a factual, 'expert', scholarly account, such as a research monograph or learned paper, has certain expectations about its form: it should present a coherent argument and organize the material into a single explanatory framework. Often, however, there is an implicit tension between the aesthetic and rhetorical demands of writing and the ethnographer's own understanding of the research enterprise. Few ethnographies, if any, are presented to the reader as 'interrogative texts' (cf Belsey 1980). Their degree of closure and coherence may nevertheless be at odds with the exploratory, reflexive spirit that informs the research.

Likewise, published accounts often present an unduly 'tidy' version of the research process. It is acceptable to publish autobiographical accounts of the conduct of fieldwork, and a number of such accounts are available (see the annotated bibliography at the end of this book for a selection). One may also present detailed reports of fieldwork practice in theses and similar texts. Such firsthand accounts often have something of a confessional tone to them, whereby the problematic, incomplete, mistaken, dubious, unethical, or uncomfortable aspects of the work are allowed to emerge. Yet these problems are rarely allowed to intrude directly on much of the main ethnographic text. They are often kept at a safe distance from the main 'findings', in an appendix, or in a separate paper. And, on the assumption of the author or the publisher that a general readership will not understand such niceties, will not appreciate their significance, or – worse – will use them to undermine the credibility of the research itself, these are precisely the kinds of issues that get excised from accounts when they are published. Such publishing practices tend to endorse a quite inappropriate distinction between 'methods' and 'findings' in a way that is especially unsympathetic to reflexive ethnography.

Reflecting on texts

We have presented a number of ideal-typical strategies for the organization of ethnographic texts. In general, we have been considering the large-scale organization of major reports, theses, monographs, and so on. At this level, it must be emphasized that few, if any, texts are in fact organized in terms of just one of the strategies we outline. An examination of a representative range of ethnographies will reveal that mixtures of the various styles – and styles that are hard to classify at all – are the norm. Different parts of the text are organized according to different principles.

As we have tried to indicate, there is no one approach to the organization of an ethnographic text that has unquestioned superiority over all others, and that can be recommended as a sure-fire guarantee of success. Moreover, each style brings with it potential pitfalls. Therefore, we do not urge the adoption of one style or another. What we do urge upon ethnographers, however, is an explicit awareness of the possibilities open to them, the various models that may be followed, and the analytic implications of their choices. As we have suggested at various points, the greatest pitfall of all seems to be the uncritical adoption of one approach or another, so that analysis and presentation are not in keeping, or so that the analysis is robbed of freshness by the use of stale textual formats.

In the course of this chapter we have attempted to outline just some considerations in the construction of an ethnography as a piece of writing. We have not attempted to offer prescriptions on 'how to do it'. The reader looking for no more than handy hints here will have been disappointed. (For one of the very few examples of practical advice to potential authors, see Spradley 1979.) Indeed, in advocating this degree of reflexivity we may have made the overall ethnographic project harder rather than easier. However, methodological sophistication is always more demanding than a lack of reflexive awareness, and we offer no apology for apparently complicating these issues.

If there is any practical advice to be formulated at this stage, it is this: be aware of the different organizations that are available for textual arrangements, think about their analytic implications, and on that basis make informed decisions. Any 'pure type' such as we have outlined, is unlikely to be adequate for most practical purposes, and the precise mix of styles will have to be determined by the possibilities and constraints of a given project. By the same token, a critical reading of existing ethnographies is to be encouraged. That is, they should be examined not only for their methodological or substantive contents, but also with a view to how they have been put together, and how their thematic coherence has been achieved. The more one learns to pay explicit attention to such features in the written work of others, the more one will be able to incorporate an informed, reflexive awareness into the production of one's own work. Ideally, such an awareness should form a part of the expertise of the fully trained researcher.

To date we lack a shared interest in such matters within the sociological community, and we also lack the basic work and the shared vocabulary to be able to progress far. To some extent, as we have indicated briefly, this understanding may be fostered by a *rapprochement* between sociologists and literary theorists. To a great extent it will be furthered by critical self-analysis by sociologists themselves. In this chapter we have been able to do little more than to commend such an approach, and to outline some relevant lines of analysis.

A concern for the organization of the written account rests not only on the sort of literary sophistication we have referred to. It also corresponds to a reflexive awareness of everyday or lay competences. It is part of our socialized competence that we are capable of organizing experience into narrative accounts, or stories, that carry their own theoretical messages and assumptions. Ryave, for instance, comments on the import of everyday story-telling:

> 'Conversationalists not only involve themselves in the relating or recounting of some event(s) but are also concerned with expressing the import, relevance, or significance of those events and/or indicating just how this significance can be appreciated in and through the way these events are recounted.'
>
> (Ryave 1979:423–24)

Likewise, Labov and Waletzky (1967), and Labov (1977) have commented on the language skills involved in the production of consequential personal narratives. Members may be more or less accomplished in the production of effective narratives, but in general the construction of these is a normal feature of the way in which everyday experience is ordered, reproduced, and shared. (See also Sacks 1972, on some features of stories.)

Here, then the researcher draws on and develops everyday competences, but, as we have been urging, this should be done in a reflexive manner. To date we have a number of aids in approaching such reflexive accounts, but we still have need of further collective and individual reflection by ethnographers. Without such activity, one of the central activities of all researchers will continue to elude scrutiny.

10

Conclusion

Our motive in writing this book was that, as ethnographers, we were dissatisfied with current accounts of ethnographic methodology. Useful as the many available texts on ethnography are, the guidance they offer is generally couched within methodological frameworks that, in our view, obscure the nature of ethnographic research and, consequently, of social scientific work in general.

We do not claim that, unlike the authors of these other texts, we have privileged access to the true nature of ethnography. In fact, in our view understanding the nature of social science is itself a process of inquiry, and thus at best involves only progress towards the truth with no absolutely conclusive means available for determining when, or if, the destination has been reached. Rather, we felt that existing attempts to conceptualize ethnography methodologically in terms of naturalism or, more rarely, positivism, failed to capture many important features of this kind of research, and distorted others. Also, through the way in which they have come to act as charters for distinct segments of the social science community, these competing paradigms have created barriers to that free flow of communication that is an essential requirement for scientific progress. We feel that the account of the logic of ethnography we provide is an advance over previous ones, but we certainly do not suggest that it is the last word on the subject; nor is it intended to represent a third paradigm.

What we offer is an alternative reconstruction of the logic of ethnography, though one that incorporates many elements from both positivism and naturalism. We start from the notion of reflexivity. This, it will be recalled, requires explicit recognition of the fact that the social researcher, and the research act itself, are part and parcel of the social world under investigation.

Following Mead (1934), we take it that a characteristic feature of human social life is our ability to view ourselves and our practices as objects in the world, and from different perspectives. This constitutes an essential condition for human knowledge. Social science represents an institutionalization of this process of reflexive understanding within the social division of labour. From this, which we take to be a rather banal fact, we draw some important implications for the nature of social science, as well as for the character and practice of ethnography.

Positivism and naturalism draw a sharp distinction between science and common sense, though they give these very different relative statuses. Positivism treats the researcher – by virtue of scientific method – as having access to superior knowledge. The radical naturalist, on the other hand, views the social scientist as incapable of producing valid accounts of events that compete with any provided by the people being studied. The latter must be accepted at face value, or at least treated as embodiments of a rationality that may be described but not endorsed or used.

If we adopt the principle of reflexivity in a thoroughgoing manner, however, this confrontation between those who claim or deny the validity of scientific knowledge by fiat is undercut. Certainly, we have no grounds for dismissing the validity of participant understandings outright: indeed they are a crucial source of knowledge, deriving as they do from experience of the social world. However, they are certainly not immune to assessment, nor to explanation. They must be treated in exactly the same manner as social scientific accounts.

The core element of the notion of reflexivity, then, is that all

social research, and indeed all social life, is founded upon participant observation. This claim is not advanced in the spirit of
methodological or theoretical sectarianism. Quite the reverse:
we are not at all convinced by arguments that suggest there are
necessarily incompatible or incommensurable paradigms of
research. While the concept of reflexivity is fundamental to
symbolic interactionism (Blumer 1969), and while we certainly
draw much from that tradition of thought, we have been at pains
to point out that what many interactionists, and others, assume
to follow from reflexivity – namely the doctrine of naturalism
– does not at all follow: indeed that the implications properly to
be drawn from it are very different. This is a point that has been
illustrated in recent years by recurrent dispute over the nature of
interactionism and its relationship to the thought of George
Herbert Mead, generally regarded as its founder (Bales 1966;
Blumer 1966; Williams 1976; McPhail and Rexroat 1980; Lewis
and Smith 1980; Stryker 1981).

Reflexivity seems to us to be incompatible with the notion of
paradigm as it is often used by social scientists, as representing a
set of theoretical-cum-political assumptions that constitute the
taken-for-granted starting point for inquiry and that cannot be
subjected to rational debate (Friedrichs 1970; Gouldner 1970;
and Harvey 1982). As we have already indicated, for the reflexive
model of inquiry, all knowledge, even that about the nature of
knowledge itself, is a construction on the basis of available evidence and is thus by its very nature fallible. This holds even
though in practice we may treat such knowledge as valid until
further notice, using it as a resource in our inquiries about other
things. Needless to say, this applies to the reflexive model itself.

An important implication of reflexivity, then, is that there
is nothing to be gained, and much to be lost, from setting
up ethnography as an alternative paradigm to quantitative
research. Reflexivity does not rule out the usefulness of quantification, though it does count against the idea, which sometimes seems to underly the practices of quantitative researchers,
that only quantitative data constitute valid knowledge. We have
tried to emphasize throughout that the general methodological
problems that ethnographers face are common to all social
research and, indeed, to practical inquiry in everyday life.
Furthermore, quantitative research offers conceptualizations

of, and strategies for dealing with, problems that can be of use to ethnographers (Evans 1983). Similarly, learning from analytic perspectives other than those of interpretive sociology or anthropology must not be blocked, the differences among theoretical approaches are rarely as fundamental as their protagonists claim, nor must they be treated as beyond argument.

In discussing various aspects of ethnography in this book we have sought to show how the notion of reflexivity can inform its practice. Where positivism has tended to reify certain procedures as 'scientific method', naturalists tend to distrust methodological thinking and discussion as rendering technical what is in fact a matter of everyday social life (Hitchcock 1982), or as attempting to fix what is essentially spontaneous and creative (Rock 1979). However, we need not deny the creative, practical nature of fieldwork and analysis, and their reliance on tacit knowledge, to argue that reflection on our experience of it, both in the field and outside, at the time and much later, can enhance our understanding and practice of ethnography. While there are often practical limits to reflexivity, and while reflection on a problem by no means always produces a solution, reflexivity is, in our view, the key to the development of both theory and methodology in social science generally and in ethnographic work in particular.

To argue, as we have, that science must not be treated as radically distinct from other forms of social activity is not, of course, to deny that it has distinctive features. Clearly, social activity is by no means homogeneous. In fact, one of the distinguishing characteristics of science for us is precisely its reflexive self-consciousness about methodology. While in everyday life we all pay some attention to methodology, to how the knowledge we have was generated, for the most part this occurs only when we run into practical problems, when our anticipations are not fulfilled. In science, by contrast, there is an obligation placed upon practitioners to scrutinize systematically the methodology by which findings, their own and those of others, were produced, and, in particular, to consider how the activities of the researcher may have shaped those findings. Paradoxically, then, reflexivity both underpins the commonality of science and common-sense while at the same time, through variation in its character, marking the one off from the other.

For us, ethnography represents one social research method among others. It is neither 'the only wheel in town' (Webb and Salancik 1966), nor a marginal 'soft' method to be used for illustrating or bolstering the findings of 'hard' experimental or survey research. It has some very definite advantages over other methods, and can be used at any phase of the process of social inquiry. It generates descriptive accounts that are valuable in their own right and it also greatly facilitates the process of theory construction. Ecological validity of the findings produced is probably better on average than that of other methods, and the diversity of data sources allows triangulation, enabling some check on, and perhaps control over, the effects of various aspects of the research process on the data. On the other hand, like all methods, ethnography also has important limitations: it cannot be used to study past events; its ability to discriminate among rival hypotheses is weak by comparison with the experiment; and, in contrast to the social survey, it is poor at dealing with large-scale cases such as big organizations or national societies.

It is perhaps too much to expect that every social scientist should become proficient in all research methods. What is important, though, is that we overcome the paradigmatic mentality and reconstruct a social science community in which work using different methods combines to further collective understanding of the social world. We believe that the principle of reflexivity provides a basis for doing this, and it is to this goal that our book is dedicated.

Annotated bibliography
of ethnographic texts

There is now a considerable, if rather poorly co-ordinated, literature on ethnographic method. We hope that this annotated bibliography will provide a useful map for travellers in this area. It is, however, severely limited in scope, covering only textbooks and collections of articles and not papers published in journals or 'natural histories' of research included as methodological appendices in research monographs. Also, of course, the annotations are simply our opinions, based on the general methodological perspective outlined in this book.

Adams, R.N. and Preiss, J.J. (eds) (1960) *Human Organization Research: Field Relations and Techniques*. Homewood, Ill.: Dorsey Press.
    Now a little dated but it includes several classic articles not easily available elsewhere such as Rosalie Wax on 'reciprocity in fieldwork' and Richardson on reporting field relationships.
Adelman, C. (ed.) (1981) *Uttering, Muttering: Collecting, Using and Reporting Talk for Social and Educational Research*. London: Grant McIntyre.
    As the sub-title indicates, this is a set of papers discussing various aspects of the treatment of talk in social, and especially educational, research.
Agar, M. (1980) *The Professional Stranger*. New York: Academic Press.
    A rather idiosyncratic view of ethnography; strong on the techniques that Agar has used extensively, especially formal semantics elic-

itation techniques. Has some interesting remarks on the funding of ethnographic research and the drafting of research proposals.

Bell, C. and Newby, H. (eds) (1977) *Doing Sociological Research.* London: Allen & Unwin.

A collection of personal accounts of sociological research, several of them ethnographic. Notable in particular for bringing out the political conflict, and the possibility of legal action, sometimes involved in social research.

Berreman, G. (1962) *Behind Many Masks: Ethnography and Impression Management in a Himalayan Village.* Monograph No. 4. Ithaca, New York: Society for Applied Anthropology, Cornell University.

An account of Berreman's research on the inhabitants of a North Indian village, focusing on the way in which his data were affected by the villagers' attempts to exercise control over the information available to him. Berreman only realized that impression management was taking place when he changed interpreters and noticed a change in the character of the data he was collecting. A classic account of very general relevance.

Bogdan, R. and Taylor, S. (1975) *Introduction to Qualitative Research Methods: A Phenomenological Approach to the Social Sciences.* New York: Wiley.

Covers basic issues in qualitative research, including life history interviewing, and presents useful extended examples from the authors' own studies. Offers relatively little by way of methodological sophistication.

Bowen, E. (1954) *Return to Laughter.* London: Gollancz.

A fictionalized account of Laura Bohannon's experiences as an anthropologist in Africa. A nice autobiographical account of issues such as 'culture shock'.

Brim, J.A. and Spain, D.H. (1974) *Research Design in Anthropology: Paradigms and Pragmatics in the Testing of Hypotheses.* New York: Holt, Rinehart & Winston.

Concerned solely with research design and of a strongly positivist cast. Illuminating none the less.

Bruyn, S.T. (1966) *The Human Perspective: The Methodology of Participant Observation.* Englewood Cliffs, NJ: Prentice-Hall.

Generally regarded as something of a classic. Very much an 'anti-positivist' text. Deals with broad theoretical issues underlying qualitative research. Has little to say on research methods and strategies at a more practical level.

Bulmer, M. (ed.) (1982) *Social Research Ethics: An Examination of the Merits of Covert Participant Observation.* London: Macmillan.

A useful collection of papers relating to just this one aspect of field research. Includes sharp debates of the ethics of several research projects that involved secret participant observation.

Burgess, R. (ed.) (1982) *Field Research: A Sourcebook and Field Manual.* London: Allen & Unwin.

The title is a misnomer since it is not in any sense a practical field manual. Nevertheless, a useful collection of materials drawn from sociology, anthropology, and history, and mixing British and American papers. The editor contributes some good editorial essays to various sections of the book and equally valuable annotated bibliographies.

Cook, T.D. and Reichardt, C.S. (eds) (1979) *Qualitative and Quantitative Methods in Evaluation Research*. Beverley Hills, Calif.: Sage.
A collection of articles for the most part concerned with the relationship between quantitative and qualitative methods. It includes articles by Becker, Campbell, and Filstead. While specifically about evaluation research, many of the issues apply equally to theoretical research.

Denzin, N.K. (1978) *The Research Act: A Theoretical Introduction to Sociological Methods*. New York: McGraw-Hill.
Discusses social research methods in the light of symbolic interactionist theory at a fairly abstract level. Places considerable faith in the value of triangulation, especially between methods. A classic attempt to reintegrate ethnography into mainstream methodology.

_____ (1978) *Sociological Methods*. New York: McGraw-Hill.
A companion volume of readings to *The Research Act*, the selection of papers reflecting its spirit and themes.

Douglas, J. D. (1976) *Investigative Social Research*, Beverley Hills, Calif.: Sage.
Offers a very distinctive and controversial approach to fieldwork methods especially from the point of view of ethics. Suggests a 'conflict' paradigm of field research, modelled on investigative journalism, and opposed to what Douglas sees as the consensus paradigm underlying much ethnography. Interesting on deception as a feature of fieldwork in contemporary society, and makes some useful points about team research. Superficial on many other aspects, and cavalier in its treatment of philosophical issues.

_____ (ed.) (1972) *Research on Deviance*. New York: Random House.
A worthwhile collection of accounts of methodological problems arising in ethnographic research on deviance, though the discussions are of more general relevance.

Epstein, A. L. (ed.) (1967) *The Craft of Social Anthropology*. London: Tavistock.
One of the very few discussions of methodological issues to be found in the British anthropological literature, deriving from the work of the Manchester School, inspired by Max Gluckman. Combines interest in both qualitative and quantitative techniques. See in particular the discussion of the 'extended case method' by van Velsen.

Filstead, W.J. (ed.) (1970) *Qualitative Methodology: Firsthand Involvement with the Social World*. Chicago, Ill.: Markham.
A more or less standard collection of papers. Includes sections on fieldwork roles, collection of data, analysis, problems of validity and reliability, ethics, methodology, and theory. Like all such readers, a useful resource, but fails to add up to a coherent view.

Freilich, M. (ed.) (1970) *Marginal Natives: Anthropologists at Work*. New York: Harper & Row.
A collection of accounts of fieldwork experience by North American anthropologists. Of varying interest; perhaps most striking is Freilich's own report of his research on Mohawk Indians in New York.

Georges, R.A. and Jones, M.O. (1980) *People Studying People: The Human Element in Fieldwork*. Berkeley, Calif.: University of California Press.
A rather strange little book on field relations that strings together many interesting anecdotes.

Glaser, B.G. (1978) *Theoretical Sensitivity*. San Francisco, Calif.: The Sociology Press.
A clarification and development of several themes in Glaser and Strauss's *The Discovery of Grounded Theory*, in particular theoretical sampling, coding, and analytic memo writing. Gives a good sense of what 'grounded theorizing' is like in practice, but still leaves some important questions unanswered, notably those surrounding theory testing.

Glaser, B. G. and Strauss, A.S. (1967) *The Discovery of Grounded Theory*. Chicago, Ill.: Aldine.
Classic discussion of the importance of and techniques for generating theory. Includes a discussion of 'theoretical sampling' and 'the constant comparative method'. While there are some highly questionable aspects of Glaser and Strauss's 'grounded theorizing' (notably the relationship between theory development and validation), there is no doubting the importance of their emphasis on theory development and the value of some of their heuristic techniques.

Glazer, M. (1972) *The Research Adventure: Promise and Problems of Field Work*. New York: Random House.
A discussion of various aspects of field relations drawing on the author's experience of doing research in Chile, and also his personal communications with many other researchers including Whyte and Liebow.

Golde, P. (ed.) (1970) *Women in the Field: Anthropological Experiences*. Chicago, Ill.: Aldine.
The experience of women fieldworkers is one case where the identity of the researcher has been treated as explicitly problematic. Gender is normally treated explicitly only as it relates to women; in this literature as in most others, men's identity is taken for granted. This book raises the issue clearly through first-hand accounts.

Green, J. and Wallat, C. (eds) (1981) *Ethnography and Language in Educational Settings* Volume V in R.O. Freedle (ed.) *Advances in Discourse Processes*. Norwood, NJ: Ablex.
An interesting set of papers, for the most part discussing methodological issues arising in research on classroom interaction. Most striking perhaps is Corsaro's account of his research on nursery school children.

Habenstein, R. (ed.) (1970) *Pathways to Data*. Chicago, Ill.: Aldine.
A collection of first-hand accounts, including some derived from major ethnographic studies, with particular emphasis on occupational, professional, and organizational research.

Hammersley, M. (ed.) (1983) *The Ethnography of Schooling: Methodological Issues*. Driffield: Nafferton.
Contains articles discussing a variety of methodological issues in ethnography, including field relations, the merits of observation versus interviewing, and the relationship between ethnography and other traditions such as conversational analysis and quantitative methodology. Deals with research on educational contexts, but the discussions have wider relevance.

Hammond, P.E. (ed.) (1964) *Sociologists at Work*. New York: Basic Books.
Essays on the conduct of eleven major North American studies, including several accounts of ethnographic projects: see in particular the contributions by Geer, Dalton, Riesman, and Fox.

Henry, F. and Saberwal, S. (eds) (1969) *Stress and Response in Fieldwork*. New York: Holt, Rinehart & Winston.
Five essays on the psychological aspects of fieldwork. Not always sophisticated in terms of sociological methods, but very worthwhile if only because this is an otherwise neglected topic in the literature.

Honigmann, J.J. (ed.) (1979) *Handbook of Social and Cultural Anthropology*. Chicago, Ill.: Rand McNally.
Huge collection of long essays covering various aspects of social and cultural anthropology (mostly North American), including methodology.

Jacobs, G. (ed.) (1970) *The Participant Observer*. New York: George Braziller.
Contains papers deriving from some well-known studies (such as Polsky on pool-room hustlers). Not organized in terms of methodological themes and issues, though the articles are interesting to read in their own right.

Johnson, J.M. (1976) *Doing Field Research*, New York: Free Press.
A readable account of many aspects of ethnographic method. Focuses particularly on the personal side of doing fieldwork, drawing heavily on the author's own experience.

Jongmans, D.G. and Gutkind, P.C.W. (eds) (1967) *Anthropologists in the Field*. Assen: van Gorcum.
An interesting collection of discussions of various aspects of anthropological fieldwork, for the most part through personal accounts of particular pieces of research. Includes Leach's 'reflections on a social survey'; Vansina on 'history in the field'; and Barnes on ethical problems.

Junker, B. (1960) *Field Work*. Chicago, Ill.: University of Chicago Press.
A particularly interesting, if little cited, book based on the author's investigations of the teaching and practice of ethnographic tech-

niques in the Department of Sociology at the University of Chicago. Includes some fascinating extracts from the fieldnotes of, amongst others, Everett Hughes.

Kaplan, A. (1964) *The Conduct of Inquiry: Methodology for Behavioral Science*. San Francisco, Calif.: Chandler.
In our view the best general philosophical account of social science methodology. A quite excellent book. Well worth reading in toto.

Lofland, J. (1971) *Analyzing Social Settings: A Guide to Qualitative Observation, and Analysis*. Belmont, Calif.: Wadsworth.
A brief and accessible guide to the conduct of ethnography, though patchy in its treatment. Poor on general methodological issues but strong on practical issues such as analysis and data collection, storage, and retrieval. A very useful treatment, thoroughly illustrated with examples.

_____ (1976) *Doing Social Life: The Qualitative Study of Human Interaction in Natural Settings*. New York: Wiley.
Takes the investigation of interactional strategies as the major focus of qualitative research. The methodological introduction is rather scrappy and disappointing, although it contains an all too rare, if brief, section on 'reporting an inquiry'. Second section provides handy extended examples from published sources.

Manners, R.A. and Kaplan, D. (eds) (1969) *Theory in Anthropology*. London: Routledge & Kegan Paul.
Contains over fifty papers covering major areas of anthropological interest, with strong emphasis on methodological and conceptual issues. Excellent overview of major authors and developments in the discipline; not particularly recommended for practical methodological advice.

McCall, G.J. and Simmons, J.L. (eds) (1969) *Issues in Participant Observation: A Text and Reader*. Reading, Mass.: Addison-Wesley.
A classic text which includes a selection of readings many of which, though now a bit dated, continue to be standard references. Areas covered: field relations, data collection, recording and retrieval, the quality of data, generation of hypotheses, evaluation of hypotheses, publication of results, and comparison of methods. For the most part, the focus is the discussion of methodological issues rather than the giving of practical advice, and the authors' standpoint verges on the positivist, though the book is none the worse for that.

Naroll, R. and Cohen, R. (1973) *A Handbook of Method in Cultural Anthropology*. New York: Columbia University Press.
Very extensive collection of articles on method and methodology in anthropology, with a good deal of emphasis on quantitative approaches.

Payne, G., Dingwall, R., Payne, J., and Carter, M. (1981) *Sociology and Social Research*. London: Routledge & Kegan Paul.
A rather inconsistent text covering a wide range of topics. Has some interesting sections on ethnography, though nothing approaching a systematic account.

Pelto, P.J. and Pelto, G.H. (1978) *Anthropological Research: The Structure of Inquiry*. Cambridge: Cambridge University Press.
Very good discussion of method in cultural anthropology. Considerable stress on measurement and quantification. Useful discussion of the 'new ethnography' (componential analysis, etc.). Good example of how anthropologists are quite happy to draw on a full range of available methods rather than becoming unduly involved in doctrinaire methodological disputes.

Powdermaker, H. (1966) *Stranger and Friend: The Way of an Anthropologist*. New York: Norton.
Autobiographical account of research in four settings: Lesu, Mississippi, Hollywood, and Northern Rhodesia.

Rynkiewich, M. and Spradley, J.P. (eds) (1976) *Ethics and Anthropology:Dilemmas in Fieldwork*. New York: Wiley.
Discussions of political and ethical issues as they arose in particular anthropological studies. Rather uneven in quality.

Shaffir, W.B., Stebbins, R.A., and Turowetz, A. (eds) (1980) *Fieldwork Experience: Qualitative Approaches to Social Research*. New York: St Martins Press.
A useful collection of personal accounts of fieldwork. For the most part the authors discuss their research in relation to methodological issues rather than simply 'telling it like it was'. A handy complement to older accounts of the ethnographic experience.

Schatzman, L. and Strauss, A. (1973) *Field Research: Strategies for a Natural Sociology*. Englewood Cliffs, NJ: Prentice-Hall.
A brief, readable, and engaging account of most aspects of fieldwork. Draws heavily on the authors' own research experience and is particularly pertinent to the ethnography of organizational settings. Recommended as an initial introduction to the field.

Schwartz, H. and Jacobs, J. (1979) *Qualitative Sociology: A Method to the Madness*. New York: Free Press.
A long, somewhat disorganized book. Contains some interesting observations on the 'reconstruction of reality' and a useful discussion of disruptive research techniques. Valuable for its emphasis on formal sociological concepts and theories.

Spindler, G.D. (ed.) (1970) *Being an Anthropologist: Fieldwork in Eleven Cultures*. New York: Holt, Rinehart & Winston.
Precisely what the title says: a collection of first-hand accounts of research by eleven cultural anthropologists.

_____ (ed.) (1982) *Doing the Ethnography of Schooling: Educational Anthropology in Action*. New York: Holt, Rinehart & Winston.
A collection of articles discussing various theoretical and methodological issues arising out of anthropological research on educational institutions in the United States. The focus varies from the micro-ethnography of the classroom to the more traditional school and community approach.

Spradley, J.P. (1980) *Participant Observation*. New York: Holt, Rinehart & Winston.

_____ (1979) *The Ethnographic Interview*. New York: Holt, Rinehart & Winston.

These two books by Spradley are very similar, both following the same step-by-step formula in the research process. In some ways excellent for their clarity, practicality, and systematic treatment of a range of techniques. Many readers will, however, find the model of culture and social life underlying them over-simplified.

Spradley, J. P. and McCurdy, D.W. (eds) (1972) *The Cultural Experience: Ethnography in Complex Society*. Chicago, Ill.: Science Research Associates.

Consists primarily of reports of ethnographic projects undertaken by students following the sort of methods advocated in the two Spradley books discussed above. Has the same limitations, but handy demonstrations of how much (and how little) can be achieved and written up in a brief ethnographic exercise as opposed to the long-term projects usually reported in the literature.

Vidich, A.J., Bensman, J., and Stein, M.R. (eds) (1964) *Reflections on Community Studies*. New York: Harper & Row.

One of the earliest collections of personal accounts of research and still among the best. Includes Whyte's methodological appendix to Streetcorner Society and an account of the Springdale controversy.

Wax, R.H. (1971) *Doing Fieldwork: Warnings and Advice*. Chicago, Ill.: University of Chicago Press.

Useful sketch of the history of ethnographic method, followed by accounts of Wax's research in three different contexts. Full of good sense and engagingly presented.

Webb, S. and Webb, B. (1932) *Methods of Social Study*. London: Longmans, Green.

One of the first methods texts. Still of some interest, especially the chapter on 'the art of note-taking'.

References

Adelman, C. (1977) On First Hearing. In C. Adelman (ed.) *Uttering, Muttering: Collecting, Using and Reporting Talk for Social and Educational Research*. London: Grant McIntyre.

Agar, M. (1973) *Ripping and Running: A Formal Ethnography of Urban Heroin Addicts*. New York: Seminar Press.

_____ (1980) *Professional Stranger*. New York: Academic Press.

Almeder, R. (1980) *The Philosophy of Charles S. Peirce: A Critical Introduction*. Oxford: Blackwell.

Altheide, D. (1976) *Creating Reality: How TV News Distorts Events*. Beverley Hills, Calif.: Sage.

Arensberg, C.M. and Kimball, S.T. (1968) *Family and Community in Ireland*. Cambridge, Mass.: Harvard University Press. (First published 1940.)

Atkinson, P. (1976) 'The Clinical Experience: An Ethnography of Medical Education.' Unpublished PhD thesis, University of Edinburgh.

_____ (1981a) *The Clinical Experience*. Farnborough: Gower.

_____ (1981b) Transition from School to Working Life. Sociological Research Unit, Cardiff: unpublished memorandum.

_____ and Heath, C. (eds) (1981) *Medical Work: Realities and Routines*. Farnborough: Gower.

Bacon, F. (1960) *The New Organon or True Directions Concerning the Interpretation of Nature*. Indianapolis, Ind.: Bobbs-Merrill. First published 1620.

Bales, R.F. (1966) Comment on Herbert Blumer's Paper. *American Journal of Sociology* **LXXI**:545–47.

Ball, S.J. (1980) Initial Encounters in the Classroom and the Process of Establishment. In P. Woods (ed.) *Pupil Strategies*. London: Croom Helm.

_____ (1981) *Beachside Comprehensive*. London: Cambridge University Press.

_____ (1982) 'Beachside Reconsidered: Reflections on a Methodological Apprenticeship'. Paper given at a conference on The Ethnography of Educational Settings, March 1982, Whitelands College, London.

_____ (1983) Case Study Research in Education: Some Notes and Problems. In M. Hammersley (ed.) *The Ethnography of Schooling: Methodological Issues*. Driffield: Nafferton.

Barbera-Stein, L. (1979) 'Access Negotiations: Comments on the Sociology of the Sociologist's Knowledge'. Paper presented at the Seventy-Fourth Annual Meeting of the American Sociological Association, August 1979, Boston.

Barrett, R.A. (1974) *Benabarre: The Modernization of a Spanish Village*. New York: Holt, Rinehart & Winston.

Barzun, J. and Graff, H. (1970) *The Modern Researcher*. New York: Harcourt, Brace & World.

Beattie, J. (1965) *Bunyoro: An African Kingdom*. New York: Holt, Rinehart & Winston.

Becker, H.S. (1953) Becoming a Marihuana User. *American Journal of Sociology* **59**:41–58.

_____ (1967) Whose Side Are We On. *Social Problems* **14**:239–47.

_____ (1967) Comment reported in R.J. Hill and K. Stones Crittenden. (eds) *Proceedings of the Purdue Symposium on Ethnomethodology*. Institute for the Study of Social Change, Department of Sociology, Purdue University.

_____ (1970) Life History and the Scientific Mosaic. In *Sociological Work*. Chicago, Ill.: Aldine.

_____ (1971) Footnote to M. Wax and R. Wax, Great Tradition, Little Tradition, and Formal Education. In M. Wax, S. Diamond, and F. Gearing (eds) *Anthropological Perspectives on Education*. New York: Basic Books.

_____ (1974) Art as Collective Social Action. *American Sociological Review* **39**:767–76.

Becker, H. S. and Geer, B. (1957) Participant Observation and Interviewing: A Comparison. *Human Organization* **XVI**:28–34.

_____ (1960) Participant Observation: The Analysis of Qualitative Field Data. In R.N. Adams and J.J. Preiss (eds) *Human Organization Research: Field Relations and Techniques*. Homewood, Ill.: Dorsey Press.

Becker, H .S., Geer, B., Hughes, E.C., and Strauss, A.L. (1961) *Boys in*

White: Student Culture in Medical School. Chicago, Ill.: University of Chicago Press.

Belsey, C. (1980) *Critical Practice.* London: Methuen.

Benney, M. and Hughes, E. (1956) Of Sociology and the Interview. *American Journal of Sociology* 61:137–42.

Bensman, J. and Vidich, A. (1960) Social Theory in Field Research, *American Journal of Sociology* 65:577–84.

Berlak, A.C., Berlak, H., Bagenstos, N.T., and Mikel, E.R. (1975) Teaching and Learning in English Primary Schools. *School Review* 83(2):215–43.

Berreman, G. (1962) *Behind Many Masks: Ethnography and Impression Management in a Himalayan Village.* Monograph 4. Society for Applied Anthropology, Ithaca, NY: Cornell University Press.

Bettelheim, B. (1970) *The Informed Heart.* London: Paladin.

Beynon, J. (1983) Ways-In and Staying-In: Fieldwork as Problem Solving. In M. Hammersley (ed.) *The Ethnography of Schooling: Methodological Issues.* Driffield: Nafferton.

Bigus, O.E. (1972) The Milkman and His Customer: A Cultivated Relationship. *Urban Life and Culture* 1:131–65.

Bloor, M. (1978) On the Analysis of Observational Data: A Discussion of the Worth and Uses of Inductive Techniques and Respondent Validation. *Sociology* 12(3):545–52.

Blumer, H. (1954) What is Wrong with Social Theory? *American Sociological Review* 19:3–10

_____ (1966) Reply to Bales. *American Journal of Sociology* LXXI:545–47.

_____ (1969) *Symbolic Interactionism.* Englewood Cliffs, NJ: Prentice-Hall.

Bogdan, R. and Taylor, S. (1975) *Introduction to Qualitative Research Methods.* New York: Wiley.

Bohannon, P. (1981) Unseen Community: The Natural History of a Research Project. In D.A. Messerschmidt (ed.) *Anthropologists at Home in North America: Methods and Issues in the Study of One's Own Society.* Cambridge: Cambridge University Press.

Booth, C. (1902–03) *Life and Labour of the People in London.* London: Macmillan.

Borhek, J.T. and Curtis, R.F. (1975) *A Sociology of Belief.* New York: Wiley.

Bowen, E. (1954) *Return to Laughter.* London: Gollancz.

Bracht, G.H. and Glass, G.U. (1968) The External Validity of Experiments. *American Educational Research Journal* 5:537–74.

Brown, R.H. (1977) *A Poetic for Sociology: Toward a Logic of Discovery for the Human Sciences.* Cambridge: Cambridge University Press.

Brunswik, E.C. (1956) *Perception and the Representative Design of Psychological Experiments.* Berkeley, Calif.: University of California Press.

Bulmer, M. (1979) Concepts in the Analysis of Qualitative Data. *Sociological Review* 27(4):651–79.

_____ (1980) Why Don't Sociologists Make More Use of Official Statistics? *Sociology* **14**(4):505-23.

_____ (ed.) (1982) *Social Research Ethics: An Examination of the Merits of Covert Participant Observation*. London: Macmillan.

Burke, K. (1936) *Permanence and Change*. New York: New Republic.

_____ (1964) *Perspectives by Incongruity*. Bloomington, Ind.: Indiana University Press.

Carey, J.T. (1972) Problems of Access and Risk in Observing Drug Scenes. In J.D. Douglas (ed.) *Research on Deviance*. New York: Random House.

Chagnon, N.A. (1977) (Second edn) *Yanomamö: The Fierce People*. New York: Holt, Rinehart & Winston.

Chambliss, W. (1975) On the Paucity of Original Research on Organized Crime. *American Sociologist* **10**:36-9.

Chomsky, N. (1968) *Language and Mind*. New York: Harcourt, Brace & World.

Cicourel, Aaron (1976) (Second edn.) *The Social Organization of Juvenile Justice*. London: Heinemann.

_____ and Kitsuse, J. (1963) *The Educational Decision Makers*. New York: Bobbs-Merrill.

Cohen, P.S. (1980) Is Positivism Dead? *Sociological Review* **28**(1):141-76.

Corsaro, W.A. (1981) Entering the Child's World – Research Strategies for Field Entry and Data Collection in a Preschool Setting. In J.L. Green and C. Wallat. *Ethnography and Language in Educational Settings*. Norwood, NJ: Ablex.

Cressey, D. (1950) The Criminal Violation of Financial Trust. *American Sociological Review* **15**:738-43.

Cronbach, L.J. (1975) Beyond the Two Disciplines of Scientific Psychology. *American Psychologist* February: 116-27.

Crowle, A.J. (1976) The Deceptive Language of the Laboratory. In R. Harré (ed.) *Life Sentences: Aspects of the Social Role of Language*. London: Wiley.

Culler, J. (1975) *Structuralist Poetics*. London: Routledge & Kegan Paul.

_____ (1981a) *The Pursuit of Signs*. London: Routledge & Kegan Paul.

_____ (1981b) Fiction, Freud and the Practice of Theory. *Times Higher Education Supplement* 14 July: 11.

Curtis, J.E. and Petras, J.W. (1970) *The Sociology of Knowledge*. London: Duckworth.

Dalton, M. (1959) *Men Who Manage: Fusions of Feeling and Theory in Administration*. New York: Wiley.

Davis, A. and Horobin, G. (eds) (1977) *Medical Encounters: The Experience of Illness and Treatment*. London: Croom Helm.

Davis, F. (1959) The Cab-Driver and his Fare: Facets of a Fleeting Relationship. *American Journal of Sociology* **65**(2):158-65.

_____ (1961) Deviance Disavowal: The Management of Strained Interaction by the Visibly Handicapped. *Social Problems* **I**:120-32.

_____ (1963) *Passage Through Crisis: Polio Victims and their*

Families. Indianapolis, Ind.: Bobbs-Merrill.

_____ (1973) The Martian and the Convert: Ontological Polarities in Sociological Research. *Urban Life and Culture* 2:333–43.

_____ (1974) Stories and Sociology, *Urban Life and Culture* 3(3):310–16.

Davis, N. J. (1974) The Abortion Consumer: Making it Through the Network. *Urban Life and Culture* 2(4):432–59.

Dean, J.P. and Whyte, W.F. (1958) How Do You Know if the Informant is Telling the Truth? *Human Organization* 17:34–8.

Dean, J. P., Eichorn, R.L., and Dean, L.R. (1967) Fruitful Informants for Intensive Interviewing. In J.T. Doby (ed.) (Second edn) *An Introduction to Social Research*. New York: Appleton-Century-Crofts.

Den Hollander, A.N.J. (1967) Social Description: Problems of Reliability and Validity. In D.G. Jongmans and P.C.W. Gutkind (eds) *Anthropologists in the Field*. Assen, Netherlands: Van Gorcum.

Denzin, N.K. (1971) The Logic of Naturalistic Inquiry. *Social Forces* 50:166–82.

_____ (1978) (Second edn) *The Research Act: A Theoretical Introduction to Sociological Methods*. New York: McGraw-Hill.

Deutscher, I. (1973) *What We Say/What We Do: Sentiments and Acts*. Glenview, Ill.: Scott Foresman.

Dexter, L. (1970) *Elite and Specialized Interviewing*. Evanston, Ill.: Northwestern University Press.

Diesing, P. (1972) *Patterns of Discovery in the Social Sciences*. London: Routledge & Kegan Paul.

Dingwall, R. (1977a) Atrocity Stories and Professional Relationships. *Sociology of Work and Occupations* 4(4):371–96.

_____ (1977b) *The Social Organization of Health Visitor Training*. London: Croom Helm.

_____ (1981) Practical Ethnography. In G. Payne, R. Dingwall, J. Payne, and M. Carter (eds) *Sociology and Social Research*. London: Routledge & Kegan Paul.

Ditton, J. (1977) *Part-Time Crime: An Ethnography of Fiddling and Pilferage*. London: Macmillan.

Dollard, J. (1937) (Third edn) *Caste and Class in a Southern Town*. New Haven, Conn.: Yale University Press.

Douglas, J. (1967) *The Social Meanings of Suicide*. Princeton, NJ: Princeton University Press.

_____ (1976) *Investigative Social Research*. Beverley Hills, Calif.: Sage.

Drass, K.A. (1980) The Analysis of Qualitative Data: A Computer Program. *Urban Life* 9(3):332–53.

Easterday, L., Papademas, D., Schorr, L., and Valentine, C. (1977) The Making of a Female Researcher. *Urban Life* 6(3):333–48.

Edgerton, R.B. (1965) Some Dimensions of Disillusionment in Culture Contact. *Southwestern Journal of Anthropology* 21:231–43.

Einstein, A. (1970) *Out of My Later Years*. Westport, Conn.: Greenwood Press.

Evans, J. (1983) Criteria of Validity in Social Research: Exploring the

Relationship between Ethnographic and Quantitative Approaches. In M. Hammersley (ed.) *The Ethnography of Schooling: Methodological Issues*. Driffield: Nafferton.

Everhart, R.B. (1977) Between Stranger and Friend: Some Consequences of 'Long Term' Fieldwork in Schools. *American Educational Research Journal* 14(1):1–15.

Festinger, L., RIECKEN, H., and SCHACHTER, S. (1956) *When Prophecy Fails*. University of Minnesota Press. (Republished 1964 London: Harper & Row.)

Fielding, N. (1982) Observational Research on the National Front. In M. Bulmer (ed.) *Social Research Ethics: An Examination of the Merits of Covert Participant Observation*. London: Macmillan.

Finestone, H. (1967) Cats, Kicks and Colour. *Social Problems* 5:3–13.

Fox, R.C. (1964) An American Sociologist in the Land of Belgian Medical Research. In P.E. Hammond (ed.) *Sociologists at Work: Essays on the Craft of Social Research*. New York: Basic Books.

Freilich, M. (1970) Mohawk Heroes and Trinidadian Peasants. In M. Freilich (ed.) *Marginal Natives: Anthropologists at Work*. New York: Harper & Row.

—— (ed.) (1970) *Marginal Natives: Anthropologists at Work*. New York: Harper & Row.

Friedrichs, R.W. (1970) *A Sociology of Sociology*. New York: Free Press.

Gamst, F.C. (1980) *The Hoghead: An Industrial Ethnology of the Locomotive Engineer*. New York: Holt, Rinehart & Winston.

Garfinkel, A. (1981) *Forms of Explanation*. New Haven, Conn.: Yale University Press.

Garfinkel, H. (1967) *Studies in Ethnomethodology*. Englewood Cliffs, NJ: Prentice-Hall.

Geer, B. (1964) First Days in the Field. In P. Hammond (ed.) *Sociologists at Work*. New York: Basic Books.

—— (1970) Studying a College. In R. Habenstein (ed.) *Pathways to Data*. Chicago, Ill.: Aldine.

George, V. and Dundes, A. (1978) The Gomer: A Figure of American Hospital Folk Speech. *Journal of American Folklore* 91(359):568–81.

Giallombardo, R. (1966) Social Roles in a Prison for Women. *Social Problems* 13:268–88.

Giddens, A. (1979) Positivism and its Critics. In T. Bottomore and R. Nisbet (eds) *A History of Sociological Analysis*. London: Heinemann.

Glaser, B. (1978) *Theoretical Sensitivity*. San Francisco, Calif.: The Sociology Press.

Glaser, B. and Strauss, A. (1964) Awareness Contexts and Social Interaction. *American Sociological Review* XXIX: 669–79.

—— (1967) *The Discovery of Grounded Theory*. Chicago, Ill.: Aldine.

—— (1968) *Time for Dying*. Chicago, Ill.: Aldine.

—— (1971) *Status Passage*. Chicago, Ill.: Aldine.

Goffman, E. (1955) On Face-Work: An Analysis of Ritual Elements in Social Interaction. *Psychiatry* **18**(3):213–31.

_____ (1959) *The Presentation of Self in Everyday Life*. New York: Doubleday.

_____ (1961) *Asylums: Essays on the Social Situation of Mental Patients and Other Inmates*. New York: Doubleday.

_____ (1963) *Behaviour in Public Places*. Glencoe, Ill.: Free Press.

_____ (1971) *Relations in Public: Micro Studies of the Public Order*. New York: Basic Books.

_____ (1972) *Interaction Ritual*. Harmondsworth: Penguin.

Gold, R.L. (1958) Roles in Sociological Fieldwork. *Social Forces* **36**:217–23.

Golde, P. (ed.) (1970) *Women in the Field: Anthropological Experiences*. Chicago, Ill.: Aldine.

Goode, W.J. and Hatt, P.K. (1952) *Methods in Social Research*. New York: McGraw-Hill.

Gorbutt, D. (1972) The New Sociology of Education. *Education for Teaching* **89** Autumn: 3–11.

Gouldner, A.W. (1954) *Patterns of Industrial Bureaucracy*. New York: Free Press.

_____ (1968) The Sociologist as Partisan. *American Sociologist* May: 103–16.

_____ (1970) *The Coming Crisis of Western Sociology*. New York: Basic Books.

Gregor, T. (1977) *Mehinaku: The Drama of Daily Life in a Brazilian Indian Village*. Chicago, Ill.: University of Chicago Press.

Gregory, R. (1970) *The Intelligent Eye*. London: Weidenfeld and Nicolson.

Guba, E. (1978) *Toward a Methodology of Naturalistic Inquiry in Educational Evaluation*. Los Angeles, Calif.: Center for the Study of Evaluation, UCLA Graduate School of Education.

Gumperz, J. (1981) Conversational Inference and Classroom Learning. In J.L. Green and C. Wallat (eds) *Ethnography and Language in Educational Settings*. Norwood, NJ: Ablex.

Hammersley, M. (1980) 'A Peculiar World? Teaching and Learning in an Inner City School'. PhD thesis, University of Manchester (unpublished).

_____ (ed.) (1983a) *The Ethnography of Schooling: Methodological Issues*. Driffield: Nafferton.

_____ (1983b) Introduction: Reflexivity and Naturalism. In M. Hammersley (ed.) *The Ethnography of Schooling: Methodological Issues*. Driffield: Nafferton.

_____ (1983c) 'The Researcher Exposed: A Natural History'. In Robert G. Burgess (ed.) *The Research Process in Educational Settings*. Lewes: Falmer

_____ (1984) Interpretive Sociology and the Macro-Micro Problem. In *Conflict and Change in Education: A Sociological Perspective*, Unit 16, Open University Course E205. Milton Keynes: Open University.

Hannerz, U. (1969) *Soulside*. New York: Columbia University Press.

Hansen, E.C. (1977) *Rural Catalonia Under the Franco Regime*. Cambridge: Cambridge University Press.

Hanson, N.R. (1958) *Patterns of Discovery*. London: Cambridge University Press.

Hargreaves, A. (1981) Contrastive Rhetoric and Extremist Talk: Teachers, Hegemony and the Educationist Context. In L. Barton and S. Walker (eds) *Schools, Teachers and Teaching*. Lewes: Falmer.

Hargreaves, D.H. (1967) *Social Relations in a Secondary School*. London: Routledge & Kegan Paul.

_____ (1977) The Process of Typification in the Classroom: Models and Methods. *British Journal of Educational Psychology* 47:274–84.

Hargreaves, D. H., Hesterr S., and Mellor, F. (1975) *Deviance in Classrooms*. London: Routledge & Kegan Paul.

Harré, R. and Secord, P.F. (1972) *The Explanation of Social Behaviour*. Oxford: Blackwell.

Harris, M. (1979) *Cultural Materialism: The Struggle for a Science of Culture*. New York: Random House.

Hartshorne, C. and Weiss, P. (eds) (1931–35) *The Collected Papers of Charles Sanders Peirce*. Cambridge, Mass: Harvard University Press.

Harvey, L. (1982) 'Chicago School Mythology'. Department of Sociology, Birmingham Polytechnic: unpublished paper.

Hawkes, T. (1977) *Structuralism and Semiotics*. London: Methuen.

Heath, C. (1981) The Opening Sequence in Doctor-Patient Interaction. In P. Atkinson and C. Heath (eds) *Medical Work: Realities and Routines*. Farnborough: Gower.

Hewitt, J.P. and Stokes, R. (1976) Aligning Actions. *American Sociological Review* 41:838–49.

Hitchcock, G. (1983) Fieldwork as Practical Activity: Reflections on Fieldwork and the Social Organization of an Urban, Open-Plan Primary School. In M. Hammersley (ed.) *The Ethnography of Schooling: Methodological Issues*. Driffield: Nafferton.

Hoffman, J.E. (1980) Problems of Access in the Study of Social Elites and Boards of Directors. In W.B. Shaffir, R.A. Stebbins, and A. Turowetz (eds) *Fieldwork Experience: Qualitative Approaches to Social Research*. New York: St Martin's Press.

Holdaway, S. (1982) 'An Inside Job': A Case Study of Covert Research on the Police. In M. Bulmer (ed.) *Social Research Ethics: An Examination of the Merits of Covert Participant Observation*. London: Macmillan.

Homan, R. (1980) The Ethics of Covert Methods. *British Journal of Sociology* 31(1):46–59.

Honigmann, J. (1970) Fieldwork in Two Northern Canadian Communities. In M. Freilich (ed.) *Marginal Natives: Anthropologists at Work*. New York: Harper & Row.

Humphrey, L. (1970) *Tearoom Trade*. Chicago, Ill.: Aldine.

Hyman, H. (1954) *Interviewing in Social Research*. Chicago, Ill.: University of Chicago Press.

Hymes, D. (1978) What is Ethnography? Sociolinguistic Paper **45**, April, Austin, Tex.: Southwest Educational Development Laboratory.

Irwin, J. (1973) Surfing: The Natural History of an Urban Scene. *Urban Life and Culture* **2**(2):131–60.

Jacobs, J.B. (1974) Participant Observation in Prison. *Urban Life and Culture* **3**(2):221–40.

Jahoda, M., Deutsch, M., and Cook, S.W. (1951) *Research Methods in Social Relations*. New York: Dryden.

Jeffery, P. (1979) *Frogs in a Well: Indian Women in Purdah*. London: Zed Press.

Johnson, J. (1975) *Doing Field Research*. New York: Free Press.

Jules-Rosette, B. (1978) The Veil of Objectivity: Prophecy, Divination, and Social Inquiry. *American Anthropologist* **80**(3): 549–70.

_____ (1978) Towards a Theory of Ethnography. *Sociological Symposium* **24**:81–98.

Junker, B. (1960) *Field Work*. Chicago, Ill.: University of Chicago Press.

Kaplan, A. (1964) *The Conduct of Inquiry: Methodology for Behavioural Science*. San Francisco, Calif.: Chandler.

Karp, D.A. (1980) Observing Behavior in Public Places: Problems and Strategies. In W.B. Shaffir, R.A, Stebbins, and A. Turowetz (eds) *Fieldwork Experience: Qualitative Approaches to Social Research*. New York: St Martin's Press.

Keat, R. and Urry, J. (1975) *Social Theory as Science*. London: Routledge & Kegan Paul.

Keiser, R.L. (1970) Fieldwork Among the Vice Lords of Chicago. In G.D. Spindler (ed.) *Being an Anthropologist*. New York: Holt, Rinehart & Winston.

Kolakowski, L. (1972) *Positivist Philosophy: From Hume to the Vienna Circle*. Harmondsworth: Penguin.

Kotarba, J.A. (1975) American Acupuncturists: The New Entrepreneurs of Hope. *Urban Life* **4**(2):149–77.

Krieger, S. (1979a) Research and the Construction of a Text. In N.K. Denzin (ed.) *Studies in Symbolic Interaction*, Vol. 2. Greenwich, Conn.: JAI Press.

_____ (1979b) The KMPX Strike (March-May 1968). In N.K. Denzin (ed.) *Studies in Symbolic Interaction*, Vol. 2. Greenwich, Conn.: JAI Press.

Labov, W. (1969) The Logic of Nonstandard English. *Georgetown Monographs on Language and Linguistics* **22**:1–31.

_____ (1972) The Transformation of Experience in Narrative Syntax. In W. Labov (ed.) *Language in the Inner City*. Philadelphia, Pa: Pennsylvania University Press.

Labov, W. and Waletzky, J. (1967) Narrative Analysis: Oral Versions of

Personal Experience. In J. Holm (ed.) *Essays on the Verbal and Visual Arts*. Seattle, Wash.: University of Washington Press.

Lacey, C. (1970) *Hightown Grammar*. Manchester: Manchester University Press.

_____ (1976) Problems of Sociological Fieldwork: A Review of the Methodology of 'Hightown Grammar'. In M. Shipman (ed.) *The Organization and Impact of Social Research*. London: Routledge & Kegan Paul.

Lazarsfeld, P. P. and Barton, A. (1951) Qualitative Measurement in the Social Sciences: Classification, Typologies and Indices. In D.P. Lerner and H.D. Lasswell (eds) *The Policy Sciences*. Stanford, Calif: Stanford University Press.

Lazarsfeld, P. P. and Thielens, W. (1958) *The Academic Mind: Social Scientists in a Time of Crises*. Glencoe, Ill.: Free Press.

LePlay, F. (1879) *Les Ouvriers Européens*. Paris: Alfred Mame et Fils.

Lerner, D. (1957) The 'Hard-Headed' Frenchman: On Se Défend, Toujours. *Encounter* 8(March):27–32.

Lever, J. (1981) Multiple Methods of Data Collection: A Note on Divergence. *Urban Life* 10(2):199–213.

Levy, D.J. (1981) *Realism: An Essay in Interpretation and Social Reality*. Manchester: Carcanet New Press.

Lewis, J.D. and Smith, R.L. (1980) *American Sociology and Pragmatism: Mead, Chicago Sociology and Symbolic Interaction*. Chicago, Ill.: University of Chicago Press.

Liebow, E. (1967) *Tally's Corner*. London: Routledge & Kegan Paul.

Lindesmith, A. (1947) *Opiate Addiction*. Bloomington, Ind.: Principia Press.

Lipset, D. (1980) *Gregory Bateson: The Legacy of a Scientist*. Englewood Cliffs, NJ: Prentice-Hall.

Llewellyn, M. (1980) Studying Girls at School: The Implications of Confusion. In R. Deem (ed.) *Schooling for Women's Work*. London: Routledge & Kegan Paul.

Lodge, D. (1977) *The Modes of Modern Writing: Metaphor, Metonymy, and the Typology of Modern Literature*. London: Edward Arnold.

_____ (1981) *Working with Structuralism*. London: Routledge & Kegan Paul.

Lofland, J. (1967) Notes on Naturalism. *Kansas Journal of Sociology* 3(2):45–61.

_____ (1970) Interactionist Imagery and Analytic Interruptus. In T. Shibutani (ed.) *Human Nature and Collective Behaviour: Papers in Honour of Herbert Blumer*. Englewood Cliffs, NJ: Prentice-Hall.

_____ (1971) *Analyzing Social Settings: A Guide to Qualitative Observation and Analysis*. Belmont, Calif.: Wadsworth.

_____ (1974) Styles of Reporting Qualitative Field Research. *American Sociologist* 9 (August):101–11.

_____ (1976) *Doing Social Life: The Qualitative Study of Human Interaction in Natural Settings*. New York: Wiley.

_____ (1980) Early Goffman: Style, Structure, Substance, Soul. In J.

Ditton (ed.) *The View From Goffman*. London: Macmillan.

Lofland, J. and Lejeune, R.A. (1960) Initial Encounters of Newcomers in Alcoholics Anonymous. *Social Problems* **8**: 102–11.

Lofland, L.H. (1966) *In the Presence of Strangers: A Study of Behaviour in Public Settings*. Working Paper **19**. University of Michigan, Ann Arbor: Centre for Research on Social Organization.

_____ (1973) *A World of Strangers: Order and Action in Urban Public Space*. New York: Basic Books.

_____ (1975) The 'Thereness' of Women: A Selective Review of Urban Sociology. In M. Millman and R.M. Kanter (eds) *Another Voice: Feminist Perspectives on Social Life and Social Science*. New York: Anchor Books.

Loizos, P. (1975) *The Greek Gift: Politics in a Cypriot Village*. Oxford: Blackwell.

Lutz, F.W. (1981) Ethnography – The Holistic Approach to Understanding Schooling. In J.L. Green and C. Wallat (eds) *Ethnography and Language in Educational Settings*. Norwood, NJ: Ablex.

Lyman, S.M. and Scott, M.B. (1970) *A Sociology of the Absurd*. New York: Appleton-Century-Crofts.

McCall, G.J. (1969) The Problem of Indicators in Participant Observation Research. In G.J. McCall and J.L. Simmons (eds) *Issues in Participant Observation: A Text and Reader*. Reading, Mass.: Addison-Wesley.

McCurdy, D.W. (1976) The Medicine Man. In M.A. Rynkiewich and J.P. Spradley (eds) *Ethics and Anthropology: Dilemmas in Fieldwork*. New York: Wiley.

McDermott, R. (1976) 'Kids Make Sense. An Ethnographic Account of the Interactional Management of Success and Failure in One First Grade Classroom': Unpublished PhD thesis, Stanford University, California.

MacIntyre, S. (1977) *Single and Pregnant*. London: Croom Helm.

McPhail, C. and Rexroat, C. (1980) Ex Cathedra Blumer or Ex Libris Mead? *American Sociological Review* **45**: 420–30.

Mackay, R.W. (1967) 'The Acquisition of Membership: Socialization in Grade One Classrooms'. Unpublished MA thesis, University of British Columbia.

Magee, B. (1972) *Popper*. London: Fontana.

Malinowski, B. (1922) *Argonauts of the Western Pacific*. London: Routledge & Kegan Paul.

_____ (1967) *A Diary in the Strict Sense of the Term*. London: Routledge & Kegan Paul.

Manning, P.K. (1980) Goffman's Framing Order: Style as Structure. In J. Ditton (ed.) *The View From Goffman*. London: Macmillan.

Martin, J. (1981) A Garbage Can Model of the Psychological Research Process. *American Behavioral Scientist* **25**(2):131–51.

Masterman, M. (1970) The Nature of a Paradigm. In I. Lakatos and A. Musgrave (eds) *Criticism and the Growth of Knowledge*. London: Cambridge University Press.

Matza, D. (1969) *Becoming Deviant*. Englewood Cliffs, NJ: Prentice-Hall.

Mayhew, H. (1861) *London Labour and the London Poor*. London: Griffin Bohn.

Mead, G.H. (1934) *Mind, Self and Society*. Chicago, Ill.: University of Chicago Press.

Measor, L. (1983) Gender and the Sciences: Pupils' Gender-Based Conceptions of School Subjects. In M. Hammersley and A. Hargreaves (eds) *Curriculum Practice: Sociological Accounts*. Lewes: Falmer.

Measor, L. and Woods, P. (1983) The Interpretation of Pupil Myths. In M. Hammersley (ed.) *The Ethnography of Schooling: Methodological Issues*. Driffield: Nafferton.

Medawar, P. (1967) *The Art of the Soluble*. London: Methuen.

_____ (1979) *Advice to a Young Scientist*. New York: Harper & Row.

Merton, R.K. (1959) Introduction: Notes on Problem-Finding in Sociology. In R.K. Merton, L. Broom, and L. S. Cottrell Jr. (eds) *Sociology Today*, Vol 1. New York: Harper & Row.

Miller, S.M. (1952) The Participant Observer and 'Over-Rapport'. *American Sociological Review* **17**: 97–9.

Mills, C.W. (1940) Situated Actions and Vocabularies of Motive. *American Sociological Review* **5** (6):439–52.

Moser, C.A. and Kalton, G. (1971) (Second edn) *Survey Methods in Social Investigation*. London: Heinemann.

Mungham, G. and Thomas, P.A. (1981) Studying Lawyers: Aspects of the Theory, Method and Politics of Social Research, *British Journal of Law and Society* **8**(1):79–96.

Nadel S.F. (1939) The Interview Technique in Social Anthropology. In F.C. Bartlett, M. Ginsberg, E.J. Lindgren, and R.H. Thouless (eds) *The Study of Society*. London: Routledge & Kegan Paul.

Nader, L. (1970) From Anguish to Exultation. In P. Golde (ed.) *Women in the Field*. Chicago, Ill.: Aldine.

Newby , H. (1977a) In the Field: Reflections on the Study of Suffolk Farm Workers. In C. Bell and H. Newby (eds) *Doing Sociological Research*. London: Allen & Unwin.

_____ (1977b) *The Deferential Worker: A Study of Farm Workers in East Anglia*. London: Allen Lane.

Okely, J. (1983) *The Traveller-Gypsies*. London: Cambridge University Press.

Olesen, V. and Whittaker, E. (1968) *The Silent Dialogue, A Study in the Social Psychology of Professional Socialization*. San Francisco, Calif.: Jossey-Bass.

Orne, M.T. (1962) On the Social Psychology of the Psychological Experiment. *American Psychologist* **17**:776–83.

Papanek, H. (1964) The Woman Fieldworker in a Purdah Society. *Human Organization* **23**:160–63.

Parker, H.J. (1974) (Second edn) *View From the Boys: A Sociology of Downtown Adolescents*. London: David & Charles.

Patrick, J. (1973) *A Glasgow Gang Observed*. London: Eyre Methuen.

258 *Ethnography: Principles in Practice*

Paul, B.D. (1953) Interviewing Techniques and Field Relations. In A.C. Kroeber (ed.) *Anthropology Today: An Encyclopaedic Inventory*. Chicago, Ill.: University of Chicago Press.

Pelto, P.J. and Pelto, G.H. (1978) Ethnography: The Fieldwork Enterprise. In J.J. Honigmann (ed.) *Handbook of Social and Cultural Anthropology*. Chicago, Ill.: Rand McNally.

Perlman, M.L. (1970) Intensive Fieldwork and Scope Sampling: Methods for Studying the Same Problem at Different Levels. In M. Freilich (ed.) *Marginal Natives: Anthropologists at Work*. New York: Harper & Row.

Piliavin, I. and Briar, B. (1964) Police Encounters with Juveniles. *American Journal of Sociology* **70**:206–14.

Platt, J. (1981) On Interviewing One's Peers. *British Journal of Sociology* **32**(1):75–91.

Plummer, K. (1975) *Sexual Stigma: An Interactionist Account*. London: Routledge & Kegan Paul.

Polanyi, M. (1958) *Personal Knowledge*. Chicago, Ill.: University of Chicago Press.

Pollert, A. (1981) *Girls, Wives, Factory Lives*. London: Macmillan.

Popper, K. (1972) *The Logic of Scientific Discovery*. London: Hutchinson.

Powdermaker, H. (1966) *Stranger and Friend: The Way of an Anthropologist*. New York: Norton.

Quine, W.V. (1960) *Word and Object*. Cambridge, Mass.: MIT Press.

Radcliffe-Brown, A.R. (1948a) *The Andaman Islanders*. Glencoe, Ill.: Free Press.

_____ (1948b) *A Natural Science of Society*. New York: Free Press.

Rees, C. (1981) Records and Hospital Routine. In P. Atkinson and C. Heath (eds) *Medical Work: Realities and Routines*. Farnborough: Gower.

Reichenbach, H. (1938) *Experience and Prediction: An Analysis of the Foundations and the Structure of Knowledge*. Chicago, Ill.: University of Chicago Press.

_____ (1951) *The Rise of Scientific Philosophy*. Berkeley, Calif.: University of California Press.

Reilly, F.E. (1970) *Charles Peirce's Theory of Scientific Method*. New York: Fordham University Press.

Rescher, N. (1978) *Peirce's Philosophy of Science: Critical Studies in his Theory of Induction and Scientific Method*. South Bend, Ind.: University of Notre Dame Press.

Riemer, J.W. (1977) Varieties of Opportunistic Research. *Urban Life* **5**(4):467–77.

Riesman, D. (1958) Interviews, Elites, and Academic Freedom. *Social Problems* **6**: 115–26.

Roberts, H. (ed.) (1981) *Doing Feminist Research*, London: Routledge & Kegan Paul.

Robinson, D. (1971) *The Process of Becoming Ill*. London: Routledge & Kegan Paul.

Robinson, W.S (1969) The Logical Structure of Analytic Induction. In G.J. McCall and J.L. Simmons (eds) *Issues in Participant Observation*. Reading, Mass.: Addison-Wesley.

Rock, P. (1973) *Making People Pay*. London: Routledge & Kegan Paul.

_____ (1979) *The Making of Symbolic Interactionism*. London: Macmillan.

Rohner, R. (1969) *The Ethnography of Franz Boas*. Chicago, Ill.: University of Chicago Press.

Rosenhahn, D.L. (1982) On Being Sane in Insane Places. In M. Bulmer (ed.) *Social Research Ethics: An Examination of the Merits of Covert Participant Observation*. London: Macmillan.

Rosenthal, R. (1966) *Experimenter Effects in Behavioural Science*. New York: Appleton-Century-Crofts.

Rosnow, R.L. (1981) *Paradigms in Transition: The Methodology of Social Inquiry*. New York: Oxford University Press.

Roth, J. (1963) *Timetables*. New York: Bobbs-Merrill.

Ryave, A.L. (1979) On the Art of Talking About the World. In H. Schwartz and J. Jacobs (eds) *Qualitative Sociology: A Method to the Madness*. New York: Free Press.

Sacks, H. (1972) On the Analyzability of Stories by Children. In J.J. Gumperz and D. Hymes (eds) *Directions in Sociolinguistics: The Ethnography of Communication*. New York: Holt, Rinehart & Winston.

_____ (1975) Everyone Has to Lie. In M. Sanches and B. Blount (eds) *Sociocultural Dimensions of Language Use*. London: Academic Press.

Sacks, H., Schegloff, E.A., and Jefferson, G. (1974) A Simplest Systematics for the Organization of Turn-Taking for Conversation. *Language* **50**:696–735.

Sahlins, M.G. and Service, E.R. (1960) (eds) *Evolution and Culture*. Ann Arbor, Mich.: University of Michigan Press.

Schatzman, L. and Strauss, A. (1955) Social Class and Modes of Communication. *American Journal of Sociology* **60**:329–38.

_____ (1973) *Field Research: Strategies for a Natural Sociology*. Englewood Cliffs, NJ: Prentice-Hall.

Schuman, H. (1982) Artifacts are in the Mind of the Beholder. *American Sociologist* **17**(1):21–8.

Schutz, A. (1964) The Stranger: An Essay in Social Psychology. In A. Schutz (ed.) *Collected Papers*, Vol. II. The Hague: Martinus Nijhoff.

Schwartz, H. and Jacobs, J. (1979) *Qualitative Sociology: A Method to the Madness*. New York: Free Press.

Scott, M.B. (1968) *The Racing Game*. Chicago, Ill.: Aldine.

Selltiz, C., Jahoda, M., Deutsch, M., and Cook, S. (1959) *Research Methods in Social Relations*. New York: Holt, Rinehart & Winston.

Sevigny, M.J. (1981) Triangulated Inquiry – A Methodology for the Analysis of Classroom Interaction. In J.L. Green and C. Wallat (eds)

Ethnography and Language in Educational Settings. Norwood, NJ: Ablex.

Sharrock, W.W. and Anderson, R.J. (1980) *On the Demise of the Native: Some Observations on and a Proposal for Ethnography*. Occasional Paper **5**, Department of Sociology, University of Manchester, Manchester.

Simons, H. (1981) Conversation Piece: the Practice of Interviewing in Case Study Research. In C. Adelman (ed.) *Uttering, Muttering: Collecting, Using and Reporting Talk for Social and Educational Research*. London: Grant McIntyre.

Sjoberg, G. and Nett, R. (1968) *A Methodology for Social Research*. New York: Harper & Row.

Skipper, J.K. and McCaghy, C.H. (1972) Respondents' Intrusion Upon the Situation: The Problem of Interviewing Subjects with Special Qualities. *Sociological Quarterly* **13**:237–43.

Smigel, E. (1958) Interviewing a Legal Elite: The Wall Street Lawyer. *American Journal of Sociology* **64**:159–64.

Speier, M. (1973) *How to Observe Face-to-Face Communication: A Sociological Introduction*. Pacific Palisades, Calif.: Goodyear.

Spencer, L. and Dale, A. (1979) Integration and Regulation in Organizations: A Contextual Approach. *Sociological Review* **27**(4):679–702.

Spradley, J.P. (1970) *You Owe Yourself a Drunk: An Ethnography of Urban Nomads*. Boston, Mass.: Little Brown.

_____ (1979) *The Ethnographic Interview*. New York: Holt, Rinehart & Winston.

_____ (1980) *Participant Observation*. New York: Holt, Rinehart & Winston.

Stein, M.R. (1964) The Eclipse of Community: Some Glances at the Education of a Sociologist. In A.J. Vidich, J. Bensman, and M.R. Stein (eds) *Reflections on Community Studies*. New York: Harper & Row.

Stimson, G.V. and Webb, B. (1975) *Going to See the Doctor: The Consultation Process in General Practice*. London: Routledge & Kegan Paul.

Strauss, A. (1970) Discovering New Theory from Previous Theory. In T. Shibutani (ed.) *Human Nature and Collective Behaviour: Essays in Honour of Herbert Blumer*. Englewood Cliffs, NJ: Prentice-Hall.

_____ (1978) A Social World Perspective. In N.K. Denzin (ed.) *Studies in Symbolic Interaction*, Vol. 1. Greenwich, Conn.: JAI Press.

Strong, P.M. (1979) *The Ceremonial Order of the Clinic: Parents, Doctors and Medical Bureaucracies*. London: Routledge & Kegan Paul.

Strong, P. (1982) The Rivals: An Essay on the Sociological Trades. In R. Dingwall and P. Lewis (eds) *The Sociology of the Professions: Medicine, Law and Others*. London: Macmillan.

Stryker, S. (1981) Symbolic Interactionism: Themes and Variations. In M. Rosenberg and R.H. Turner (eds) *Social Psychology: Sociological Perspectives*. New York: Basic Books.

Sudman, S. (1974) *Response Effects in Surveys: A Review and Synthesis*. Chicago, Ill.: Aldine.

Sudnow, D. (1965) Normal Crimes. *Social Problems* **12**:255–76.

_____ (1967) *Passing On*. Englewood Cliffs, NJ: Prentice-Hall.

Sullivan, M.A., Queen, S.A., and Patrick, R.C. (1958) Participant Observation as Employed in the Study of a Military Training Program. *American Sociological Review* **23**(6):660–67.

Suttles, G.D. (1968) *The Social Order of the Slum*. Chicago, Ill.: University of Chicago Press.

Sykes, G. (1958) *The Society of Captives: A Study of a Maximum Security Prison*, Princeton, NJ: Princeton University Press.

Thomas, W.I. (1967) *The Unadjusted Girl*. New York: Harper & Row. First published 1923, Boston, Mass.: Little, Brown & Co.

Thomas, W.I. and Znaniekci, F. (1927) *The Polish Peasant in Europe and America*. New York: Alfred Knopf.

Tinbergen, N. (1972) *The Animal and its World*. Vol. 1. London: Allen & Unwin.

Toulmin, S. (1972) *Human Understanding*. Oxford: Clarendon Press.

Turnbull, C. (1973) *The Mountain People*. London: Cape.

Turner, R.H. (1962) Role-Taking: Process Versus Conformity. In A.M. Rose (ed.) *Human Behaviour and Social Processes*. London: Routledge & Kegan Paul.

Von Wright, G.H. (1971) *Explanation and Understanding*. London: Routledge & Kegan Paul.

Walker, R. (1981) On the Uses of Fiction in Educational Research. In D. Smetherham (ed.) *Practising Evaluation*. Driffield: Nafferton.

Walker, R. and Adelman, C. (1972) *Towards a Sociography of Classrooms*. Final Report, SSRC Grants HR 996/1 'The Analysis of Classroom Behaviour', and HR 1442/1 'The Long-Term Observation of Classroom Events Using Stop-Frame and Cinematography'. London: Centre for Science Education, Chelsea College.

Warren, C.A.B. (1972) Observing the Gay Community. In J.D. Douglas (ed.) *Research on Deviance*. New York: Random House.

_____ (1974) *Identity and Community in the Gay World*. New York: Wiley.

Warren, C.A.B. and Rasmussen, P.K. (1977) Sex and Gender in Field Research. *Urban Life* **6**(3):349–69.

Wax, R. (1971) *Doing Fieldwork: Warnings and Advice*. Chicago: University of Chicago Press.

Webb, E.J. and Salancik, J.R. (1966) The Interview or the Only Wheel in Town. *Journalism Monographs* **2** November: 1–49.

Webb, S. and Webb, B. (1932) *Methods of Social Study*. London: Longmans Green.

Werthman, C. (1963) Delinquents in Schools: A Test for the Legitimacy of Authority. *Berkeley Journal of Sociology* **8**(1):39–60.

West, W.G. (1980) Access to Adolescent Deviants and Deviance. In W.B. Shaffir, R.A. Stebbins, and A. Turowetz (eds) *Fieldwork Experience: Qualitative Approaches to Social Research*. New York: St.Martin's Press.

Whitten, N. (1970) Network Analysis and Processes of Adaptation among Ecuadorian and Nova Scotian Negroes. In M. Freilich (ed.) *Marginal Natives: Anthropologists at Work*. New York: Harper & Row.

Whyte, W.F. (1953) Interviewing for Organizational Research. *Human Organization* 12:15–22.

_____ (1981) (Third edn) *Street Corner Society: The Social Structure of an Italian Slum*. Chicago, Ill.: University of Chicago Press.

Wieder, D. (1974) *Language and Social Reality: The Case of Telling the Convict Code*. The Hague: Mouton.

_____ (1974) Telling the Code. In R. Turner (ed.) *Ethnomethodology*. Harmondsworth: Penguin.

Willer, D. (1967) *Scientific Sociology*. Englewood Cliffs, NJ: Prentice-Hall.

Williams, R. (1976) Symbolic Interactionism: Fusion of Theory and Research. In D.C. Thorns (ed.) *New Directions in Sociology*. London: David & Charles.

Willis, P. (1977) *Learning to Labour: How Working Class Kids Get Working Class Jobs*. Farnborough: Saxon House.

_____ (1981) Cultural Production is Different from Cultural Reproduction is Different from Social Reproduction is Different from Reproduction. *Interchange* 12(2–3):48–67.

Wilson, T.P (1971) Normative and Interpretive Paradigms in Sociology. In J.D. Douglas (ed.) *Understanding Everyday Life*. London: Routledge & Kegan Paul.

Wintrob, R.M. (1969) An Inward Focus: A Consideration of Psychological Stress in Fieldwork. In F. Henry and S. Saberwal (eds) *Stress and Response in Fieldwork*. New York: Holt, Rinehart & Winston.

Wolff, K.H. (1964) Surrender and Community Study: The Study of Loma. In A.J. Vidich, J. Bensman, and M.R. Stein (eds) *Reflections on Community Studies*. New York: Wiley.

Woods, P. (1979) *The Divided School*. London: Routledge & Kegan Paul.

_____ (1981) Understanding Through Talk. In C. Adelman (ed.) *Uttering, Muttering: Collecting, Using and Reporting Talk for Social and Educational Research*. London: Grant McIntyre.

Wright, M. (1981) Coming To Terms with Death: Patient Care in a Hospice for the Terminally Ill. In P. Atkinson and C. Heath (eds) *Medical Work: Realities and Routines*. Farnborough: Gower.

Young, M.F.D. (ed.) (1971) *Knowledge and Control: New Directions in the Sociology of Education*. London: Collier-Macmillan.

Zelditch, M. (1962) Some Methodological Problems of Field Studies. *American Journal of Sociology* 67:566–76.

Zerubavel, E. (1979) *Patterns of Time in Hospital Life*. Chicago, Ill.: University of Chicago Press.

Zimmerman, D.H. (1969) Record-Keeping and the Intake Process in a Public Welfare Agency. In S. Wheeler (ed.) *On Record: Files and Dossiers in American, Life*. New York: Russell Sage Foundation.

Zimmerman, D.H. and Wieder, D.L. (1977) The Diary: Diary-Interview Method. *Urban Life* 5(4):479–98.

Znaniecki, F. (1934) *The Method of Sociology*. New York: Farrar & Rinehart.

Zorbaugh, H. (1929) *The Gold Coast and the Slum*. Chicago, Ill.: University of Chicago Press.

Name index

Subject index

abstractness of research problems, 34
access, 54–76; deception, 68–72;
    entry to settings, 56–63;
    gatekeepers, 63–8; obstructive and
    facilitative relationships, 72–6
accounts, 105–26, 133–35, 190
advice, lack of, 27–8
age, researchers, 87–8
alien culture, 88–92
analysis: and narration, separating,
    221–23; concepts, generating,
    177–81; concepts, types, and
    indicators, 184–95; process of,
    174–206; respondent validation,
    195–98; substantive and formal,
    34–9; theories and comparative
    method, 200–04; triangulation,
    198–200; types of theory, 204–06;
    typologies, developing, 181–84
analytic concepts, 226
'analytic induction', 18, 201–04
'analytic interruptus', 182, 201
analytic notes and memos, 164–67
anonymity, researcher, 56–8
anxiety, fieldwork, 100–03
appearance of researchers, 78–81

'artificial' settings, see positivism;
    ecological validity
audience, 123, 188–92, 227–29
audio-taping, 245, 157–63
autobiographical records, 129–31
'awareness contexts', 182–84

bias, 130–31
biographical records, 129–31
borrowed concepts, 179

cards, punched, 171
'career' perspective, 219
cases, selection of, 45–53
categories, 50–1, 168–70, 180.
    182–84
change in research problems, 32–3
character of field notes, 151
Chicago School, 9, 23, 42, 127–28
chronology in writing, 217–20
clothes, researcher's, 78–80
coding records, 169–72
colleges, studies on, 72, 97; see also
    university
commonsense, see naturalism
community studies, 42–3